Wheels In The Head

Educational Philosophies of Authority, Freedom, and Culture from Socrates to Human Rights

SECOND EDITION

Joel Spring

State University of New York
College at New Paltz

LEA Lawrence Erlbaum Associates
Taylor & Francis Group

New York   London

Originally published by The McGraw-Hill Companies, Inc.

Copyright © 2006 by Lawrence Erlbaum Associates, Inc.

Freelance cover deigner: Erin V. Scott

Cover illustration: Cathy Hull

Library of Congress Cataloging-in-Publication Data

Spring, Joel H.
    Wheels in the head : educational philosophies of authority, freedom, and culture from Socrates to human rights / Joel Spring — 2nd ed.
       p. cm.

Includes bibliographical references and index.

ISBN 0-8058-6131-9 (softcover : alk. paper)

1. Education—Philosophy—History. 2. Education—Social aspects. 3. Education—Political aspects. 4. Critical pedagogy. 5. Free schools. I. Title.
LB14.7.S67 1999
370'.1—dc21   98–24367
                                                  CIP

Printed in the United States of America
10 9 8 7 6 5 4 3 2

Dedication and Note on the Title

This book is dedicated to Max Stirner (1806–1856), whose phrase "wheels in the head" serves as its title. Stirner warned that control of the dissemination of ideas through schools was fast becoming an important means of domination by the modern state. He believed that an idea becomes a wheel in the head when the idea owns the individual rather than the individual owning the idea. In his classic volume *The Ego and His Own: The Case of the Individual Against Authority* (1845), Stirner writes about wheels in the head: "The thought is my own only when I have no misgiving about bringing it in danger of death every moment, when I do not have to fear its loss as a loss for me, a loss of me."[1]

Stirner's warnings against ideological domination by governments and public school systems eventually destroyed his relationship with his intellectual colleague Karl Marx. Stirner claimed that ideologies, such as communism and liberalism, have the power to dominate individual actions even to the point of self-destruction. For Stirner, an idea truly becomes a wheel in the head when a person is willing to die for it. Stirner's warnings went unheeded in the nineteenth and twentieth centuries as countless lives were lost in the defense of the ideas of communism, socialism, fascism, imperialism, Nazism, and all other isms.

[1]Max Stirner, *The Ego and His Own: The Case of the Individual Against Authority*, trans. Steven T. Byington (New York: Libertarian Book Club, 1963), p. 342.

Contents

Part 2
DISSENTING TRADITIONS IN EDUCATION

Part 3
THE POLITICS OF CULTURE

Part 4
THE POLITICS OF GENDER

Preface

In a new chapter concluding this second edition, I propose a solution for the authoritarian tendencies of government-operated schools. This solution is a legally binding right to an education that includes an education in human rights. I treat human rights as claim rights that obligate all members of society to protect the rights of each other. This definition of rights requires an active and empowering relationship between individuals, and society and government. In this new chapter, I specify the meaning of a right to an education and the rights to be taught. Based on the Universal Declaration of Human Rights, my list includes economic and social rights along with political rights. In addition, I provide a resolution to the conflict between cultural differences and human rights doctrines. My "wheel in the head" is the moral duty to protect one's own human rights and the human rights of others.

For many years, I have searched for a means of conducting government-operated schools that are free of the controlling influences of politicians, business elites, and special interest groups. The problem for any school is that outside groups want to influence the content of instruction. Political despots want the glories of their regimes taught in history and civics classes. Business elites want the schools to be pervaded with doctrines favorable to their economic concerns. Special interest groups want to ensure that their religious, moral, and social doctrines are either included or not questioned in classroom instruction. Government-operated schools tend to serve the interests of groups outside the school rather than the desires and interests of the student.

The subservience of schools to outside ideological forces creates a major problem for democratic societies. Outside groups try to influence the future choices of students. All pretense of freedom of thought is lost in the classroom. It is difficult to find when, in the history of U.S. schools, freedom of thought reigned in classrooms. A true democracy requires the intellectual freedom to make choices about political decisions. Is intellectual freedom possible after twelve years of ideological management in public schools? Also, the uniformity of the school curriculum leaves the student with little to think about. To be meaningful, intellectual freedom requires an exposure to a diversity of ideas. Uniformity and not diversity is the hallmark of most government school systems.

I believe that an important problem in the relationship between democracy and schooling can be overcome if government schools are required to adhere to basic human rights doctrines. Again, I want to emphasize that my use of rights doctrines extends beyond political rights. For instance, everyone should have a right to education, adequate medical care, proper nutrition, work, and housing, along with the right to free speech and to choose one's government leaders. As claim rights, this means that everyone has a duty to ensure the fulfillment of these rights for others. Traditionally, schools have taught liberty rights which require only that individuals and government do not interfere with the exercise of liberty. Liberty rights provide the right to do something, such as the right to free speech, without the obligation of ensuring that all people can actually exercise that right. As claim rights, students are taught that they should protect their own right and the rights of others to free speech, democratic governance, education, medical care, housing, work, and other essential rights. Until schools are required to fulfill a duty to protect human rights and teach others to protect human rights, schools will remain authoritarian rather than democratic institutions.

Acknowledgments

My thanks to those reviewers who read and commented on the original manuscript for the first edition. Chief among these are Nicolas Appleton, Arizona State University; Barry Bull, Indiana University; Bryan Deever, Georgia Southern University; Wendy Kohli, Louisiana State University; Gerald Reagan, Ohio State University; and Edward Stevens, Ohio University.

For the second edition, I relied on the sage criticism of Richard Brosio, Ball State University. Professor Brosio wisely criticized me for not articulating a philosophy of education in the first edition. I have attempted to correct this shortcoming by developing a human rights approach to education in this new edition.

Joel Spring

PART ONE

Autocratic and Democratic Forms of Education

CHAPTER 1

Education and the Authoritarian State

My goal is to find a means for making schools sources of freedom and political power in contrast to institutions of social control and political despotism. By the end of this book, I conclude that the answer is constitutional amendments or international treaties guaranteeing that all human beings have a right to an education that includes an education in human rights. In this context, human rights includes political, social, and economic rights and imposes an obligation on all human beings to protect the rights of others.

Understanding my conclusion requires an intellectual trip through a variety of ideas regarding schooling, political despotism, democracy, freedom, culture, gender, and human rights. Each of these topics identifies obstacles to achieving freedom and political power. For instance, this chapter examines how governments can use schools to maintain political despotism. Chapter 2 explores the unresolved problem for democratic governments of providing public schooling that is free of political interference. There is a long history of radical alternatives to despotic forms of education. Analyzed in Chapters 3 to 5, these radical alternatives provide important insights into the possibilities and problems in creating liberating schools. Any system of schooling, as discussed in Chapters 6 and 7, encounters problems of cultural differences. In addition, there has been a long history of discussions, as examined in Chapters 8 and 9, of schooling and the politics of gender and the family. In recent years, the philosophy of Paulo Freire has provided the most promising method for linking education with political freedom. However, I find Freire's philosophy seriously flawed by its assumptions about human psychology and consciousness. In Chapter 11, I explain how human rights doctrines as claims on society and government can make schools a source of freedom and political power.

PLATO: EDUCATION AND THE REPUBLIC

Plato's *Republic* provides clues to the role of education in an authoritarian state. In the *Republic*, Socrates explores the meaning of justice and the ideal state. A key feature of the ideal state is the education of citizens and rulers. Education is used as a method for determining a person's place in society and teaching people to accept those places. The censorship of literature and the manipulation of historical instruction are justified as the means of creating social harmony. In addition, the education of rulers is considered the key to assuring that wisdom rules society. Throughout the book, Socrates draws parallels between the psychological organization of the individual and the organization of the state. In other words, education serves the purpose of organizing the state in two ways: It puts each person in his or her correct place in the social hierarchy and it assures the right relationships among faculties of the human mind. In the end, Socrates rejects the democratic state and democratic person for the rule of wisdom. Philosopher-kings are to rule society, while individual wisdom is to control human passions.

The methodology of *The Republic*, the Socratic dialogue, is based on the premise that the knowledge of truth is within each individual, and the role of dialogue is to help the individual discover truth. For instance, in *Meno*, Socrates demonstrates this point by asking a young boy a series of questions that lead the boy to an understanding of how to determine the length of a diagonal of a square. The boy is never told how to determine the length of the diagonal but is asked questions that lead to the discovery of the correct answer.[1]

In *The Republic*, the parable of the cave is used to explain the Socratic method. In the parable of the cave, Socrates asks his listeners to imagine that humanity is similar to a group of people chained together in the bottom of a cave. The chains are arranged in a fashion that forces the people to stare at the cave wall and denies them the ability to turn around. Behind them is a fire, and in front of the fire objects are passed that cast shadows on the cave wall. Forced to see only the shadows, the chained individuals believe the shadows represent reality.

Socrates argues that humanity is similar to the chained individuals in the cave because they mistake the shadows of truth for actual truth. The goal of education is not to tell the individuals in the cave what truth is but to help them see the real objects. Eventually, education will help the individual to emerge from the cave and see "the good." Socrates argues that most teachers think that understanding is not in the individual and that their job is to put it into the person "as they were putting sight into blind eyes."[2] But, Socrates argues in the context of the parable, the power of understanding is already within the individual, and the educator should not try to put sight into blind eyes but should turn eyes so that they can see the good.

As Socrates uses the term, "the good" is a combination of the power that creates truth and the ability to know truth. In Socrates' words, "Then that which provides their truth to the things known, and gives the power of knowing to the knower, you must say is the idea or principle of the good, and you must conceive it as being the cause of understanding and of truth in so far as known. . . ."[3] In his plan for educating philosophers, understanding of the good is achieved after the learner progresses through a study of earthly images and objects to a study of ideas and ideals. Existing in the world of ideals are concepts such as perfect beauty and perfect justice. The good is the source of these ideals and the means by which humans can know them.

Therefore, experiencing the good opens the door, according to Socrates, to a knowledge and understanding of ideals. Experiencing the good makes it possible for a person to understand perfect justice, and that person would then be qualified to rule a just state. To know the good means that an individual also knows what is best for all people. Therefore, knowledge of the good would qualify a person to define what is best for all people, what is called the common good. According to this reasoning, it would be logical to conclude that persons who know the common good should be the rulers.

In *The Republic* only the rulers know the good. For Socrates, the ideal state is ruled by philosopher-kings who are selected because they are born with intellectual abilities that can be educated to know the good. This argument gives important power to the rulers. Any state that claims that only the rulers have access to the truth provides a justification for totalitarianism. For instance, in justifying the dictatorship of the Communist party, Lenin argued that the Communist party was the vanguard of the working class and represented the class consciousness of the workers. Therefore, the dictatorial control by the Communist party was justified because it represented truth as it was supposed to be present in the working class. In Germany, Hitler argued that the Nazi party represented the true spirit of the German people. This claim of access to truth resulted in dictatorial control and mass terrorism.

In *The Republic,* the claim of access to the good is used to justify the right of philosopher-kings to lie to the population and to spread myths that justify the social order. Rulers are allowed to lie, according to Socrates, because they know what is true and best for the people. Socrates states: "Then for the rulers of the city . . . it is proper to use falsehood, to deal with enemies or indeed with citizens for the benefit of the city."[4] Of course, Socrates argues, no one else should be allowed to lie.

One of the important myths to be spread by the rulers was designed to make people accept their social position. Of course, any myth of this type serves the purpose of reducing social discontent and justifying the power of the rulers. In the myth of the metals, Socrates proposed telling the population that people were a mixture of gold, silver, iron, and brass. Those most fit to rule were composed primarily of gold and therefore were the most precious. The guardian soldiers were composed primarily of silver, while farmers and workers were composed of iron and brass.

An important thing about this myth is that if people believe it, then they believe a person's place in society is the result of inherent qualities. For instance, a person might believe that it is right for a ruler to control because that ruler is made of superior metals. One could argue that intelligence tests served the same function in the early twentieth century. People were told that some persons were better than others because of their high scores on intelligence tests. People might also accept their lowly places in society because of low scores on intelligence tests.

The myth of the metals also served as a justification for the maintenance of hereditary social classes. Socrates argues that gold parents will tend to produce gold children, and brass parents will most often beget brass children. Ideally, Socrates maintains, similar metals should breed with each other. Of course, some children of gold parents will be born brass, and some children of brass parents will be gold. When this occurs, children who are unlike their parents are to be placed in their proper social class.

As stated in *The Republic*, an important role of the educational system is the determination of the mixture of metals within each child. Initially, there should be a determination of who should be placed among the farmers and workers and who should be educated. In other words, boys and girls who are considered to be composed of silver or gold are to be given an education. Out of this group, a decision would be made as to who should be educated to be a philosopher-king.

Important to the first stage of education is the right of rulers to control the type of knowledge disseminated to the population. The first stage of education, according to Socrates, should involve gymnastics for the body and music for the soul. In this case, music includes literature and history. Socrates argues that the stories told to children must be carefully censored so that the children are molded by the opinions the rulers want future citizens to hold. Of most importance, the child should be taught that heroes and gods are always good. In other words, the role of censorship is to provide ideals to guide the child. Rulers, Socrates argues, know what poets should write, and they should not tolerate the creation of fables that develop wrong opinions.

In addition, Socrates states, since one cannot know the truth about ancient things, then one "should make it useful."[5] The idea of making history useful to the state continues to the present. Socrates is correct that one can never know the exact "truth" with regard to historical events, and, consequently, one can select or interpret historical material to serve political purposes. History continues to be a means of building national myths and winning patriotic allegiance from citizens.

After education in music and gymnastics, students are to undergo a series of tests to determine their fitness to be educated as philosopher-kings. While the types of tests proposed by Socrates are quite different from contemporary tests, the idea is basically the same. Some form of standard is used to determine one's place in the social system. In a fashion similar to the myth of the metals, the creation of a standard serves to hide basic inequalities in the social system. When the content of a test is declared a standard, people can be led to believe that the test is objective and right. Failure to pass the test can lead to the doubting of one's self-worth, while passing it contributes to a sense of self-worth. In the case of *The Republic*, the tests are designed to determine who should be educated to be philosopher-kings. Of course, this means that the tests are designed to maintain a particular type of social system and political structure.

The plan for educating philosopher-kings is designed to bring the student to an understanding of the ultimate truth. The education begins with the study of arithmetic for its practical value and because it causes a student to think about the abstract meaning of numbers. The goal is to help the student see truth—not to teach truth. According to Socrates, the study of the abstract meaning of arithmetic helps to turn the eye away from the shadows of existence to the light of the good. The same purpose is served by the study of plane and solid geometry, which follows the study of arithmetic. Both subjects have a practical dimension, and they also help to turn the student's eyes to the abstract world of the good. This is also the purpose of studying astronomy after solid geometry. And, of course, the education concludes with the study of philosophy.

The education of philosopher-kings, the organization of the republic, and Socrates' concept of the ideal individual all deal with a fundamental problem for the state—the control of seemingly irrational emotions. In the West, the Platonic or Socratic tradition clearly separates reason and emotions and places a higher value on reason. The ideal within this tradition is for individuals to overcome and control their emotions and focus on a life of the mind. Physical desires, particularly sexual desires, are to be controlled or shunned.

It is for the above reasons that Socrates rejects the democratic state. In making the parallel between the individual and the state, Socrates argues that desires come to control the democratic person in the same fashion as individual desires control the democratic state. A democratic person, in Socrates' argument, is a person ruled by desires as opposed to wisdom or spirit. For Socrates, democracy eventually deteriorates into a slave state ruled by a tyrant. The democratic individual eventually deteriorates into an individual controlled by the strongest emotion—sexuality.

On the other hand, in Socrates' ideal state, wisdom or philosopher-kings rule with the aid of guardians to assure proper behavior by the citizenry. Within the ideal individual, wisdom aligns itself with the spirit to control the desires. The goal of education is to produce philosopher-kings to control the masses and to educate the philosopher-kings so that higher truth controls individual physical desires.

Giving a higher value to abstract truth or wisdom than to physical desires creates, I would argue, the possibility of the worst form of slavery. Within this framework, individuals can be asked to sacrifice their physical needs to a supposed greater abstract good. Of course, average citizens are not supposed to have the ability to understand this greater good. And if they are taught that physical desires should be suppressed, then they must also question any negative feelings they may have about sacrificing their physical pleasure to higher goals.

Therefore, the educational system in *The Republic* is designed to control the individual by teaching myths and censored literature, by teaching history lessons made "useful" to the goals of the state, and by teaching that the highest ideal is for individuals to suppress their physical desires in the service of the good. The myths, fables, and history lessons are directed at shaping the content of the mind and building the right ideals. What is most difficult for the state to control—emotions and desires—are to be brought under control by teaching that they should be sacrificed for a higher ideal.

The educational system's role in maintaining the stability of social classes is directly related to Socrates' concept of justice. Socrates' search for the ideal republic was for the purpose of finding the meaning of justice. A key part of the concept of justice is the concept of virtue. Socrates defines virtue as people and parts of the mind doing what they were intended to do. In other words, the virtue of an individual born to be a farmer is to be a farmer. According to the myth of the metals, all humans have some particular role that they are best fitted to play in society, such as guardian, worker, farmer, or philosopher-king. People who are fulfilling their roles are living in a state of virtue.

Also, the virtuous person has each mental faculty playing its proper role. Similar to the state, Socrates divides the mental faculties into wisdom, spirit, and desires. In paralleling the structure of the state to the human mind, Socrates equates philosopher-kings with wisdom in the mind, guardians with human spirit, and the masses of humanity with individual desires. In the virtuous person, according to Socrates, all mental faculties are to fulfill their proper function and work harmoniously together. Therefore, the virtuous person has wisdom using spirit to control desires. This is similar to the ideal state, where philosopher-kings use guardians to control the masses.

Therefore, justice, according to Socrates, is a combination of harmony and virtue. Harmony occurs when all citizens are working together doing what they are best fitted to do for society. Harmony also exists within the individual when all faculties cooperate in fulfilling their proper functions. The just state and the just individual are both virtuous and harmonious.

It is in this search for justice that Socrates provides the early model for the role of education in the state. Many of his proposals are reflected in actions of the modern state. Most modern educational systems serve the function of sorting individuals into what is supposed to be their proper social place, and, through the use of some form of the myth of the metals, individuals are taught to accept the correctness of this sorting process. Most modern educational systems make the teaching of literature and history useful to the goals of the state. In addition, attempts are made to teach the individual to sacrifice for some greater good that is often defined by the state. Most modern educational systems teach the correctness of obedience to the state's rulers.

In harsher terms, one could describe this process as "get into line, accept the job the system has given you, believe that the job is the best one for you, submit to the wisdom of the rulers, and be willing to make physical sacrifices for the greater good." Of primary importance is believing in one's own inferiority to the rulers. Once people accept their inferiority, then they can willingly and with gratitude allow the state to dictate their actions and thoughts. In the context of a world ruled by global corporations, workers accept their places and are willing to sacrifice for the good of the company. And, because they believe in the goodness of the corporation and in their own inferiority to managers, workers allow managers to dictate their actions and thoughts.

ANTON MAKARENKO: EDUCATION AND THE MODERN AUTHORITARIAN STATE

Although all of the elements of the educational system in *The Republic* are present in arguments regarding the role of education in the modern authoritarian state, one aspect of Socrates' plan has received the most attention. This is the important role of education in creating a willingness on the part of the population to fight for the preservation of the state. In *The Republic*, gymnastics and music are the basic education of the guardian or soldier class. Socrates' ideal is for soldiers to be strong and high spirited. To be gentle with his own people, the guardian should be educated, according to Socrates, to be a lover of wisdom. Of course, in the case of *The Republic,* a lover of wisdom is also a lover of the ruling class since only the philosopher-kings have access to the good.

Similarly to modern armies and police forces, the guardian class must internalize and accept the laws of the state. Education is the means of causing this internalization. Socrates compares this educational process to the dyeing of cloth. After describing the best method of ensuring that the colors do not wash out, he argues that by educating the guardian class in music and gymnastics "we were only trying to find a contrivance to make them, under our persuasion, receive the laws like a dye, as thoroughly as possible."[6]

In the modern state, patriotic exercises serve the function of building allegiance to the state and its laws. The thorough internalization of the law advocated by Socrates has, in the modern state, depended on the building of emotional attachments. Socrates did not advocate this approach because of his desire to subjugate emotions to wisdom. Guardians were to be true to the laws of the state because of their love of wisdom. In the modern state, patriotic exercises such as flag salutes, playing or listening to patriotic music, marching, and relating of national histories are intended to create an emotional attachment to the state or, in other words, love of country. Of course, most modern educational systems are designed to put these emotions into every student's breast.

In many cases, the use of education for military purposes is tied to the protection of economic systems. Within the global village, this military protection could be extended to international corporations. An early example of the linkage between education, militarism, and protection of an economic system can be found in the writings of the major advocate of the laissez-faire state, Adam Smith. In *Inquiry into the Nature and Causes of the Wealth of Nations* (1776), Smith argues that the best economic system is one based on private ownership without government interference. In Smith's reasoning, the best method of distributing economic goods and ensuring economic growth is to allow individuals to act in their own self-interest and compete in a free market.

Despite Smith's advocacy of minimal government interference, however, he believed that government should provide some form of education for the poor to maintain a "martial spirit" among the people. He argues for the benefit of martial spirit: "Where every citizen had the spirit of a soldier, a smaller standing army would surely be requisite."[7]

Similar to Socrates, Smith was in search of a method of organizing society. Unlike Socrates, Smith was concerned about the effects of the factory system. Smith argued that educating the factory worker was necessary to help relate individual interests to the interests of the state. Specifically, he was concerned that "in the progress of the division of labour, far greater part of those who live by labour . . . comes to be confined to a very few simple operations, frequently to one or two." The specialization of the factory, Smith argues, causes the modern worker to be "as stupid and ignorant as it is possible for a human creature to become." Therefore, the factory system, according to Smith, makes workers incapable of judging the interests of their country and "unless very particular pains have been taken to render him otherwise, he is equally incapable of defending his country in war."[8]

What is most surprising about Smith's argument regarding education is that it takes place in a defense of what is apparently a minimalist role for the state. But, of course, the state does have the role of protecting the free enterprise economic system. In other words, Smith is arguing that while the free market economic system requires minimum government intervention, the economic system itself does need to be protected. In other words, the role of the state is to defend the free market from outside interference, including war.

In this context, the role of education is to prepare people to defend the economic system by overcoming its negative effects on workers. According to Smith's reasoning, the modern worker is rendered useless to the state by the factory system but is made useful to the state by the educational system. Critics of free market economics might argue that Smith proposed educating workers to defend a state whose role is to protect an economic system that exploits those same workers. In other words, Smith's argument is that workers should be educated to defend their own exploitation.

In the twentieth century, the use of education to protect an economic system and an authoritarian state can most clearly be found in communist governments. In the nineteenth-century writings of Karl Marx, very little space is given to the issue of education. Karl Marx briefly referred to education in *Capital* (1867) in what was to become known as the great principle of polytechnical education. Like Adam Smith, Marx was concerned about the crippling effects of the factory system. He felt that long periods of repetition of a task in a factory made a worker unable to adapt to changes in technology. Marx wanted the replacement of the specialized worker with "the fully developed individual, fit for a variety of labours, ready to face any change of production, and to whom the different social functions he performs, are but so many modes of giving free scope to his own natural and acquired powers."[9] Marx went on to praise the development of technical schools, which combined the study of technology with the practical handling of the implements of work. Referring to the English Factory Act, Marx stated that though it "is limited to combining elementary education with work in the factory, there can be no doubt that when the working class comes into power, as inevitably it must, technical instruction, both theoretical and practical, will take its proper place in the working-class schools."[10] Therefore, Marx was primarily interested in providing workers with an education that would give them the ability to adapt to changing industrial conditions.

After the 1917 revolution, the new Soviet constitution embodied Marx's principle of a polytechnical form of education. The constitution called for "free, compulsory general and polytechnical [familiarizing in theory and practice with the main branches of production] education for all children of both sexes up to 16 years of age, close linking of instruction with children's socially productive labor."[11] But with the rise to power of Joseph Stalin in the 1920s, the communist state became more authoritarian, as did the educational system. In the early 1930s, polytechnical education was abandoned for a system that put heavy emphasis on academic subjects. Under Stalin's rule, Anton Makarenko became the leading theorist of communist education.

Makarenko wrote: "The profound meaning of educational work . . . consists in the selection and training of human needs . . . A morally justified need is, in fact, the need of a collectivist, that is, a person linked with his collective by his sense of the common aim, of the common struggle, by the living and certain awareness of his duty toward society."[12] Makarenko believed that the most important educational goal was making people part of the collective by teaching them to subordinate self-interest for the good of the group.

While Socrates wanted authority to be placed in the hands of philosopher-kings, Makarenko wanted it placed in the hands of the collective. In this context a collective could be the Soviet state or a factory, farm, or other organization. It was assumed that the collective created a common class consciousness among its members. The Communist party represented the collective consciousness of the working class. Therefore, in the context of Makarenko's arguments, subordination of self-interest to a local factory or farm collective is subordination to the Soviet state.

Makarenko developed his educational philosophy while dealing with communities of homeless and delinquent children. As a means of controlling the children, he instituted a military-type organization with uniforms and brigades. The organization permeated the life of the community with bugle calls, salutes, a system of ranks, and industrial shops organized along military lines.

The military commune reflected Makarenko's concept of the collective. Everyone had an assigned place to work for the good of the total organization, and allegiance to the group was a combination of military discipline and the fighting and nationalistic spirit represented by the modern army.

Makarenko rejected self-discipline and self-organization as a basis of group life. He believed that the group should be formed by conscious discipline because socialist society knows the kind of individual it wants the educational system to produce. "We all know perfectly well, I reasoned, what sort of human being we should aim at turning out. Every class-conscious worker knows this too. Every Party member knows it well."[13] The problem, Makarenko states, was not what was to be done but how to do it. In other words, conscious discipline was needed to mold the individual into the ideal socialist.

Makarenko compared education for a disciplined collective to the factory process. He wrote: "At any rate it was clear to me that many details of human personality and behavior could be made from dies, simply stamped out en masse, although of course the dies themselves had to be of the finest description, demanding scrupulous care and precision."[14]

Conscious disciplining of human beings for collective existence was the hallmark of Makarenko's thinking. In his popular handbook for parents he made the distinction between children treated as flowers and children treated as fruit trees. Those treated as flowers were admired and allowed to bloom in any manner. Those treated as fruit trees required that one "dig, water, get rid of the caterpillars, prune out the dead branches."[15] He reminded his readers of Stalin's words: "People should be reared with care and attention as a gardener rears his chosen fruit tree."[16] Makarenko told parents that the family must function as a collective unit to prepare the child to participate in the greater collective society: "The decisive factor in successful family upbringing lies in the constant, active, and conscious fulfillment by parents of their civic duty toward Soviet society."[17]

CONCLUSION: CHARACTERISTICS OF EDUCATION IN THE AUTHORITARIAN STATE

Makarenko's idea of disciplined collectivism represents a key element in the role of education in the authoritarian state. A common theme from the time of Plato to the present is educating citizens to sacrifice themselves for the good of the state.

Using education to train individuals to sacrifice for the common good is premised on the belief that the common good can be defined by some element of the state. In Plato's *Republic*, philosopher-kings define the common good, while in Makarenko's Soviet state the role was given to the Communist party. Of course, people must be taught to believe that the ruling group has the ability and the authority to know the common good. This type of education is aided by the use of patriotic exercises and the development of martial spirit, both of which are designed to link personal emotions to a belief in the ability of the state to proclaim the common good. In other words, people learn to love to sacrifice their self-interest for the common good as defined by the state.

Of course, the flaw in this argument is the belief that particular individuals or groups have the ability and authority to know what is good for the rest of the population. In most cases, what is defined as the common good is really what is good for the group making the definition. When the Nazi and Communist parties of the twentieth century declared their conceptions of the common good, they were, of course, definitions of the common good that supported the continued role of those parties. If a group of wealthy individuals controls the state, then they will define the common good in such a way that it supports their continued wealth. In this situation, the people are taught to love making sacrifices to support a system that guarantees the continued wealth and powers of the monied class. In fact, if properly educated, they might develop such strong emotional feelings that they are willing to die to protect the ideals established by this wealthy group, just as others have been educated to sacrifice themselves to protect a particular ruling class and its ideology.

The need of the state to develop a willingness in the population to die for the ideals of the state is closely linked to the authority of the state to define the "good person." Often authoritarian states declare the psychological characteristics of the ideal person and make the development of those psychological characteristics a goal of the educational system. Both Plato and Makarenko emphatically stated that a particular type of person should emerge from the educational system. Plato wanted a personality in which wisdom used spirit to control desires, and Makarenko wanted a socialist personality in which individual desires were inseparable from the needs of the collective. In both cases, individual personality was developed to meet the needs of the state.

As part of developing a personality that will support and love the state's definition of the common good, the authoritarian state is interested in people accepting and internalizing the laws of the state as being good and right. This involves both education about the laws of the state and the creation of a desire to want to conform to those laws. As Socrates stated, the goal is for the laws to be absorbed by people in the same manner as cloth absorbs dye. In this situation, individual actions are to be inseparable from the dictates of the law. For instance, a person might be taught that the law requires conformity to the judgments of the ruler and that the law is always good and just. In this situation, questioning the law is the same as questioning the ability of rulers to know what is good for all people.

Creating these emotional attachments to the will of the authoritarian state requires censorship and manipulation of history. The content of instruction is censored so that the information given to the student conforms to the dictates of the state. In addition, as Socrates recommended, literature is censored so that only the right moral ideals are presented to students and the teaching of history is made useful to the state. History instruction in the authoritarian state is designed to shape historical images in the minds of students that will lead them to believe in the past glory and rightness of the state and its rulers. Further, historical instruction aids in the development of patriotism and a willingness to sacrifice for the common good.

Along with developing a willingness to sacrifice for the common good, the authoritarian state uses the educational system to fit people for particular places in the social order. Students are taught to accept their assigned social positions and the differences between social classes as good and just. This means that, if an educational system determines that a person should be working at a menial, low-paid task, the individual will accept that position as good and just. That person will also accept the idea that it is good and just for other people to earn more money and do more interesting work.

Achieving this goal requires convincing people that a standard exists that can be used to judge where a person should be placed in the social order. Of course, this standard is one that guarantees that the rulers will always be shown to be the most fit to rule. In modern times, standardized tests are used to measure a person's abilities and interests as a means of determining her or his place in the social order. Of course, this requires educating people to believe that standardized tests are fair and just even though they might be designed to show the inferiority of most people to the rulers.

In summary, the authoritarian state uses educational systems to shape knowledge and emotions as a means of winning total allegiance from the people. The key to this process is teaching people to believe that the state has the ability and authority to know what is good for the people and that the state can establish standards for measuring individual worth. In the authoritarian state, people are taught to love and protect the state, its rulers, and its laws. People are educated to accept and love their place in the social order and to believe that they should sacrifice for the common good. The educational system of an authoritarian state wants to produce common citizens who are willing to die to protect the very state and social system that condemn them to a life of slavery and exploitation.

NOTES

1. *Meno* in *Great Dialogues of Plato*, trans. W. H. D. Rouse (New York: Mentor Books, 1956), pp. 43–49.
2. *The Republic* in *Great Dialogues . . .*, p. 316.
3. Ibid., p. 308.
4. Ibid., p. 186.
5. Ibid., p. 181.
6. Ibid., p. 228.
7. Adam Smith, *The Wealth of Nations* (New York: Modern Library, n.d.), pp. 735–739.
8. Ibid., pp. 734–736.
9. Karl Marx, *Capital: A Critique of Political Economy* (New York: Modern Library, 1936), p. 534.
10. Ibid.
11. Maurice Shore, *Soviet Education: Its Psychology and Philosophy* (New York: Philosophical Library, 1947), p. 129.
12. A. S. Makarenko, *The Collective Family: A Handbook for Russian Parents* (New York: Doubleday Anchor, 1967), p. 32.
13. Anton Makarenko, *The Road to Life* (Moscow: Foreign Languages Press, 1955), Vol. 3, p. 265.
14. Ibid., p. 267.
15. A. S. Makarenko, *The Collective Family: A Handbook for Russian Parents* (New York: Doubleday Anchor, 1967), p. 14.
16. Ibid.
17. Ibid.

CHAPTER 2

Educational Problems in a Democratic State

Democratic governments are faced with two major problems in establishing schools. The first is the ability of elected officials, special-interest groups, and the majority of voters to control the content of instruction. When these controls are exerted, freedom of ideas, an essential quality for a democratic school, is not possible. The second problem is identifying a source of authority that will determine what should be taught in government-operated schools. The problem for a democratic state is that individuals and groups might influence the educational system to assure that ideas supporting their political and economic interests are implanted in the minds of children. These influences over the educational system could be damaging to the exercise of democratic rights. For instance, political leaders might require that all children be taught to believe in political principles that support the continued power of the existing regime. If this education is effective, voters educated in this manner will reelect their rulers. The purpose of elections under these conditions is not the selection of rulers but an affirmation by voters of their loyalty to the existing government.

Therefore, the control of schools is an important issue in a democratic society because of the potential influence on the future political decisions of children. What people think and know influences their decisions at the ballot box. Whenever a government runs a school system, the possibility exists that elected rulers might try to perpetuate their power by influencing the knowledge and attitudes disseminated by the school system. In other words, they might use schools to indirectly control the decisions of future citizens. In addition, special-interest groups such as business and labor might try to control the educational system to ensure that future voters will elect politicians who favor their interests.

Ideally, citizens in a democratic state should be free of any outside coercion in selecting their leaders. While coercion can involve direct threats and rewards for voting for particular candidates, it can also involve influences on what voters think. At this point in time, most government schools are coercive institutions. Compulsory education laws require children to attend school, and governments mandate what will be taught to students. Students are coerced into learning particular behaviors, knowledge, and values through a system of rewards and punishments that includes academic grades, grades for behavior, and the granting of credentials.

The problem for a democratic society is limiting the coercive power of the school in determining the future political decisions of students. Amy Gutmann, whom I will discuss in the next section of this chapter, argues that this goal can be achieved by making freedom of ideas, or what she calls the nonrepression of ideas, a guiding principle of the educational system. In her philosophy of a democratic education, the principle of freedom of ideas would limit the influence of a majority of voters or special-interest groups on the minds of students. Another approach to this problem is to argue that a particular method of instruction will ensure that schools will not coerce students into adopting particular political beliefs and values. This solution, which I discuss after examining Gutmann's proposals, is best represented by the ideas of John Dewey and Henry Giroux.

The solutions offered by Amy Gutmann, John Dewey, and Henry Giroux highlight the second major problem for education in a democratic state: Who or what will be the source of authority for defining what should be taught in government-operated schools? In the authoritarian state, rulers claim knowledge of the public good as their source of authority for determining the content of instruction. At first glance, one might argue that the majority of voters in a democracy should be the authority for determining what is taught in schools. But Amy Gutmann wants to restrict the power of the majority of voters to limit free expression in schools. Dewey and Giroux want schools to implement a critical methodology that might or might not be supported by all citizens. In the final section of the chapter, I will discuss this question in the context of the issues raised by Gutmann, Dewey, and Giroux.

AMY GUTMANN: NONREPRESSION AND NONDISCRIMINATION

Amy Gutmann defines a democracy as a state in which all adult members share in the ruling of society.[1] Gutmann is concerned with both the power of the majority and the power of special-interest groups and politicians to restrict freedom of ideas and to use education to dominate others. In a democratic society it is possible that a majority of the citizens might decide to limit free thought and expression and establish laws and institutions that restrict the rights of minority groups. It is also possible for the majority of the population to decide that ideas disseminated in public schools should be carefully censored and that certain groups should be denied an education.

Gutmann is concerned about preventing this kind of abuse of power by a majority of the population. For Gutmann, two of the hallmarks of a democratic education are the protection of freedom of ideas and nondiscrimination. Her goal is to determine what political structure is needed to protect these democratic ideals. Her search for this ideal political structure begins with a consideration of four possible political models for education, which she refers to as "the family state," "the state of families," "the state of individuals," and "the democratic state."

The first model, the family state, is based on Plato's *Republic*. The basic goal of education in the family state is to unite all people and teach them to desire a common concept of the good life. Gutmann's main objection to the family state is the power of the state to define what is good—in other words, giving the power to philosopher-kings to determine the good. She argues that there is no objective definition of good and that how a person defines what is good is relative to the education received and the choices made by that individual. In other words, in her reasoning, for each individual the good life is one that is according to that individual's standards. Therefore, she rejects a political structure for education that lets the rulers of the state determine what is good and thus what should be taught to students.

The second model is what Gutmann calls the state of families, in which individual families, as opposed to the philosopher-kings in the family state, make the decisions about the best education for their children. Arguments supporting the state of families, Gutmann states, are similar to arguments given for educational choice in the 1980s and 1990s. She points out two factors that characterize these arguments: the desires to limit state power over the education of children and to gain more power for each family to pass on its way of life to its children. In the framework of this definition of choice, parents would be allowed to choose the type of schooling for their children that is compatible with individual family values.

Gutmann finds the state of families inconsistent with the ideal of a democratic education, because some families might want to pass on to their children ideals that are undemocratic. History, she argues, suggests that without state regulation families might teach children to disrespect certain people and to support restriction of their freedom of thought. She contends that, like the state, families do not have knowledge of the good and therefore should not be allowed to impose their ideal of the good life on their children. Therefore, she dismisses both the family state and the state of families as a source of democratic education.

In Gutmann's third model, the state of individuals, which is based on arguments by John Stuart Mill in *On Liberty*, education prepares children to make their own choice of the good life. This requires that education avoid imposing on children any particular concept of the good life. In addition, the educational system must give the child the ability to make choices between different concepts of the good life. The key is that the educational system remain neutral. According to Gutmann, this is impossible because values play an important role in decisions about what should be taught and how it should be taught.

Gutmann's major criticism of the state of individuals is that the ideal of free choice is a particular definition of the good life. In other words, the ideal of free choice is not a neutral concept of the good life. For instance, most religious groups would reject this concept because they advocate the imposition on children of a concept of the good life based on religious values. Other citizens might argue that other sets of values should be imposed on children. In other words, a position in favor of allowing children to choose is not in itself a neutral position. And, in an argument similar to the one used against the state of families,

Gutmann opposes giving people free choice because they might choose an education that passes on values that are contrary to the interests of a democratic state.

Since neutrality is not a possibility, Gutmann argues for a "democratic state of education," her fourth model. She contends that in the democratic state, education must be committed to "conscious social reproduction"; in other words, it must consciously seek to prepare citizens who will maintain a democratic state. This means preparing children to participate actively in the sharing of power and the shaping of society.

Of course, there is still the problem of families and individuals claiming that conscious social reproduction of particular values undermines their own values. For instance, religious and political dissenters might object to the teaching of values that are in conflict with their religious or political beliefs. Gutmann answers this objection in the framework of democratic control. She argues that democratic control allows all people the opportunity to participate in the control of the educational system and to shape that system according to their own values. The ability to participate depends on the existence of a democratic state, which, in turn, depends for its continuation on conscious social reproduction through education. Therefore, for Gutmann, conscious social reproduction through education makes it possible for the critic of the educational system to participate actively in trying to change it. Her response to the person who objects to conscious social reproduction is thus: "The kind of character you are asking us to cultivate would deprive children of that chance [to collectively shape society], the very chance that legitimates your own claim to educational authority."[2]

Therefore, the source of authority for an educational system in a democratic state is the democratic process itself. Gutmann rejects majority rule, the philosopher-king, the family, and the individual as sources of truth for shaping a democratic education. But, of course, her argument raises the issue that some person or group must define the educational requirements for maintaining a democracy.

Interestingly, Gutmann does not propose that all people participate in deciding the educational requirements for democracy. Her fear is that majority control might restrict freedom of thought and promote discrimination. In the end, with support from other philosophers whom she cites, Gutmann defines the basic requirements for a democratic education as nonrepression and nondiscrimination.

Basic to democracy, she argues, is the capacity to deliberate among alternative concepts of the good life. Simply stated, a democratic educational system allows and enhances the ability of future citizens to consider alternative ways of personal and political life. In this context, the principle of nonrepression means that a democratic educational system will not repress students' consideration of different concepts of the good life. A democratic education must preserve freedom of thought.

The second principle, nondiscrimination, places some limits on freedom of choice. She argues that educators have the authority to teach children racial, ethnic, and religious tolerance because "these virtues . . . constitute the kind of character necessary to create a society committed to conscious social reproduction."[3] In other words, allowing consideration of alternative concepts of the good life does not mean that education remains neutral. Rather, it is based on certain values that are to be transmitted by the schools. According to Gutmann, a democratic education should not only avoid discrimination but should also teach values that reduce discrimination in the rest of society.

For Gutmann, then, nonrepression and nondiscrimination are limits to be placed on democratic authority over education. In other words, control by the majority and the influence of special-interest groups are limited by these two principles. Democratic control is not allowed to interfere with students' consideration of different versions of the good life, nor is it allowed to use the educational system to discriminate against a particular group of people.

Of course, most existing states that claim to be democratic do not operate on the principle of nonrepression. In the United States, educational authorities have shown little concern about repression of discussion and little support for freedom of ideas about alternative modes of the good life. In fact, freedom of thought has never been a governing principle of the educational system. Often, majority rule results in the censorship of classroom material and the teaching of values representing only one definition of the good life. When special-interest groups disagree, they pressure schools to ensure that their values regarding the good life become part of the curriculum.

Therefore, the problem for Gutmann is creating a political structure for education that allows democratic control but limits the authority of the state to repress freedom of ideas and to discriminate against any particular group of people. The major problem in establishing a democratic educational system is to safeguard the principle of nonrepression. Nondiscrimination is not the same kind of problem since it is protected by the U.S. Constitution. How do you keep people from destroying the principle of nonrepression in a democratic education? Gutmann's answer is teachers. Teachers, she argues, must be governed by "democratic professionalism." She writes, "The professional responsibility is to uphold the principle of nonrepression by cultivating the capacity for democratic deliberation."[4] In addition, she maintains, the principle of nonrepression should be the guiding principle of teachers' unions. In the framework of democratic professionalism, teachers would ensure that students discuss alternatives to the good life.

There are two problems with Gutmann's reasoning: establishing the authority for imposing nonrepression and nondiscrimination as the basic principles of a democratic education, and relying on teachers' professionalism to maintain nonrepression in the schools. Her source of authority for the principles of nonrepression and nondiscrimination seems to be herself and other political philosophers. She does not claim that these principles were decided by democratic vote or that they have been proven necessary in some type of social experiment. The only support she claims for her position is found in footnotes to her writings citing other writers on politics and education. In this context, she gives herself as much claim to knowing truth as the philosopher-kings in *The Republic*.

In addition, it is difficult to imagine a situation where all teachers agree that democratic professionalism involves the protection of nonrepression. But without such agreement, it is possible that only teachers with certain values would be recruited into teaching and that teachers would become the arbiters of the meaning of nonrepression. Unfortunately, Gutmann does not suggest a political structure that would truly protect the principle of nonrepression from majority rule and the influence of special interests.

But even with these problems in Gutmann's reasoning, her ideals of nonrepression and nondiscrimination are important for a democratic society that requires all citizens to be able to deliberate about political issues. Both John Dewey and Henry Giroux would agree with Gutmann's emphasis on the need for nonrepression. Each suggests classroom methods for developing citizens who will be able to participate critically in democratic deliberations. But, like Gutmann, they do not suggest any viable political structure for assuring that schools adhere to educational methods that produce a critical citizenry. In addition, neither Dewey or Giroux has an answer to the dilemma of schools imposing a form of critical thinking on those people who do not want this type of education. It is the dilemma faced by Gutmann when she proposes maintaining the principle of nonrepression even if some students and parents object.

JOHN DEWEY: EDUCATING DEMOCRATIC CITIZENS

Writing most of his educational works in the late nineteenth and early twentieth centuries, John Dewey struggled with some of the same issues discussed in Chapter 1 regarding Adam Smith and Karl Marx. All three were concerned with the negative effects on workers of the modern industrial system. Dewey wanted to resolve these industrial issues within the context of a democratic political system. He believed a democratic society provided the conditions for the type of critical thinking required for the progress of civilization. Like Gutmann, Dewey argues in a somewhat circular fashion. Within Dewey's framework of thought, critical thinking is necessary for the survival of a democratic society and a democratic society is necessary for the exercise of his form of critical thinking.

Dewey advocated increasing the role of schools to deal with the effects of industrialization and urbanization. Dewey wanted the school to become the new social center of urban industrial society. He believed that the specialization of industry and the growth of large urban centers destroyed a sense of community and alienated people from one another. To counter these trends, he wanted the school to serve as a social center that would knit together the urban community by providing space for community gatherings, creating a sense of interdependence, and building a spirit of cooperation.[5]

His advocacy of an increased role for schooling reflects his belief that the survival of democracy and civilization are dependent on teaching a particular form of critical thinking and on building a spirit of cooperation. Influenced by evolutionary theory, Dewey believed it was necessary for the school to change and adapt to modern urban industrial conditions. This adaptation, according to Dewey, required a stronger role for the school in the control of the distribution of ideas and in the shaping of behavior.

Dewey's concept of critical thinking is rooted in the concept of the social construction of knowledge, as opposed to the Socratic concept that knowledge is a reflection of some ideal form or created by a divine being. For instance, Socrates would argue that arithmetic is a reflection of some ideal system of numbers and the purpose of studying arithmetic, besides its practical value, is to lead the learner to an understanding of some form of ultimate truth. Dewey, on the other hand, would argue that arithmetic developed because humans needed to solve particular types of problems. In other words, arithmetic, for Dewey, was not derived from some ideal form but was created through social interaction.

For instance, in the Socratic dialogue *Meno* discussed in Chapter 1, the young boy learned the diagonal of the square by being asked a series of questions. The assumption is that truth is in the individual and that to see it only requires turning the eyes in that direction. In the Dewey school, however, learning to count is tied to a concrete social situation. Young children are asked to set the table for a midmorning snack. In order to do this, the children have to count the number of students and then the number of spoons to be placed on the table. In the process, students learn that counting originated out of social necessity and that it serves a socially useful function.[6]

Religious groups might object to Dewey's arguments regarding the social construction of knowledge because it challenges the idea of a god as the source of truth. Throughout the twentieth century, religious groups, particularly fundamentalists, have objected to the idea of moral values being socially constructed. For these groups, moral values are created by a god and remain immutable through time. Dewey, on the other hand, argues that moral values are a product of particular social situations. Moral systems develop because society needs some method of regulating behavior to maintain social order.

The difference between Dewey and religious groups over the origin of moral values highlights a central aspect of his form of critical thinking. For religious groups, moral values established by a god are immutable and humans should not attempt to change them. For Dewey, since moral values serve a particular social function, they should be changed or abandoned when they no longer serve that function. The value of any changes in or additions to moral values should be determined by their ability to achieve a particular objective. For instance, if the concern is to decrease crime rates, then existing moral values should be tested as to their effectiveness in preventing crime. If it is found that existing moral values are not preventing crime and new moral values are required, then the new moral values should be tested regarding their ability to reduce crime.

Therefore, the form of critical thinking Dewey argues is necessary for a democracy involves an understanding of the social construction of knowledge and the ability to test and judge the value of new forms of knowledge. Consequently, history is at the heart of Dewey's instructional methodology. It is through the study of history that students learn how and why knowledge and institutions were created.

Dewey wants history to be integrated into the teaching of all subjects. He objects to teaching young children subject matter, including science, in a form organized by contemporary adults. He wants subject matter to be tied to a particular social problem. For instance, young children might be interested in the topic of milk. A Deweyian instructor might guide the children in investigating the history and evolution of human use of milk, the chemistry of milk, agricultural practices used in producing milk, the value of milk, the treatment used to sterilize milk, and the distribution of milk to consumers. In the process of this study, students would learn history, chemistry, arithmetic, economics, sociology, agriculture, and biology. All of the knowledge learned in these disciplines would be tied to a particular social situation. In addition, students would learn why humans changed their methods of production and distribution of milk as they learned more about biology and health issues.

Another important element in the Dewey method is basing instruction on the interests of the child. Dewey believes that learning is a product of individual interest. In addition, he wants to educate self-motivated people who would actively pursue knowledge and work for beneficial social change in a democratic society. For instance, the above example of the study of milk would originate in an expression of interest by the students in this topic.

Other aspects of Dewey's methods are related to concerns about the effects of urban industrial society. Dewey believes modern industry requires cooperation among workers and cooperation in solving economic and social problems. Consequently, Dewey made a big show of eliminating individual desks from the classroom and replacing them with tables for group work. Unlike Makarenko, who advocated disciplined collectivism (as discussed in Chapter 1), Dewey wants the spirit of cooperation to be developed through group work in the classroom.

Another method Dewey advocates for developing a spirit of cooperation is to encourage students to understand the interdependence of society. Like Adam Smith and Karl Marx, Dewey believes specialization in the factory had negative effects on workers. He argues that factory workers were alienated from their work because they did only one specialized task in the manufacturing process, such as operating a machine that puts heels on shoes. This repetitious and specialized labor did not give the worker the same feeling of accomplishment that could be gained from making the whole product. In addition, factory workers had little understanding of the social usefulness of their labor. In contrast, the old-time shoemaker made the whole shoe and saw customers wear the shoes. The old-time shoemaker gained satisfaction from making the whole product and could witness the social value of his work by seeing others use his products.

According to Dewey, the teaching of interdependence is supposed to heighten understanding of the social usefulness of work. Even if workers only put heels on shoes, they would have a knowledge of the social usefulness of their labor, gained through understanding the interdependence of society. Learning about the social construction of knowledge is supposed to convey to students a knowledge of the interdependence of society. This is also to be accomplished through group work in the classroom.

Dewey also believes that in industrialized societies factory workers experience a separation between thought and action. Factory workers operate machines but do not know or think about the theory behind their actions. In this situation, according to Dewey, workers experience a fragmentation of their power, becoming appendages of a factory machine rather than controlling and giving direction to the machine. Dewey writes in *Democracy and Education* that the separation of liberal education from industrial and professional education is a result "of a division of classes into those who had to labor for a living and those who were relieved from this necessity." Workers, he argues, have no insight into the social aims of their work, and consequently the "results actually achieved are not the ends of their actions, but only of their employers."[7]

Therefore, the citizens in Dewey's ideal democratic society both understand the social usefulness of their work and are able to relate theory to practice. In addition, they understand that knowledge and institutions are products of particular social conditions and needs, and they are willing to change when ideas and institutions become outmoded. Citizens in Dewey's democracy cooperate in testing new ideas and institutions to determine their value to the progress of civilization.

From Dewey's perspective, democracy is necessary for the advance of civilization because it allows for this type of critical thinking. If individuals are not willing to adapt their ideas and institutions to new social and environmental conditions, then, according to Dewey's reasoning, humanity faces the possibility of stagnation or extinction.

On the reverse side of the argument, the continued existence of democracy, according to Dewey, depends on citizens being critical thinkers. Without an understanding of social and economic conditions and how to change them, the average citizen faces the possibility of eventual slavery to an economic elite. The continued existence of democracy, Dewey argues, depends on a citizenry that actively participates in the construction and reconstruction of society. Therefore, Dewey's proposed form of education is necessary for the continuation of democracy and the progress of civilization.

In the end, Dewey faces the same problems as Gutmann: How do you ensure, in a democratically controlled school system, that a particular—in this case Dewey's—method prevails? One could argue that a person educated according to Deweyian methods would support only an educational system that educates other children by the same method. But this does not answer the question of how to organize the political structure of education to ensure that Dewey's methodology is used in all public schools.

There is also the issue of the source of truth. How do we know that Dewey is correct? Dewey seems to think he derived the truth through his reasoning about history and society. Does this mean that Dewey is the source of truth? Or does it mean that philosophers are the source of truth? Dewey would probably respond that truth is relative to a given social situation. If his ideas work, then they should be used. If they are no longer viable, then they should be discarded. In this case, the decision might be made by a democratic majority or by implementing findings of experiments conducted by social scientists.

Another problem is that of imposition. A weakness in Gutmann's arguments is that the educational system she advocates can force people who do not believe schools should promote consideration of alternative definitions of the good life to be educated in institutions that practice nonrepression. In the context of Dewey's thought, it hardly seems democratic to force students to learn a method to which they might object. What about people who believe that a god is the source of truth? Are they to be forced into educational institutions that teach a method of critical thinking that is in opposition to that belief? Implied in Gutmann's and Dewey's arguments is the idea that the school must be authoritarian in demanding a certain type of education in order to maintain a democratic state.

HENRY GIROUX: CRITICAL PEDAGOGY

In the 1980s and 1990s, Henry Giroux expanded on Dewey's concepts of critical thinking and democracy. Like Dewey, Giroux believes that knowledge originates in social interaction. In addition, Giroux goes beyond Dewey in his argument that social relationships must be understood in the context of power. Knowledge and institutions are created to solve social problems, but the type of solution is dependent on who has the most power. For instance, slavery might be considered a product of a desire by Europeans to cultivate agricultural products in North and South America. Of course, this analysis of the social construction of slavery is trivial when compared to the human suffering and inequality that resulted from slavery. The only true way of understanding the social construction of slavery, Giroux would argue, is in the fact that Europeans had the power to enforce a system of slavery. For many Europeans, slavery became a legitimate way of developing North and South America. In addition, Europeans developed theories of racial inferiority to justify the enslavement of Africans and Native Americans. Therefore, within this framework of thought, the historical origins of theories of racial inferiority must be understood as resulting from relations of power.

For Giroux, the primary task of education is to help students understand the social construction of knowledge in the framework of power. The method of achieving this goal is critical pedagogy. The final aim of the process is the empowerment of the student and ultimately the empowerment of all citizens. Empowerment, in Giroux's words, means "the process whereby students acquire the means to critically appropriate knowledge existing outside their immediate experience in order to broaden their understanding of themselves, the world, and the possibilities for transforming the taken-for-granted assumptions about the way we live."[8] In other words, students are empowered when they gain the knowledge and critical understanding required to improve the social and economic conditions of the world. At the heart of empowerment is the search for methods of eliminating social injustice and decreasing inequalities in power.

Of course, a consideration of power relations is crucial for a democratic state that claims to share power with all people. Inequalities in power occur because of differences in wealth, social status, occupation, gender, and race. In a democratic society, these differences can give some people more power than others in influencing political decisions. Certainly, wealth provides greater access to political candidates and provides greater opportunity for influencing legislation. Anyone looking at a picture of the U.S. Senate might conclude that being a white male improves a person's ability to become a senator.

For Giroux, critical pedagogy gives people the ability to participate in a democratic state and the tools to equalize the distribution of power. Also, a democratic state is necessary for the exercise of critical thinking. Therefore, in reasoning similar to Dewey's, Giroux argues that there is a close interdependence between critical thinking and the democratic state. Simply stated, one cannot exist without the other.

Giroux's concept of democracy extends to all spheres of life. He argues that not only government but schools, corporations, and other institutions should be sites of democratic struggle. Teachers, students, workers, parents—all citizens— should struggle in all institutions that affect their lives to eliminate inequalities in power and human injustice.

In this context, the school, as a site of democratic struggle, should be shaped by attempts to promote justice and eliminate inequality of power. Critical pedagogy is a method that prepares all citizens for participation in the democratic state and prepares students to participate in this democratic struggle within the school and in other public spheres of life. In other words, critical pedagogy is both a method for maintaining a democratic state and the means by which the school becomes a democratic public institution.

As an instructional method, critical pedagogy gives a voice to all participants. In general, the goal is to help people understand why they think the way they do. That is, the method helps people understand how the social construction of knowledge determines what people believe is true and how they interpret their surrounding world. For instance, consider the preceding example of the development of theories of racial inferiority in order to justify slavery. People might grow up believing these theories are true and act according to these beliefs. Without questioning these beliefs, people might operate on unquestioned assumptions that cause inequality between races. Critical pedagogy would let people give voice to their beliefs, whatever their source, and then engage in a dialogue about the origins of these racist theories. A possible result of such critical dialogue would be an understanding that those beliefs originated in a justification by those with power of European acts of slavery.

The importance of providing a voice for all people is illustrated in a classroom situation described by Giroux. The example is meant to illustrate his concern about teachers who ignore student voices that they feel are not politically correct. In his example, a middle-class teacher is horrified at the sexism of male students. The teacher tries to correct this situation by showing feminist films and distributing feminist literature.[9]

In this situation, Giroux argues, male students react with scorn and resist being converted to the feminist viewpoint. The concept of resistance is important to Giroux's theory of critical pedagogy. For Giroux, people are not passive. They cannot be easily manipulated. He argues that people do resist their own exploitation. But resistance may not be a positive act. For instance, students from low-income families may believe that schools are not operating for their benefit. Consequently, they resist schooling by creating an oppositional culture that openly defies school authorities through vandalism, disrupting the classroom, and rejecting all forms of learning. Obviously, this form of resistance is not, in the long run, necessarily beneficial to the student. For instance, doing poorly in school might condemn a student from an impoverished family to a life of continued poverty. And, of course, these students greet with open hostility and scorn any attempts to lecture them on the value of schooling. From the standpoint of critical theory, the oppositional culture of students must be taken as legitimate and students must be given an opportunity to voice their ideas on schooling. In a critical dialogue there would be a search for why students think and act the way they do about schools. If this search for meaning is between students and teachers, then teachers must also reveal the sources of their own beliefs about schooling and students. There is no assumption in the dialogue between the two groups that either has the correct vision of what is wrong and what should change. From the dialogue between students and teachers there might emerge methods for changing schools, as well as for changing teachers' and students' attitudes toward equalizing student participation in school.

In the example of sexism in the classroom, Giroux argues that the feminist teacher's initial failure was in assuming the self-evident correctness of her political position and, consequently, assuming an authoritative role and dictating to students what she viewed as the correct attitude. This denied students the opportunity to explore their own experiences and to investigate their own feelings about sexual equality. Thus, the real message sent to students by the teacher in the example is that school is a place where teachers attempt to impose values on students. Such dictating of politically correct values about sexism only increases student resistance to the school's attempt to impose these values. On the other hand, Giroux argues, a real dialogue in which students' views are taken as legitimate expressions of experience breaks down resistance. The dialogue should lead to an understanding by both students and teachers of the origins of their beliefs about sexism and to attempts to deal with the problem.

An important part of this type of dialogue involves what Giroux calls the language of possibilities. Advocates of critical pedagogy are very interested in language and discourse. Language provides the tools for naming the world, thinking, and framing interpretations of experience. Similar to knowledge in general, language is socially constructed in the context of power relations. If, for instance, the term "culturally disadvantaged" is used to describe African Americans, Puerto Ricans, and other dominated groups in the United States, then one might think that these groups are either without a culture or that their culture is inferior to other cultures in some ways. People, including those to whom the term is applied, might incorporate the term into their thinking and speech. The result would be a marginalization of those groups. If "culturally disadvantaged" becomes part of the discourse of African Americans, they might internalize a belief in their inferiority and include this belief in conversations with others. Critical pedagogy applied to this situation would result in a dialogue about the origins of the term "culturally disadvantaged" and the power relationships implied in the term. For instance, consider the difference in meaning between "culturally disadvantaged" and "dominated cultures." "Dominated cultures" refers to those racial and ethnic groups that were forced to submit to the government of the United States, such as African slaves, Native Americans, Puerto Ricans, and Mexican Americans who lived in the Southwest at the time the United States took over this territory from Mexico. The use of "dominated cultures," as opposed to "culturally disadvantaged," thus conveys a different meaning and frames discussions in a different way.

The same issue is involved in Giroux's use of the term "language of possibilities." He would argue that our language inherently conveys the sense that people are passively manipulated by power and have little power to improve the human condition. But intentional use of the "language of possibilities" would frame discussions to emphasize that social change is a product of human action and to empower people to see themselves as being able to change the course of history. The language of possibilities would provide a basis for discourse that would lead people to understand their power to limit inequalities in the distribution of power through democratic struggle.

Just as Gutmann placed responsibility on the teacher for protection of nonrepression in the classroom, Giroux places responsibility on the teacher for the implementation of critical pedagogy. Rather than acting as technicians carrying out a preplanned curriculum, Giroux argues, teachers should be transformative intellectuals who engage their students in critical dialogues. He argues also that teacher-training institutions should be in the business of conducting critical dialogues with future teachers to prepare them for entering the classroom.

Of course, the training and role of the teacher must be considered in the context of Giroux's concept of democracy. Democracy, as he uses the term, must be a part of daily life. For Giroux, democracy is the quest to reconstruct in a way that provides greater equality of power. Consequently, teachers must engage in democratic struggles within all public spheres in which they are active—in teacher-training institutions, teachers' unions, professional organizations, and the school and classroom.

Like Gutmann's and Dewey's theories, Giroux's theories also can be criticized for imposing a value system—in this case, critical pedagogy—on students who might not want to adopt that style of thinking. The objections might come most strongly from those religious groups I noted earlier in this chapter, who believe that a god has proclaimed the correct way to live. For the same reasons that these groups might object to Gutmann's principle of nonrepression of thinking about alternatives to the good life and to Dewey's belief that truth and knowledge are products of social relationships, they would raise similar objections to critical pedagogy.

Giroux dismisses the charge of imposition as a "theoretically flawed position that represents nothing less than a flight from serious politics and an apology for the status quo." "Serious politics" in this case means "changing those forms of economic and political power that promote human suffering and exploitation."[10] In other words, he is saying that opposition to critical pedagogy as an imposition is a political position that supports the continued inequalities in power. For instance, if Baptists object to critical pedagogy because it questions the authority of God, then Giroux might argue that their religious beliefs are maintaining the status quo and hindering attempts to end exploitation and human suffering. Of course, this assumes that religious objections are rooted in maintaining inequalities as opposed to being based on deeply held and possibly true religious beliefs.

In addition, Giroux argues that critical pedagogy does not involve imposition since everyone is given a voice. For instance, all of our hypothetical religious groups would have an equal right to express their ideas and beliefs in any critical dialogue. But since these religious groups might not believe in the social construction of knowledge, they might not believe in the basic premises of a critical dialogue. Therefore, according to critical theory, even if they were given a voice, it would be necessary to impose the methodology of critical pedagogy on the dialogue taking place. Logically, it would seem, the only way to say that critical pedagogy is not being imposed on groups who may not accept it for religious reasons is to assert that these religious beliefs are not valid and should be open for critical examination.

Of course, this raises the issue of who should have the power to decide the validity of either critical pedagogy or religious beliefs. Indeed, who should decide that critical pedagogy is the best method of eradicating inequalities? Historically, other ideologies have also proclaimed methods of reducing inequalities in society. Who should decide which methodology—be it a socialist revolution or critical pedagogy—is the best road to a democratic society? Despite Giroux's claims, critical pedagogy does contain a set of beliefs about the origins of human action and knowledge that are contrary to beliefs held by others. Requiring students to participate in critical pedagogy is an imposition of a particular set of beliefs. Indeed, there is always the possibility that critical pedagogy is wrong in both its assumptions and its methods.

CONCLUSION: THE PROBLEMS OF EDUCATION IN THE DEMOCRATIC STATE

This analysis of Gutmann, Dewey, and Giroux highlights the major problems raised by the existence of government-operated schools in a democratic state. Because education can influence the political decisions people make, there is the danger that politicians, special-interest groups, or a majority of citizens might try to use the school system to influence future political decisions made by students when they become voting citizens later in life. In this sense, schools can be a means of political control. On the other hand, knowledge and thinking skills are important aids in making good political decisions in a democratic society.

The central question is this: How can a school system in a democratic state be constructed to ensure that it is not used to control the political decisions of citizens and, at the same time, ensure that it does provide citizens with the knowledge and skills they need in order to make good decisions?

Gutmann, Dewey, and Giroux all answer this question by arguing for principles and methods that limit democratic authority over the school. The problem is that, although the decision to use these principles and methods might be democratically decided, they still place constraints on what is taught in schools in democratic states. In other words, the democratic decision-making process itself is limited. For example, Gutmann would argue that democratic decision making should be limited by the principle of nonrepression. Operating on the principle of nonrepression, schools, no matter what is decided regarding the content taught, would still promote and allow the consideration of alternatives to the good life. This principle, according to Gutmann, would ensure the maintenance of freedom of ideas, and it would ensure that no fixed idea of either the good or the truth would dominate the classroom. This would limit the possibility of using the school to control political decisions. Dewey and Giroux argue that their methods ensure that any subject matter will prepare students for making decisions in a democratic state. In this case, a democratically determined curriculum would not serve the interests of any particular group of citizens, because the methodology of instruction will ensure that any content serves the purposes of democracy. And according to Dewey and Giroux, once citizens exercise critical thinking a democratically determined curriculum will be truly democratic.

These ideas raise the question: What is the source of authority for deciding that the principle of nonrepression should govern a school system or that a particular methodology should govern instruction?

Gutmann would not allow the democratic process to decide that nonrepression should govern schools. In fact, she specifically wants to protect the principle of nonrepression from any interference by a democratic majority. Her only source of authority for the establishment of the principle of nonrepression appears to be herself and other philosophers. The same is true of the critical methodologies proposed by Dewey and Giroux. In addition, they might argue that once citizens adopt their proposed methods of critical thinking they would then democratically support the use of those methods in schools.

These issues bring us back to the discussion of education in an authoritarian state. In many ways, Gutmann, Dewey, and Giroux are philosopher-kings announcing the truth that should govern the educational system. Personally, I like the ideas of nonrepression and the promotion of freedom of thought in a democratic state. But others might argue that schools in a democratic state must educate citizens according to a prescribed morality and teach obedience to laws decided upon by the majority. The problem is this: How does a democratic state decide which argument is correct? How does a democratic state decide which methods will be best for democracy? For example, how does a democratic state decide that Giroux's methods may be best for reducing inequality in the distribution of power? What happens if Giroux is wrong? What if there are better methods of accomplishing the same goals?

This discussion leads to the central question: Who or what should be the source of authority in a democratic state regarding methods and content of instruction?

The answer to this question requires that we consider the issue of imposition. Throughout this chapter I have discussed the possible objections of religious groups to instruction based on nonrepression and on the methodologies of Dewey and Giroux. Gutmann, Dewey, and Giroux might respond that their principles and methodologies allow for the expression of religious views in the democratic process and that therefore they support the concept of religious pluralism. However, these arguments lead to a contradiction, because they completely neglect the fact that the principle of nonrepression and the proposed critical methodologies are not neutral with regard to religious values. Many religious people believe that there is one correct definition of the good life, and they do not want their children to consider others. Most religions believe that a god, not human beings, is the source of knowledge and truth. The only way of accepting the principle of nonrepression and the critical methodologies of Dewey and Giroux as components of a government school system in a democratic state is to reject the basic principles that govern most religions. Again, it can be asked: Where is the source of authority for imposing ideas on students in government-operated schools that might be contrary to their religious beliefs? What democratic power do religious groups have to educate their children in their own beliefs?

We are left with the question: Should a government-operated school system in a democratic state impose particular values, methods of instruction, and curricula on citizens?

NOTES

1. Amy Gutmann's major work is *Democratic Education* (Princeton: Princeton University Press, 1987).
2. Ibid., p. 39.
3. Ibid., p. 40.
4. Ibid., p. 76.
5. John Dewey, "The School as Social Center," *National Education Association Proceedings 1902* (Ann Arbor, Mich.: NEA, 1902), pp. 373–383.
6. For a description of the activities of the Dewey School, see Katherine Camp Mayhew and Anna Camp Edwards, *The Dewey Schools: The Laboratory School of the University of Chicago 1896–1903* (New York: D. Appleton-Century, 1936).
7. John Dewey, *Democracy and Education* (New York: The Free Press, 1966), pp. 250–261.
8. Henry A. Giroux, *Schooling and the Struggle for Public Life: Critical Pedagogy in the Modern Age* (Minneapolis: The University of Minnesota Press, 1988), p. 189.
9. Ibid., pp. 164–165.
10. Ibid., p. 68.

PART TWO

Dissenting Traditions in Education

CHAPTER 3

Traditions of Dissent to Government Education

Many people have criticized the authoritarian state for using schools to teach future citizens to love and protect the state, its rulers, and its laws. An important point of criticism is the ability of government schools to convince students that the state has the competence and authority to know what is good for all people. In addition, critics object to instruction which convinces citizens that they have a duty to sacrifice their needs and desires for the common good. Critics of education in the democratic state wonder if government-operated schools should impose particular values, methods of instruction, and knowledge on future citizens. Ideally, in a democratic state, political choices are made without coercion. However, imposition of ideas in government-operated schools can have a coercive influence on the future political decisions of students. Therefore, in both the authoritarian and democratic states, there exists the potential for government-operated schools to be used to control the population by shaping the ideas and values of citizens.

Concern about government-operated schools limiting freedom of thought and creating uniformity of ideas began as early as the seventeenth and eighteenth centuries. Inspired by the scientific revolution, some people began to argue that freedom of thought was essential for the development of science and, consequently, for the material advancement of society. For instance, political philosopher William Godwin rejected government-operated schools because of the potential of government officials to use schools to perpetuate their political power. And Max Stirner expressed concern that any form of education might result in the planting of controlling ideas, or wheels in the head, in the minds of citizens. Nineteenth-century liberals, such as John Stuart Mill, wondered if government schools were a new form of political despotism.

ROBERT MOLESWORTH AND *CATO'S LETTERS*: FREEDOM, OBEDIENCE, AND SCIENCE

Early libertarian writers were concerned that state education could be used as a means for gaining the obedience of citizens and limiting freedom of thought. Written in the seventeenth century, Robert Molesworth's *An Account of Denmark as It Was in the Year 1692* examines the role of education in making citizens obedient to the state. In Denmark, Molesworth found, citizens were made obedient to the state through schools operated by a state-supported religion. Using logic similar to Plato's justification of philosopher-kings in *The Republic*, religious leaders in Denmark argued that the rulers were inspired by God and, consequently, had access to the truth. Therefore, religious groups could preach a doctrine of submission and obedience to both heavenly and earthly rulers. Molesworth writes that the rulers considered that it was in their interest to have the absolute obedience of their citizens and that this could be gained by enslaving people's spirits. Since religious leaders depended on the rulers for support, Molesworth claims, they too backed the idea of gaining the absolute obedience of citizens. According to this argument, since education was a function of the state and operated by religious orders, then one of the primary goals of the schools was teaching absolute obedience.

Molesworth writes that the combination of state and religious governance of education resulted in the frequent recommendation that students submit to "the Queen of Virtues, Viz. Submission to Superiors, and an entire blind Obedience to Authority."[1] Molesworth also claims that the educational system causes people to forget that government is a product of human action—not divine intervention. By making government appear divine in origin, religiously controlled education can teach obedience to government as if it were obedience to divine authority. Such education taught "that the people ought to pay an Absolute Obedience to a limited Government; fall down and worship the Work of their own Hands, as if it dropt from Heaven."[2]

Molesworth clearly recognizes that the authoritarian state can maintain power by claiming access through religion to some form of higher truth. He believes that, in order for education to contribute to liberty and freedom, it must be separated from religion. He calls for the professor to replace the priest and for education to be free of religious dogma in service to the state.

Molesworth's study contributed to a general discussion of freedom with his two friends John Trenchard and Thomas Gordon. These discussions resulted in a broad defense of freedom of ideas and learning. Trenchard and Gordon's essays were distributed between 1720 and 1723 as *Cato's Letters* and were reprinted many times during the subsequent twenty-five years. Their essays, which are considered a primary source for the justification of the American Revolution, provided topics for endless political discussion in public houses on both sides of the Atlantic Ocean.[3]

The essays place the issue of freedom of thought in the context of the progress of civilization. In making the link between social progress and freedom, the *Letters* state that a country needs freedom because without it there can be no growth in human wisdom and invention and, consequently, no progress in economic development. In the *Letters*, freedom of thought and speech is declared a right that should be abridged only to protect the freedom of others: "Without Freedom there can be no such Thing as Wisdom; and no such Thing as public Liberty, without Freedom of Speech: Which is the Right of every Man, as far as by it he does not hurt and control the Right of another." This one limitation on freedom, Trenchard and Gordon declared, "is the only Check which it ought to suffer, the only Bounds which it ought to know."[4]

In linking freedom of thought and speech to human progress, the authors argue that humans in their original state of nature contented themselves with "the Spontaneous Productions of Nature," but these "spontaneous" supplies proved insufficient to support increasing numbers of humans. Consequently, humans began to apply their minds to developing better methods of production. The result was differing degrees of prosperity between nations because of different levels of advancement in the state of learning, which allowed more advanced nations to enjoy greater productivity. Wisdom and art, Gordon and Trenchard argue, promote prosperity, which in turn provides full employment, economic well-being, and a general elevation of the spirit and culture of a people. If advancement of wisdom and learning fails to occur, unemployment will come and result in human misery.[5]

The equation made in *Cato's Letters* between freedom of ideas and the good life is this: Freedom of thought and speech promotes wisdom, which in turn provides the basis of prosperity and the elimination of the crime that arises from hunger and poverty. Within the framework of this argument, tyranny must be avoided because it hinders the growth of wisdom, prosperity, and social happiness.

Taken together, Molesworth's arguments and *Cato's Letters* provide a defense of free thought and speech in the context of the survival of civilization. The authors fear that if religious groups and the state demand absolute obedience and limit freedom of thought, a nation's ability to feed, clothe, and house its people will decrease. In the framework of these arguments, if education took place in an environment free of ideological restraints, particularly those of religion, it would be the source of material benefits for society.

From Molesworth's perspective, schools operated by religious groups would clearly place ideological restraints on education. On the other hand, it is still necessary to ask whether or not a secular education administered by the state, even if it does not have ties to religion, can be free of ideological restraints.

In the eighteenth century, this question was taken up by a group of English political thinkers, scientists, inventors, and early industrialists who placed their faith in the beneficence of science and industrial progress. Called the Commonwealth men, they included Matthew Boulton, James Watt, Erasmus Darwin, Samuel Galton, and Joseph Priestly. They objected to government-provided systems of education as a threat to intellectual freedom. English historian Brian Simon writes about Joseph Priestly and this group of intellectuals: "In common with . . . all other dissenters, Priestly was adamantly opposed to education becoming a function of the state. Should it do so, it would not achieve the object he desired, on the contrary, it would be used to promote uniformity of thought and belief."[6] Priestly used concrete examples to prove the negative effects of government-controlled schools, including attempts of Oxford University to discourage the reading of John Locke's *Essay on Human Understanding*.

Priestly believed that any group that gained control of the educational system could greatly increase its power over the rest of society. He argued that education should encourage free inquiry and inspire the love of truth and that state-endowed education would be more committed to instilling a particular set of religious, moral, or political principles than to training the mind for the free use of reason.

Historian Caroline Robbins summarizes Priestly's ideas: "The chief glory of human nature, the operation of reason in a variety of ways and with diversified results, would be lost. Every man should educate his children in his own manner to preserve the balance which existed among the several religious and political parties in Great Britain."[7]

Priestly's arguments touch on several points made by Amy Gutmann. From Priestly's standpoint, the protection of nonrepression or freedom of thought is not possible in a government-operated school system because political leaders want to impose their own educational agendas. For Priestly, it would be hard to imagine a government not trying to fulfill its policies through its own school system. Of course, one could argue, as Amy Gutmann does, that nonrepression could be government policy.

Thus, Amy Gutmann would object to Priestly's proposal for a "state of families" in which parents educate their children according to their beliefs. She would argue that family control could result in parents educating children in undemocratic values and the possible repression of freedom of thought. On the other hand, Priestly believed that diversity is necessary for freedom of thought. He advocates that children be educated in a variety of political and religious traditions. It is these differences that provide the basis for a meaningful free exchange of ideas. In other words, from Priestly's perspective, there is no meaningful freedom of thought if everyone thinks the same things.

It is important to note Priestly's possible objection to Gutmann's dismissal of the family as the source of educational authority. Priestly doesn't care if parents educate children to accept a particular set of religious and political values as long as not everyone is educated into the same set of values. According to this argument, the issue of freedom of thought is an issue for education only when government education represses freedom of thought in order to create uniformity of thought among citizens. It is, rather, an issue for the political functioning of society. This can be stated another way: Priestly accepts the right of people not to believe in freedom of thought and to educate their children in that belief, but he also believes the political system should allow freedom of thought and speech, which, in turn, would allow some people to argue against freedom of thought. In this context, people should be free to speak and think whatever they want. Diversity of ideas would make this freedom meaningful.

Thus, these early libertarians, suspicious of state-operated schools, were rooted in a belief in the importance of freedom of thought and speech to the advancement of civilization. State-operated education, in their minds, would hinder these freedoms by teaching according to a political agenda and creating uniformity of thought.

WILLIAM GODWIN: LEARNING TO LOVE UNJUST LAWS

For some early libertarian-anarchists, freedom of thought and speech was important for establishing and maintaining equality of political power among citizens. Within this framework, tyranny contributes to human unhappiness by continuously threatening physical harm and crushing human desires. The combination of arguments for freedom as necessary to the advancement of civilization through science and as necessary to human happiness provided a strong attack on the authoritarian state. As I discussed in Chapter 1, the authoritarian state is often justified by claims that rulers have access to truth or wisdom that should be used to control the actions of citizens. For Socrates, freedom would mean that citizens no longer act according to the wisdom of the philosopher-kings, and the consequence would be the destruction of justice and the psychological health of citizens. Therefore, claims that freedom is necessary to human happiness completely undercut arguments that human happiness can be achieved only by obeying the dictates of a wise ruler.

The issue of state-controlled education is not only important in libertarian-anarchist discussions of the advancement of civilization through science; it is also important in discussions of the contribution of freedom of thought and speech to equalizing political power and increasing human happiness. Born in England in 1756, political philosopher William Godwin analyzed the role of state education in a society where power was shared equally. Living in the eighteenth and early nineteenth centuries, Godwin worried that monarchies would be replaced by a new ruling elite. He believed that changing the form of government meant very little as long as any government existed that could be used in the interests of a controlling group. Godwin wanted a society where each person could be sovereign, rather than a republican society with periodic changes in the ruling class.

Godwin, like the previously discussed libertarians, believed that progress depended on the free exercise of human reason. He feared that the two most striking phenomena of his time—the rise of the modern state and the development of national systems of education to produce citizens for that state—would have the effect of dogmatically controlling and stifling human reason. In a pamphlet issued during his brief attempt to establish a school in 1783, he argues that the two major means by which power can be exerted over people are government and education. The most powerful of these two methods of control is education, because "government must always depend upon the opinion of the governed. Let the most oppressed people under heaven once change their mode of thinking, and they are free."[8] Government, he argues, gains its legitimacy from the recognition by and acceptance of people. Control of public opinion through government schools results in continued public support of that government. Therefore, Godwin maintains, despotism and injustice can continue to exist in any society in which human reason is controlled within the walls of the schoolhouse.

Godwin explores the role of national education in maintaining political power in his study of government, *Enquiry Concerning Political Justice*. In this book, he warns that "before we put so powerful a machine [education] under the direction of so ambiguous an agent [the state], it behooves us to consider well what it is that we do. Government will not fail to employ it, to strengthen its hands, and perpetuate its institutions." From his perspective, the content of any national education would be shaped by the dictates of political power. He argues, in words that would ring true for authoritarian states of the twentieth century, that "the data upon which their conduct as statesmen is vindicated, will be the data upon which their instructions [in school] are founded."[9]

Godwin's criticism of government schools reflects his general suspicion of government. First, Godwin argues that political institutions favor control by the rich and widen the differences between the rich and the poor. Legislation and taxation, he contends, tend to protect the property of the rich. In this framework, law is administered by governments to the advantage of those with economic power. In this case, government schools are used to teach citizens to obey the laws favoring the wealthy and to accept them as wise and just.

Second, Godwin believes the growth of large, centralized states results in the promotion of values—such as a quest for national glory, patriotism, and international economic and cultural competition—that provide little benefit to the individual citizen. In Godwin's words: "The desire to gain a more extensive territory, to conquer or hold in awe our neighboring states, to surpass them in arts or arms, is a desire founded in prejudice and error . . . . Security and peace are more to be desired than a name at which nations tremble."[10] According to Godwin's reasoning, national education is used to support chauvinistic patriotism and the political and economic power of the state.

Another important part of Godwin's argument is that freedom of thought and speech is necessary for the evolution of better forms of government. Since people constantly improve their reasoning power and their understanding of nature, he contends, their understanding of the best form of government is constantly changing. On the other hand, this process of change is impeded by constitutions and political institutions, which tend to make laws permanent. This hinders the unfolding of people's understanding of how life should be regulated. Government schools contribute to retarding the development of new forms of government by teaching students to revere the constitution and laws of the state. Godwin writes: "It is not true that our youth ought to be instructed to venerate the constitutions, however excellent; they should be led to venerate truth; and the constitution only so far as it corresponds with their uninfluenced deductions of truth."[11] In addition, Godwin believes that if national systems of education had existed in the past, then progress in developing new forms of government would have been seriously hindered.

Besides hindering the evolution of new forms of government, Godwin believes that national schools are used to convince citizens to accept unjust laws. Most people, he argues, can understand that certain crimes are injurious to the public. Those laws which stand outside the realm of reason and have to be taught rather than understood are usually laws which give advantages to some particular group. For example, he argues, reason teaches him that he should not strike his neighbor, but it does not teach him that he should obey laws supporting the manufacturing of woolens in England or a law forbidding the printing of the French constitution in Spain. In his words, "all crimes that can be supposed to be the fit objects of judicial administration, are capable of being discerned without the teaching of law."[12] According to this reasoning, government-operated schools can be used to teach the value of laws that are beneficial to one segment of society but not in the self-interest of the majority of people.

Godwin's fear that government-operated schools would reduce human happiness by retarding the development of new forms of government, by perpetuating political power and wealth, and by convincing the population of the justice of unjust laws led him to declare: "Destroy us if you please; but do not endeavor, by a national education, to destroy in our understandings the discernment of justice and injustice."[13]

MAX STIRNER: WHEELS IN THE HEAD

In contrast to early libertarian-anarchist concerns about the negative effects of government schools, Max Stirner worried that any form of education has the potential to restrict freedom of thought. Stirner, whose real name was Johann Kaspar Schmidt, was a poor German schoolteacher who during the 1840s attended meetings of the Young Hegelians in Berlin with Karl Marx. In 1842, Marx published Stirner's important article "The False Principle of Our Education." In 1845, Stirner completed his book *The Ego and His Own*, which so upset Marx that he later devoted a large section of *The German Ideology* to an attack on Stirner.

Amy Gutmann would place Stirner in the category of "state of individuals" because of his contention that the method of education should allow for individual choice of belief. Stirner believes that individuals should at all times make their knowledge and beliefs subservient to their own needs and desires. Gutmann rejects this argument because it is contrary to the idea she supports, that a democracy requires an acceptance of nonrepression and nondiscrimination. Stirner would argue that this idea might be necessary for the functioning of a democratic state, but it is not necessarily linked to individual happiness. The only true test of the value of a particular idea or belief, Stirner would argue, is its value not to the state but to the individual. For instance, the state might support the teaching of a particular idea or belief because it reflects the needs and desires of the ruling elite. In this situation, the idea or belief might not be beneficial to the individual citizen. This reasoning is similar to Godwin's objection to government schools teaching laws that might be contrary to the interests of most citizens.

For Stirner, the test of whether a person selects an idea or belief—as opposed to it being planted in the mind by an outside force such as schools—is the ability of that person to get rid of that idea or belief. Stirner writes, "The thought is my own only when I have no misgiving about bringing it in danger of death every moment, when I do not have to fear its loss as a loss for me, a loss of me."[14]

Stirner refers to any thought that an individual cannot give up as a "wheel in the head." For Stirner, an idea or belief that is a wheel in the head owns the individual, as opposed to thoughts that individuals own and can use for their own benefit. A wheel in the head controls individual will and uses the individual, rather than being used by the individual.

Ownership of self, Stirner argues, means elimination of wheels in the head. He elaborates on this theme in *The False Principle of Our Education* by making a distinction between a "freeman" and an "educated man." For the educated person, knowledge is used to shape character; it becomes a wheel in the head that allows the person to be possessed by the church, state, or humanity. For the free person, knowledge is used to facilitate choice. "If one awakens in men the idea of freedom," Stirner writes, "then the freemen will incessantly go on to free themselves; if, on the contrary, one only educates them, then they will at all times accommodate themselves to circumstances in the most highly educated and elegant manner and degenerate into subservient cringing souls."[15]

According to Stirner's distinction, for the free person, knowledge is the source of greater choice, but for the educated person, knowledge is the determiner of choice.

The major problem with modern society, Stirner believes, is the existence of vast numbers of educated people as opposed to free people. "Man," Stirner warns, "your head is haunted; you have wheels in your head! . . . An idea that has subjected the man to itself."[16] The problem for Stirner is how to achieve ownership of self as opposed to political liberty. Stirner objects to the idea of political liberty, because it means freedom only for institutions. "Political liberty," he writes, "meant that the polis, the State, is free; freedom of religion that religion is free, as freedom of conscience signifies that conscience is free; not, therefore, that I am free from the State, from religion, from conscience, or that I am rid of them."[17]

The real source of power in society, Stirner contends, is institutions that own the inner life of the individual. In the past, the church fulfilled the mission of guiding and dominating the mind. In this context, as indicated by the above quote, freedom of religion means freedom for religion to control human minds, as opposed to Stirner's concept of freedom, which would give individuals power to make the choice to be free of religious beliefs. Religion and politics, according to Stirner, gain power by their ability to establish imperatives, or wheels in the head, to direct the actions of individuals. Stirner writes, "Under religion and politics man finds himself at the standpoint of should: he should become this and that, should be so and so. With this postulate, this commandment, everyone steps not in front of another but also in front of himself."[18]

Echoing Godwin's reasoning, Stirner argues that the power of the state to dominate the mind is necessary for gaining obedience to the law. The modern state causes laws to be internalized in the individual, so that "freedom" merely means freedom to obey the laws that one has been taught. It is the dream of government schoolmasters, according to Stirner, to end disobedience to the state through the internalization of laws in government-controlled classrooms.

Stirner writes, in one of his finest passages, "Here at last the domination of the law is for the first time complete. 'Not I live, but the law lives in me.' Thus I have really come so far to be only the vessel of its glory. Every Prussian carries his gendarme in his breast, says a high Prussian officer."[19] According to Stirner, placing a gendarme in the breast (or a wheel in the head) is the goal of the modern state. In this condition, individuals feel free from the direct control of the state, but they are being indirectly controlled by the wheels in their heads.

Stirner believes the state can control citizens not only by implanting ideas but also by placing ideals in their minds. For Stirner, there are two levels of wheels in the head. The first level takes people through their daily lives. At this level, the wheels in the head make people go to church and pay taxes because that is what they are taught to do. On the second level are ideals—ideals that drive people to sacrifice themselves for the good of the state, that make them try to be Christ-like, that make them give up what they are for some unrealizable goal. It is this realm of ideals, Stirner argues, that supports religion and governments. Patriotism and religious fervor are the results of people being possessed by ideals.

Ideals gain possession of people, Stirner argues, because of a confusion between what is thinkable and what is possible. Just because one can think that all people can be good does not mean that it is possible for all people to be good nor that they ought to be good. Yet it is precisely this "sleight of mind," Stirner suggests, that occurs: "It was thinkable that men might be obedient subjects." Since it was thinkable, it was possible, "and further because it was possible to men . . . therefore they ought to be so."[20]

From this point of view, people in the modern world are driven creatures who sacrifice what they are for some ideal of what they ought to be. People do not own themselves but are owned by what they ought to be. The church tells people they ought to be like Christ, the state tells them that they ought to be good citizens, and the liberal politician tells them that they ought to give all to the cause of humanity. People cannot find themselves because they are surrounded by images of what they ought to be. "Man is not the individual," Stirner writes, "but man is a thought, an ideal, to which the individual is related not even as the child to the man, but as a chalk point to a point thought of."[21]

The ideals created to support dominant institutions become the moral imperatives of society. In the past, according to Stirner, the dominant institution was the church with its handmaiden, the priest; in the nineteenth century it was the state and its preacher, the schoolmaster. In modern times, therefore, the state defines the ideals of society. Of course, these ideals serve the interests of the rulers of the state, who in turn ensure that these ideals are taught to citizens through government schools. For instance, the state might establish an ideal for citizenship that includes a willingness to die to protect the state. This ideal is taught in government schools through nationalistic histories and literature and patriotic exercises. If effectively taught, Stirner argues, the ideal will be a wheel in the head driving citizens to sacrifice their own well-being for the good of the state.

In this context, belief in the rightness of the state is the main problem for modern times. If people become citizens and live for the state, Stirner contends, then the state can sanctify all actions. The state can justify killing when it occurs in defending the state or in punishing those who violate state laws. As an instrument of power for a ruling elite, the state turns the desires of the ruling elite into law and declares it just to kill during the protection and execution of these laws. Therefore, if the ruling elite kills through the instrument of the state, it is called justice. If a citizen kills in retaliation, it is a crime.

Stirner believes that the only way to counteract domination by wheels in the head is for people to gain knowledge and beliefs through actions of individual will, as opposed to acquiring knowledge and beliefs through schooling. In other words, the possession of knowledge and beliefs should be a function of what is useful to the individual. All ideas and actions are to be judged according to their value to the person. For example, Stirner makes a distinction between learning a religious catechism at an early age and making a choice later in life to join a church. On the one hand, being taught to believe in a religion at an early age puts a wheel into the head that is difficult to lose. Religion becomes, as Stirner states, "An idea that has subjected the man to itself." On the other hand, if one chooses a religion through the exercise of reason based on relevant knowledge and free of any belief about what ought to be, that belief is owned by that person. If one owns the thought, Stirner argues, one can get rid of it. It does not own the person.

Stirner's solution to the problem of the modern state is to replace it with a Union of Egoists—a social organization of free individuals in which there is no sacrifice to meaningless abstractions. Social institutions would be based on the needs of each individual. When their usefulness ended, so would they. This will be possible, Stirner argues, when knowledge becomes a vehicle for self-ownership, a tool by which people make choices about what is useful to them.

It is interesting to compare Stirner's arguments with those of John Dewey and Henry Giroux as described in Chapter 2. Both would agree with Stirner that people should not be dominated by ideas and beliefs that serve to perpetuate inequality in the distribution of political power. They would also agree that people should be able to cast aside ideas and beliefs when they no longer serve the individual. And they would agree that people should be free so that they can continually participate in the reconstruction of society.

While there might be agreement on these points, Stirner would probably reject both of their concepts of critical thought as planting wheels in the head. As I argued in Chapter 2, Dewey's and Giroux's instructional methods are each based on a particular concept of the origin of knowledge. Since neither the methods nor their underlying assumptions have ever been proved, the possibility of creating better methods of equalizing power in a democratic society exists. Therefore, any instruction that places the methodology into the mind of students could create a situation in which the methodology and the ideal behind it dominate the mind. Rather than people owning critical methodologies, they are owned by the methodologies imposed on them. To avoid this problem, Stirner would argue, students must choose the methodology so that they own it. In this way, people would be able to rid themselves of the methodology when it is no longer useful. In other words, Stirner would argue against the imposition of any methodology, even one that claims to free people, because people cannot be free if they are controlled by particular ideals, ideas, and methods of thinking.

Stirner might also criticize Dewey and Giroux for being schoolmasters who confuse what is thinkable with what is possible. For instance, for Dewey and Giroux it is thinkable that their methods of critical thinking will assure that government schools will prepare people to reconstruct society and to struggle against inequality in the distribution of power. But is it possible? Is it possible that government schools in a democratic state will adopt the methods of Dewey and Giroux? For instance, in the United States there is nothing to suggest that public schools would adopt these methods. Even though discussion of Dewey's ideas continues, there has been no wholesale adoption of his methodology. In fact, it is hard to imagine, given the important influence of the business community on American schools, that Giroux's critical pedagogy would be let into the schoolhouse door. It is unlikely that, under the present political structure of public education in the United States, schools would become dedicated to eliminating inequalities in power and wealth.

Therefore, by confusing what is thinkable with what is possible, Stirner might argue, Dewey and Giroux have created ideals that merely help to perpetuate the current system of education and inequality. For instance, if people struggle to get critical pedagogy into public schools even when it is not possible to achieve that goal, they are indirectly supporting the continued existence of those schools by perpetuating the belief that government schools can be organized to reduce inequalities in power. From Stirner's point of view, schools run by the government will always operate according to the dictates of a ruling elite and can never be made democratic or be a means for equalizing power. From this standpoint, Stirner might argue, what Dewey and Giroux really accomplish is the continued domination in the minds of citizens of beliefs that government-operated schools can accomplish these goals.

CONCLUSION: JOHN STUART MILL: DESPOTISM OVER THE MIND

Summarizing many of the early libertarian-anarchists' attitudes, John Stuart Mill declares in *On Liberty* (1859) that state education "establishes a despotism over the mind."[22] In words that might have been written by any of the early libertarian-anarchists, Mill states: "A general State education is a mere contrivance for moulding people to be exactly like one another: and . . . the mould in which it casts them . . . pleases the predominant power in the government, whether this be a monarch, a priesthood, an aristocracy, or the majority of the existing generation."[23]

Mill's statement highlights fears that government-operated school systems will be used by political rulers to perpetuate their power. Libertarian-anarchists fear that schools will teach obedience and submission to political rulers and the acceptance of unjust laws. Even in a democratic state a majority of the population might use schools to impose their beliefs. Also, libertarian-anarchists, such as Max Stirner, worry that schools will teach ideals that support political rulers and do not serve the interests of the individual. In addition, there is a fear that a state education that serves the interests of a political elite will limit freedom of thought and speech and, consequently, hinder the development of new knowledge. In turn, the slow growth of new knowledge will retard the advance of civilization and, according to Godwin, the development of new political forms.

The concerns of these early libertarian-anarchists raise important questions regarding the relationship between the state and education. Is it possible to organize a government school system that does not serve the interests of a ruling elite? Is it possible in a democratic state to organize government schools so that they do not hinder the free development of knowledge? Mill tried to answer these questions in the context of a representative democracy. By representative democracy, Mill means a form of government under which people elect representatives to vote on laws and to administer them. This system (which is the system in the United States) is different from a direct democracy, under which people vote directly on legislation. In fact, Mill warns that people often confuse representative democracy with "self-government" and "the power of the people over themselves." Mill argues that representative democracy is not self-government, because it really means that each individual is governed by all the rest of the people—the will of the people. What the will of the people actually means, Mill claims, is either the will of the majority or the will of the most active part of the population. The distinction between "the majority" and "the most active" is important when you consider that in many representative democracies, only a fraction of the eligible population votes. What often happens is that the will of the majority is in reality the will of the most active or the most powerful.

To avoid the possibility of education serving the interests of a political elite or a majority, Mill proposes making education a responsibility of the family. Of course, Mill believes that education is an important element in maintaining political liberty, and therefore he proposes that governments make families comply with a requirement to educate their children by requiring public examinations of children to determine if they can read. In addition, Mill proposes state aid to families to defray educational expenses. If a child fails the reading examination, Mill recommends that the parents be forced to pay a fine and to send the child to a private school at their own expense. In addition, Mill proposes public examinations in a variety of subjects; a person would receive a certificate after passing these examinations.

Of course, there is the possibility of government influence through the control of the content of the public examinations. Mill thought this could be avoided by confining public examinations to facts and science. However, as Amy Gutmann points out in her criticism of Mill, objectivity is not possible in education. Even the selection of facts to be tested reflects a value position. What facts are important enough to include on a public examination? Some set of values must be used in selecting such facts.

Mill would reject Gutmann's argument that his reliance on individual and family choice would narrow the education of some students and create the possibility that some children will be educated in undemocratic ideas. Similar to Priestly, Mill argues that a great danger is state education "moulding people to be exactly like one another." Mill accepts diversity, even if it means that some people think undemocratic things. Mill also shares with Priestly the belief that freedom of thought and speech is meaningful only if there is a diversity of ideas. Therefore, these early libertarian-anarchists are willing to abolish government control of the content of education, because they accept the idea that diversity of beliefs provides substance to freedom of speech and thought and do not believe such diversity is possible in government-operated schools. Gutmann will not relinquish government control because she does not accept the idea of democratic diversity. From her standpoint, the democratic state can survive only if all children are exposed to the same set of democratic values.

Early libertarian-anarchists raised serious issues regarding the role of government-operated education systems by recognizing that control of ideas is an important source of power and domination. In addition, they believed government-operated schools would be used to maintain inequalities in wealth. Their solution was separation of state and education to avoid the tyrannical use of knowledge to control citizens.

NOTES

1. Robert Molesworth, *An Account of Denmark as It Was in the Year 1692* (Copenhagen: Rosenkilde and Bagger, 1976). No pages in the preface are numbered; all quotations are taken from the preface.
2. Ibid.
3. Bernard Bailyn, *The Ideological Origins of the American Revolution* (Cambridge, Mass.: Harvard University Press, 1967).
4. *Cato's Letters: Unabridged Reproduction of 6th Edition 1755*, ed. Leonard Levy (New York: Da Capo Press, 1971), Vol. I, p. 96.
5. Ibid., Vol. II, pp. 306–309.
6. Brian Simon, *Studies in the History of Education, 1780–1870* (London: Lawrence & Wishart, 1960), pp. 34-35.
7. Caroline Robbins, *The Eighteenth-Century Commonwealthman* (Cambridge, Mass.: Harvard University Press, 1959), p. 350.
8. William Godwin, "An account of the Seminary . . . At Epsom in Surrey," in *Four Early Pamphlets* (Gainesville, Florida: Scholars' Facsimiles and Reprints, 1966), p. 150.
9. William Godwin, *Enquiry Concerning Political Justice and its Influence on Morals and Happiness* (Toronto: University of Toronto Press, 1946), Vol. II, p. 302.
10. Quoted in George Woodcock, *William Godwin* (London: Porcupine Press, 1946), pp. 63–73.
11. Godwin, *Enquiry Concerning Political Justice*, Vol. II, pp. 302–303.
12. Ibid., Vol. II, p. 304.
13. Ibid.
14. Max Stirner, *The Ego and His Own: The Case of the Individual Against Authority*, trans. Steven Byington (New York: Libertarian Book Club, 1963), p. 342.

15. Max Stirner, *The False Principle of Our Education*, trans. Robert H. Beebe (Colorado Springs: Ralph Myles, 1967), p. 23.
16. Stirner, *The Ego and His Own*, pp. 106–107.
17. Ibid.
18. Ibid., p. 242.
19. Ibid., p. 52.
20. Ibid., pp. 330–335.
21. Ibid.
22. John Stuart Mill, *Utilitarianism, Liberty, and Representative Government* (New York: Dutton, 1951), p. 88.
23. Ibid.

CHAPTER 4

Free Schools

By the end of the nineteenth century, criticisms of government-operated schools sparked the development of alternative forms of education. Libertarian-anarchists organized schools that emphasized freedom of thought as a necessary condition for the progress of society. In addition, they criticized state schools for creating uniformity of thinking. In alternative schools, uniformity of ideas was to be replaced by diversity of ideas. They believed that diversity of ideas was a necessary condition for freedom of thought. People had to have something to think about before they could truly experience freedom in their thinking. And, of course, they rejected the idea of government-operated schools because of the possibility that political leaders would use education to perpetuate their power.

Most of these schools were eventually called "free schools." The term "free school" has several meanings. During the early twentieth century, it primarily referred to a school offering an education that was free of imposition of ideas and beliefs on students—using Stirner's words, a school that opposed placing wheels in the head. "Free" also meant free of a compulsion to learn. In these early free schools, children were free to learn anything they wanted. Therefore, the source of authority over what should be learned was placed in the hands of the students. With the development of the most famous of the free schools, Summerhill, in the 1920s, the meaning of "free" also included freedom from authoritarian families, sexual freedom, and freedom for women from male domination.

In addition, free schools try to make knowledge a function of individual needs. This goal is in sharp contrast to educational systems, as I discussed in Chapter 1, of authoritarian states. In authoritarian states, the knowledge disseminated through schools is useful to the state and its rulers, not necessarily the individual. Also, students are taught to sacrifice themselves to the common good as it is defined by the rulers of authoritarian states. Free school leaders, as I will discuss in this chapter, believed that the strength of totalitarian governments in the twentieth century was derived from their power to convince citizens that their rulers had access to knowledge of the common good and that, therefore, citizens should sacrifice themselves to the dictates of the state.

Many free school advocates are libertarian-anarchists who reject any possibility of reforming government-operated schools because these schools primarily serve the interests of a ruling elite. A leader of the early free school movement in the United States and famous anarchist, Emma Goldman, expressed concern about the imposition of ideas and beliefs by both state education and parents.

Even radical parents, she argues, must avoid the imposition of their beliefs on children. Goldman warns parents that the "boy or girl, overfed on Thomas Paine, will land in the arms of the Church, or they will vote for imperialism only to escape the drag of economic determinism and scientific socialism, or that they . . . cling to their right of accumulating property, only to find relief from the old-fashioned communism of their father."[1]

EMMA GOLDMAN AND FRANCISCO FERRER: RATIONAL AND RADICAL EDUCATION

Goldman rejected state education and advocated educational methods that would not put wheels into the head. The early model for this type of free school, and one championed by Goldman, was Francisco Ferrer's Modern School in Spain. Ferrer's execution by the Spanish government on charges that he was responsible for a rebellion in Barcelona sparked the development of the free school movement in the early twentieth century in the United States and throughout Europe. Exemplifying the desire to avoid any imposition of ideas or ideals on the child, Ferrer, when organizing the Modern School in the 1890s, searched for nondogmatic books for its library. Frustrated in his search, he opened the library without a single volume.

Ferrer argues that the way to avoid imposing ideas and ideals is for the teacher to plant germs of ideas that can be developed by individual reason. Similar to many nineteenth-century thinkers, Ferrer had faith that science can provide objective ideas that can be turned into ideals. "The work of man's cerebral energy is to create the ideal," Ferrer writes, "with the aid of art and philosophy. But in order that the ideal shall not degenerate into fables, or mystic and unsubstantial dreams . . . it is absolutely necessary to give it a secure and unshakable foundation in the exact sciences."[2]

From Ferrer's perspective, education should not be designed to make people religious or good citizens. Any such goal is dogmatic because it is imposing an ideal of what ought to be. It is for this reason that there were no rewards or punishments in Ferrer's Modern School. "Since we are not educating for a specific purpose," Ferrer writes, "we cannot determine the capacity or incapacity of the child."[3] In other words, in an educational process with no particular goal or end, children cannot be rewarded or punished because there is nothing to be rewarded or punished for. In addition, since there are no goals, then there is no standard by which the student can be graded.

Of course, despite his claims to the contrary, there were goals in Ferrer's Modern School. And these goals prove Amy Gutmann's point that no form of education can be truly objective. Ferrer's objectives can be considered another type of wheel in the head. Ferrer states his objectives: "It must be the aim of the rational schools to show the children that there will be tyranny and slavery as long as one man depends upon another, to study the causes of the prevailing ignorance, to learn the origin of all the traditional practices which give life to the existing social system, and to direct the attention of the pupils to these matters."[4]

Ferrer suggests methods of instruction that reflect both these goals and the goal of teaching that knowledge develops in a social context. For example, Ferrer states that the teaching of arithmetic should be placed in the context of an economic system that distributes goods fairly to all people. "In a word," Ferrer writes, "the Modern School wants a number of problems showing what arithmetic really ought to be—the science of the social economy (taking the word economy in its etymological sense of 'good distribution')."[5]

In this context, Ferrer gives a special meaning to the concept of objectivity. A fact or idea becomes objective if it can be used to increase human freedom and equality. For instance, Ferrer argues that arithmetic taught using examples from existing economic systems would serve the function of indoctrinating students into those systems. On the other hand, arithmetic presented as a tool for creating a more just organization of the economy is knowledge that individuals can use to free themselves.

Emma Goldman's concern with the teaching of history provides another example of this approach to instruction. Goldman criticizes traditional history instruction: "See how the events of the world become like a cheap puppet show, where a few wire-pullers are supposed to have directed the course of development of the entire race."[6] This approach to history, she argues, conditions people to be passive while rulers, governments, and great men lead society. In contrast, she advocates emphasizing the ability of all people to act and shape the course of events. From her perspective, traditional history instruction enslaves humanity to authoritarian institutions. In contrast, history taught from the premise that all people can be active agents teaches people that they have the power to shape the future.

Clearly, this instructional approach places wheels into the heads of students—albeit different wheels than those imposed by government-operated educational systems. Stirner would certainly object to the manipulation of arithmetic and history to impart certain attitudes about the economic and political system. On the other hand, as I discussed in Chapter 2, Henry Giroux would support the idea of making education consciously political in its content as long as the goal is equality of power—a goal that would be acceptable to libertarian-anarchists.

Therefore, while claiming to avoid imposition, this type of free school does try to impart a content that is radically different from that of government-operated schools. In general, the political content is designed to counter the state's efforts to win political obedience from citizens. And, of course, the content is to be conveyed without punishment, compulsion, or examinations.

LEO TOLSTOY: A LITTLE BIT OF GOD IN ALL OF US

During the same period that Ferrer was organizing the Modern School, the famous Russian author and anarchist Leo Tolstoy struggled with the issue of education. As a Christian anarchist, Tolstoy believed that freedom is necessary to avoid the imposition of ideas and beliefs and to allow the emergence of the goodness of God in each person. Like other anarchists, he feared the control of minds by the power of state education.

Tolstoy resolved the problem of how to teach without putting wheels into the head by making distinctions between the concepts of culture, education, instruction, and teaching. He defines "culture" as the total of all social forces shaping individual character and "education"—which is to be avoided—as the conscious attempt to give people a particular type of character and habit. The important difference between culture and education, Tolstoy argues, is compulsion.[7]

Based on this distinction between education and culture, Tolstoy argues that instruction and teaching contribute to culture when they are free from compulsion. On the other hand, when they are imposed on students, they are a means of education. He defines "instruction" as the transmission of one person's information to another and "teaching" as instruction in physical skills. Education, which he wants to avoid, occurs when instruction based on what the teacher thinks is necessary is forced on the student.

Therefore, according to Tolstoy, learning should be a process of culture and not of education. The school should practice noninterference, which means granting students the freedom to learn what they want and avoiding teaching students what they do not want or need.

Tolstoy pointed to museums and public lectures as examples of schools based on the idea of noninterference: They are consciously planned to achieve a certain goal, but the user is free to attend or not to attend. In contrast, state schools and universities, which use a system of rewards and punishments and limit areas of study to achieve particular goals, compel students to learn certain things.

Tolstoy defines a school of noninterference or, using another term, a noncompulsory school, as one without a planned program where teachers can teach what they want and students can study what they want. The noncompulsory school is not interested in how its teaching is used or what effect it has on the students. As Tolstoy defines the terms, a school should be a place of culture, not education.

Tolstoy's solution highlights the general direction of libertarian-anarchist thought about how to achieve an education that does not impose specific ideas and beliefs on students. There was a growing recognition that it is impossible to teach without conveying ideals and beliefs—that knowledge cannot be presented objectively. Since some type of ideas and beliefs underlies all knowledge, the solution to providing an education that does not impose particular ideas and beliefs is to give teachers and students the freedom to teach and to learn whatever they want. In this manner, an education can be consciously political without imposing beliefs and ideals because students are free to study or not study, to accept or reject, a particular body of knowledge.

This solution offers an important answer to Amy Gutmann's criticism of the state of individuals discussed in Chapter 2. She argues that imposition of ideas and beliefs cannot be avoided, and therefore education should consciously pass on democratic values. She does not consider the option to avoid imposition by allowing students to choose what they want to study. She would likely reject the option of student choice on the same terms that she rejects family choice. Student choice, she would probably argue, might lead to learning that is too narrow as well as a choice to learn undemocratic values or to reject the principle of nonrepression. On the other hand, libertarian-anarchists such as Joseph Priestly would argue that diversity is more important to freedom than instilling the same democratic values in everyone. These libertarian-anarchist concepts of noncompulsory education and diversity in ideas and beliefs are important for countering Gutmann's argument that educational choice for families and students cannot be part of a democratic education because maintenance of a democratic state requires a conscious inculcation of democratic values.

In the above argument for noncompulsory education, the source of educational authority is located in the student and not in the state. This is one solution to the question of who should decide what students should learn. In the authoritarian state, the source of educational authority is the rulers or, in the case of Socrates, the philosopher-kings. For Gutmann, Dewey, and Giroux, as I discussed in Chapter 2, the source of educational authority appears to be themselves and other philosophers. In addition, Gutmann rejects the majority of voters as a source of educational authority in a democratic state, because the majority might decide to teach nondemocratic values. In contrast to these positions, the free school movement locates educational authority in the individual. Individuals are free to decide what they want to learn and how they want to learn it.

THE MODERN SCHOOL AT STELTON

Noncompulsory learning was a central feature of the version of the Modern School that was established in the United States in 1915 in Stelton, New Jersey. In addition, the founders of this school were concerned about the influence of business on state schools. Thus, the Modern School at Stelton wove together the concerns of nineteenth-century libertarian-anarchists, who tended to concentrate on the problem of rulers using state education to assure the continued obedience of citizens, with emerging concerns among twentieth-century libertarian-anarchists about modern corporations turning state schools into factories for producing compliant workers.

The problem of state schools serving the interests of industry was brought to the forefront in the United States with the organization of the Modern School. While many Americans in the 1890s and early twentieth century had heard of Ferrer's school, it was his article reprinted in 1909 in *Mother Earth* that made his ideas familiar to American radicals. In the article, Ferrer argues that control of the school system is one of the main sources of political power. He states, "Governments have ever been careful to hold a high hand over the education of the people. They know, better than anyone else, that their power is based almost entirely on the school. Hence they monopolize it more and more." In the past, he argues, governments could maintain control of the people by keeping them in a state of ignorance. But with international industrial competition this was no longer possible. The current popularity of state-controlled education, Ferrer argues, is because it can be used as an instrument of control by the state and by industry. In words that echo those of other libertarian-anarchists, Ferrer states, "The organization of the school, far from spreading the ideal which we imagined, has made education the most powerful means of enslavement in the hands of the governing power to-day."[8]

Responding to Ferrer's message and spurred to action by his execution, a mixed group of American radicals, including anarchists, socialists, and single taxers, met in New York in 1910 to initiate the creation of a Modern School. The leaders of the modern school movement in the United States were the anarchists Emma Goldman and Alexander Berkman, who toured the country raising money for the school. Until 1915, the school was housed at various locations in New York City and offered a variety of courses for adults and children on topics such as Esperanto, art, sex hygiene, and physiology. In 1915, the school moved to Stelton, New Jersey, where it became a leading center of free school education. The school sent its message around the country in an educational journal, *Modern School Magazine.* In 1925, the Modern School Association, realizing its role as a model for other free schools, published a history of the school.

The educators in the modern school movement shared a belief that government-operated schools were a new form of despotism. For instance, in 1925 Harry Kelly, chairman of the first board of management of the Modern School at Stelton, states in retrospect about the founding of the school, "We saw then and we see now, that the public school system is a powerful instrument for the perpetuation of the present social order with all its injustice and inequality . . . and that, quite naturally, whatever is likely to disturb the existing arrangement is regarded unfavorably by those in control of the public schools." Kelly claims that since the primary purpose of public schools is to perpetuate the authority of those in power, "From the moment the child enters the public school he is trained to submit to authority, to do the will of others as a matter of course, with the result that habits of mind are formed which in adult life are all to the advantage of the ruling class." Reflecting the concern about business control of public schools, Kelly argues that schools destroy initiative and individuality "except in the narrow fields where these qualities can increase the efficiency of the capitalist machine."[9]

This opposition to domination of public schools by big business was a major theme at the Modern School at Stelton. Alexis Ferm, the coprincipal of the school, argued that when workers originally struggled for the establishment of public schools, they were concerned with equalizing economic opportunities. Consequently, when they won their schools, they thought they had solved their children's future economic problems. But the workers failed, Ferm argues, because they turned schools over to government authorities without retaining any control over the educational process. Workers forgot, Ferm writes, "that the authorities were the very exploiters of labor against whose encroachments upon their liberties the workers were organized to defend themselves."[10] Consequently, the education of workers' children in public schools resulted in

these children failing to understand the school's reactionary role a
sity for questioning its real purpose.

According to members of the modern school movement, the
derstand the role of the school in serving the interests of ruling a
industry results in workers not understanding how their minds have been do...
inated and how they are exploited by the economic system. By conditioning students to submit to authority, the public schools turned out workers completely obedient to the needs of capitalism. James Dick, one of the most dedicated teachers at Stelton, argues that a powerfully persuasive and controlling device used by public schools is the promise of economic advancement. He writes, "The seductive atmosphere of 'prosperity' is too much for him [the worker], and the lethal chambers of governmental scholastic career for his child is the real solution to his salvation."[11]

The organizers of the Modern School at Stelton believed that public schools control minds through both the content taught and the process of education. Alexis Ferm argues that public schools assume that a course of study can be established for the student's "own good." This means, according to Ferm, that students are not given a choice but must depend on the advice and decisions of authorities. "It is considered," he writes, "that his [the students'] choice would not be any good anyhow and that he should be taught to accept things without question, to admire our captains of industry, our Presidents who bring us prosperity, our army and navy and our religions."[12] Thus in public schools the process of education is that of teaching children to be obedient to the authority of government and economic leaders. What public school students really learn, Ferm argues, are the rules and methods for getting through school. These rules and techniques are not related to real learning and critical thinking. In fact, they teach subservience. This is why, Ferm maintains, parents cannot counteract the influence of the public schools by exposing their children to subject matter different from that learned in school. The only solution is to remove children from public schools and place them in free schools.

To achieve its goals, the Stelton school was organized around the principle of noncompulsory education, as defined earlier in this chapter. For example, if children wanted to study art, they went to the art teacher for instruction. This freedom was tempered by the nature of the courses taught at Stelton. Obviously, many of these courses, like those at Ferrer's Modern School, taught consciously radical ideas. It would have been difficult to find a teacher at Stelton who believed in the economic and political ideology that supports the status quo. However, children were free to ask questions and teachers were free to direct them to materials that supported a conservative political position.

Freedom at Stelton was tempered not only by conscious radicalism, but also by the Stelton community's concept of the role of the teacher. For the organizers of Stelton, avoiding imposition of ideas and beliefs did not mean a passive role for the teacher. Teachers at Stelton were supposed to actively help students make choices. This role for the teacher was promoted in the Stelton school by Elizabeth Ferm, who before the establishment of Stelton

was involved in the development of kindergartens, in various political movements, and in writing education articles for *Mother Earth.* She worried that
teachers would confuse self-determination for the child with passivity for the
educator. There is a difference, she argues, between people who want to make
children into something and people who want to help children determine for
themselves what they want to be. Educators should be active, not passive,
participants in the child's quest for self-expression. The role of the educator
is to give meaning to self-expression—to help students learn how to be their
own authority and also how to accept the usefulness and necessity of help
from others.

This instructional approach added another dimension to attempts to provide an education that does not put wheels into the head. Students were free
to choose whatever they wanted to learn, but once the student made a choice
the teacher would consciously guide the student to self-awareness and self-
ownership. In other words, the teacher would help the student learn to use the
subject matter, as opposed to being controlled by it. This instructional methodology, along with the radical political orientation of much of the instruction at
Stelton, was determined by teachers. However, students were still free to
choose to attend the school and to study what they wanted.

Attendance at Stelton was voluntary, of course. Parents and children (depending on the child's age) were well aware of the political orientation and the
instructional philosophy of the Stelton school. Therefore, their selection of
Stelton represented a conscious political choice as opposed to state education
imposing a particular political philosophy and method of instruction regardless
of parents' and children's preferences.

A. S. NEILL AND WILHELM REICH: FREE SCHOOLS AND FREE SEX

The school is only one source of the imposition of ideas on children. Another
source is the family. For many twentieth-century advocates of free schools, the
primary problem with the traditional family structure is the inequality and oppression of women. According to the founder of Summerhill, A. S. Neill, the oppression of women creates an authoritarian atmosphere in the family that results
in the development of an authoritarian personality in the child. His argument
links the twentieth-century movement for female equality with the free school
movement. Therefore, from the perspective of A. S. Neill, the founder of the most
famous of the free schools, modern educational problems include the imposition
of values both by the state and by the authoritarian family.

When Neill established Summerhill in England in the 1920s, a major influence on his thinking was a popularized version of Freudian psychology. In the
1920s, Neill dreamt of spreading the free school idea through the world; he even
wrote to Henry Ford to suggest the production of school caravans to carry
Summerhill's message to other countries. In the 1930s, he blended a concern
with economic problems with Freudianism. During these years he met Freud's

student Wilhelm Reich, who provided Neill with the psychological theory on which to base the work of Summerhill. Under Reich's influence, Neill began to link the existence of authoritarian institutions with the existence of state education, female inequality, sexual repression, and the authoritarian family. By the 1950s, Summerhill had become the major model for free schools and a primary influence on the development of free schools in the United States in the 1960s and 1970s.

In founding Summerhill, Neill wanted to provide a means of saving the world from crime, despair, and unhappiness. Influenced by Freud, Neill believed that the source of world problems, and the major problem in the education of children, is the repression of natural drives. In *The Problem Child* (1927), Neill states, "I believe that it is moral instruction that makes the child bad. I find that when I smash the moral instruction a bad boy has received he automatically becomes a good boy."[13]

Neill's rejection of moral instruction gives a different twist to the concern about imposition of ideas and beliefs. Neill believed that imposition of moral ideas creates antisocial behavior. More precisely, the cause of the antisocial behavior, according to Neill, is the conflict between the "life force," which is part of human nature, and the self created by moral instruction. In this conflict, the self that is molded by moral instruction controls the desires and needs, or life force, of human nature. Human actions, Neill argues, can be seen as a product of the tension between these two components. If moral instruction is too controlling, people strike out against the world and become antisocial. Neill illustrates this phenomenon with two examples: a mother whose suppression of a child's selfishness ensures that the child will be selfish and a person who steals because of repressive moral instruction in childhood. In an imaginary dialogue with a "Mrs. Morality," he tells this symbolic figure of authority, "I believe there would be more honesty in the world if policemen were abolished. . . . It is the law that makes the crime."[14]

In the 1930s and 1940s, Neill's contact with psychoanalytical leader Wilhelm Reich provided him with a broader theoretical base for his argument. When Neill first met Reich in 1937, he said, "Reich, you are the man I've been looking for for years, the man who joins up the somatic and psychological. Can I come to you as a student?"[15] When Reich moved to the United States in the late 1930s, Neill became a frequent visitor and began writing books that justified the existence of Summerhill in the framework of Reich's psychoanalytical arguments.

Understanding Reich's concepts of the individual and the authoritarian state helps clarify Neill's intentions in operating Summerhill. Both Neill and Reich wanted people to own themselves and to be self-regulating, as a means of eliminating economic oppression and authoritarian states. A major concern of Reich was to provide a psychological explanation for the existence of authoritarian states, particularly Nazi Germany. Similarly to Neill, he believed that the imposition of moral instruction is destructive to society.

Reich argued that individuals who have an authoritarian character structure want to be controlled by authoritarian institutions, and that this type of character structure is caused by authoritarian child-rearing methods and sexual repression. He hoped that people would dispense with the irrationalism of politics and government and organize a "work-democracy" based on self-regulating character structures. His dream was of a society free of all authoritarian institutions—including the political state—one in which social relationships evolve from economic organizations created by workers.

Reich developed a psychoanalytic framework in which sexual repression is linked with a general repression of pleasure. According to his theory, sexual repression results in sexual anxiety, which then causes a general anxiety about having pleasure, and this, in turn, results in the development of hostile and authoritarian character traits. Aggression and anxiety about experiencing pleasure, Reich argues, are always found together, just as the capacity to experience pleasure and nonaggressive character traits are also always found together. In comparing sadistic and nonsadistic character traits, Reich writes, "The mildness and kindness of individuals capable of genital satisfaction was striking in contrast. I have never seen individuals capable of genital satisfaction who had sadistic character traits."[16]

Neill was attracted to the revolutionary nature of Reich's argument because it held out the hope of being able to plan a system of education and an organization for society that would eliminate hostility and authoritarianism. Reich's arguments also provide a method of analyzing the linkage between political structures and educational and child-rearing practices. For instance, he argues that the existence of authoritarian political structures can be traced to sexual repression within the family. In *The Mass Psychology of Fascism*, Reich uses this argument to explain the acceptance of Nazism in Germany, and in *The Sexual Revolution*, he contends that this explains how general repression in Soviet society caused the collapse of the dreams of the Communist revolution. Thus, according to Reich, in both Nazi Germany and Stalinist Russia, repression leading to anxiety about the experience of pleasure resulted in people seeking refuge in authoritarian institutions, including the authoritarian state.

For Reich, removing this anxiety requires a freeing of the character structure. Therefore, he argues, the primary aim of a revolutionary movement should be to free the individual character structure. Reich dismissed the idea of using psychotherapy to change the character structures of an entire population, because the amount of time and the number of analysts required for such treatment would be impossible to provide. The only real hope, he maintained, is prevention of repression, which would mean ridding society of repressive sexual morality and the patriarchal, authoritarian family structure.

Reich's emphasis on revolutionary institutional changes reflects the distinction he made between reactionary and radical psychology. For instance, he argues that reactionary psychology would explain why people steal when they are hungry or strike when they are exploited "in terms of supposed irrational motives; reactionary rationalizations are invariably the result." On the other hand, radical psychology would try to explain "why the majority of those who are hungry don't steal and why the majority of those exploited don't strike."[17]

Therefore, the question for the radical psychologist with regard to the development of totalitarian states in Germany and the Soviet Union is this: Why

do people accept authoritarian rule? For Reich, this question r？
question: Why are people willing to work in authoritarian an？
organizations?

The answer Reich gave to these questions in *The Mass Psychology* ．，
provided A. S. Neill with a strong justification for the work at Summerhill. ．．
Nazi Germany, Reich argues in the book, the existence of the patriarchal family
promoted nationalism and militarism. The emotional core of ideas concerning
the homeland and the nation, Reich contends, were the ideas of mother and family; the mother is the homeland of the child and family is a nation in miniature.
Reich quotes Nazi leader Goebbels: "Never forget that your country is the
mother of your life." And on Mother's Day, Reich reports, the Nazi press declared: "She—the German mother—is the sole bearer of the idea of the German
nation. The idea of 'mother' is inseparable from the idea of being German."[18]

Reich argues that the patriarchal family is the primary educational institution for training children for an authoritarian state. In the patriarchal family, the
father functions as the representative of authority of the state and exerts authority over the wife. In turn, the wife exerts authority over the children.
Involved in this authority structure is the repression of sexuality, particularly in
children. Reich argues that children become targets for the hostility and cruelty
that results from their parents' own sexual repression. For parents, and especially mothers, children become the only content of their lives. Children, according to Reich, "play the role of household pets whom one can love but also
torture."[19] The repression and domination by husbands often causes mothers to
find an outlet for their own dissatisfactions in sadistic forms of love toward their
children.

According to Reich, the repression of sexuality and the existence of sadistic
love in the family causes children to develop a general anxiety about having
pleasure. Because of this fear of pleasure, Reich argues, people seek refuge in the
security of authoritarian institutions. This is why workers continue for years in
jobs that provide no pleasure. This is why citizens continue to seek and tolerate
authoritarian governments that provide them only with pain.

In addition, Reich argues that militarism becomes a substitute gratification
for sexuality: "The sexual effect of a uniform, the erotically provocative effect of
rhythmically executed goose-stepping, the exhibitionistic nature of militaristic
procedures, have been more practically comprehended by a salesgirl or an average secretary than by our most erudite politicians."[20] The forces of political reaction recognize this appeal, Reich contends, and design flashy uniforms and
display recruiting posters that emphasize "foreign adventure" with the underlying implication of sexual freedom.

Reich believes the Nazi party was well aware that its support was grounded
in the negative effects of the family and sexual repression. People depended on
Hitler in the same way that they depended on their fathers. The German fascist,
Reich maintains, gave strong support to the family as the backbone of the nation
and attempted to assure that sexual acts associated reproduction with the national interest and not with pleasurable gratification. Reich quotes Adolf
Hitler's 1932 statement that a woman's ultimate aim should be the creation of a

family: "It is the smallest but most valuable unit in the complete structure of the state. Work honors both man and woman. But the child exalts the woman."[21]

The solution for overthrowing the authoritarian state, Reich concludes, is to eliminate the authoritarian personality structure that is willing to support it. This would mean eradicating the conditions that form authoritarian personalities. First on the agenda is to put an end to the patriarchal family. Second, the demise of the patriarchal family would require establishing social, economic, and political equality between men and women. And last, the conditions for sexual freedom should be established.

Reich's platform for social change directly affected A. S. Neill's conception of the purpose of Summerhill. While at Reich's institute in Maine during the late 1940s, Neill rewrote and condensed his earlier works by weaving in Reichian arguments. His idea that repressive morality produces hostility, aggression, and unhappiness was bolstered by Reich's concept of pleasure anxiety.

Neill agreed with Reich that creating a world free of authoritarianism and aggression depends on total freedom for children. Neill claims that Reich often chided him for not going as far as encouraging adolescent sexual relations at Summerhill. "I told him," Neill writes, "that to allow a full sex life to adolescents would mean the end of my school if and when the government heard about it."[22]

In advocating freedom for children, Neill makes a distinction between freedom and license. "Freedom" means freedom from moral teachings, not the right to commit any action. In response to the question of what he would do if a boy were pounding nails into a grand piano, Neill states, "It doesn't matter if you take the child away from the piano so long as you don't give the child a conscience about hammering nails."[23] In other words, he argues that one can stop people from doing something without making it a form of moral punishment. Another example Neill used is of a child leaving a tool out in the rain. In this case, the rain is harmful to the tool but not morally good or bad in an abstract sense. To provide freedom for children means providing them with the opportunity to grow up without an internalized moral authority or conscience.

Neill's concept of freedom is very close to Stirner's idea of ownership of self. Neill writes, "To give a child freedom is not easy. It means that we refuse to teach him religion or politics or class-consciousness." Freedom is the right to own or choose one's own ideals and beliefs; the function of a free school is to provide the opportunity to make these choices. "No man," Neill argues, "is good enough to give another his own ideals."[24]

In the 1930s, when Neill became more politically aware, he linked the question of freedom to political and economic conditions. In 1939, Neill wrote *The Problem Teacher*, which details the relationship between education and political and economic systems. In this book Neill states in blunt terms, "The State schools must produce a slave mentality because only a slave mentality can keep the system from being scrapped." In Germany and Italy, at the time Neill was writing, national schooling meant fascism, while in England, Neill argues, it means preparing each generation to fit into a capitalist economy. From his perspective, English schools produce a slave mentality and rob the working class of effective leadership. "The master stroke in . . . educational policy," Neill writes, "was the secondary school, the school that took children of the working class to white-collar jobs in clerking, teaching, doctoring and the other professions. Thus it robbed the workers of its best men and women."[25]

Reflecting the influence of Reich, Neill portrays the patriarchal family as the source of economic and political problems. In addition, Neill links the practices of the home with those of the school. The home, Neill argues, is the state in miniature, and since the home provides training in obedience it is strongly supported by the state. In turn, the power of the school is based on its reproduction of family life. "Theoretically one would think that schooling is an antidote to family influence. It isn't: it is family life on promotion."[26]

Neill drew parallels between the father as head of a nuclear family and the teacher as head of a family of forty or more children. In fact, the situation within the school might be worse than in the family, Neill argues, because the teacher does not necessarily feel the love most fathers feel for their children. Within the school the teacher represents the hostile side of the father. "And this is true of the disciplinarian," Neill writes, "for he has no love to give out, only hate."[27]

The answer to the problem of the oppressive, patriarchal family, Neill argues, is Summerhill and the free family. Living away from their families at Summerhill, children could escape repression. In *The Problem Family*, Neill makes a distinction between the free and the unfree family. Of course, the unfree family is the patriarchal family. In contrast, the free family is based on equality between the mother and father, which eliminates the chain of authority and repression from father to mother to child. Consequently, children in the free family are freed from the internalized authority produced by moral discipline. "In [many] families many parents do it," Neill writes, "and there are quite a lot of children living today who will never spank a child or moralize about sex or give a fear of God."[28] The free family, Neill argues, will have a major impact on society. People will demand similar freedom in the workplace, in politics, and in schools.

Until families are made free, Neill believes, an option is attendance at a free school. Writing in 1944, he expresses hope that a socialist state would create a national system of boarding schools that would be similar to Summerhill. "Naturally," he writes, "I want to specify that such a school will be a free school, with self-government and self-determination of the individual child, that is, I visualize a nation of Summerhills."[29]

Neill and Reich share a vision of a world of self-regulated individuals who will not tolerate nor seek a life within authoritarian institutions. Both believe the world's evils would disappear with changes in child-rearing practices that would transform human character. Their arguments add a psychological dimension to Stirner's concept of self-ownership and to the ideology of the free school movement.

Stirner and those associated with the establishment of the Stelton school never entertained the possibility that people might seek authoritarian institutions to fulfill some personal psychological need. They assumed that the maintenance of an authoritarian state depends on implanting beliefs and ideals in citizen's minds, and on tying emotions to symbols of the state. In this framework, people support an authoritarian state because they are taught to love the state, to internalize the laws of the state, and to accept the ideals of the state as their own. While not dismissing these ideas, Neill and Reich added the idea that the development of particular character structures can determine whether an individual wants an authoritarian state or democratic state.

Consequently, the Summerhill model extends the meaning of "free school." In this model of the free school, children are not dominated by particular ideals and morality because they are free to study whatever they want, whenever they want to. In addition, the teacher takes an active role—when a student chooses that teacher—in guiding students to an awareness of how to gain self-ownership. Also, children are free to study subject matter that is consciously political. Furthermore, all forms of oppression, including inequality between sexes, are banned from free schools. And, of course, children are free to pursue pleasure so that they will be free of anxieties about having pleasure. As a result, they will demand a world that provides them with pleasure.

The importance of the pursuit of pleasure is central to arguments against the authoritarian state. The authoritarian state asks citizens to sacrifice pleasure for the ideals and the good of the state. Reich and Neill, however, assumed that citizens raised to be free of the authoritarian character structure will refuse to make those sacrifices. They will reject the idea that they exist to serve the state. They will demand that the state exist to serve them.

CONCLUSION: WHAT WOULD SOCRATES THINK?

The goals of the free school movement are in complete opposition to those set forth by Socrates in *The Republic* (see Chapter 1). Socrates wants individual desires to be controlled by the wisdom of philosopher-kings. The individual desires of all citizens are to be subservient to some form of ultimate truth that can be discerned only by the rulers of society. The worst possible scenario for Socrates is when sexual desires are let loose. Socrates argues that the just state and the just individual can exist only when people are taught to sacrifice themselves for some ultimate good.

In the free school movement, educational authority is given to each individual, rather than to philosopher-kings. This difference in the source of educational authority is reflected in different concepts about the uses of knowledge. For the free school movement, knowledge serves the purpose of helping people to be free and happy. For instance, in examples previously cited in this chapter, arithmetic is taught in the context of planning an economy that would fairly distribute wealth and goods, while the teaching of history focuses on the power of the people to change and to build new social and political institutions. In contrast, Socrates believed that the purpose of teaching history is to teach ideals that would guide future actions, and arithmetic was to be one step on the road to understanding some form of ultimate truth.

The free school movement turns the Socratic argument on its head. The Socratic tradition says that people should not be able to choose how they want to conduct their lives and how they want to be governed. Rather, people will be happy only when taught to accept the rule of the philosopher-kings and to sacrifice themselves for ideals. On the other hand, for the free school movement, the just state is one in which people are free to pursue their own pleasures, including fulfillment of their sexual desires. The free school movement emphasizes the need to avoid planting ideals in children's minds so that they will be able to choose according to their own pleasure. The free school movement seeks a nonauthoritarian society in which people will be free to determine the type of economic and political organizations they want based on the goals of individual pleasure and happiness. In this society, people will not be asked to sacrifice their personal needs and desires for a god, a state, or a ruler.

NOTES

1. Emma Goldman, "The Child and Its Enemies," *Mother Earth*, Vol. I, No. 2, (April 1906), pp. 12–13.
2. Francisco Ferrer, *The Origin and Ideals of the Modern School*, trans. Joseph McCabe (New York: G. P. Putnam's Sons, 1913), p. 29.
3. Ibid., p. 76.
4. Ibid., pp. 86–89.
5. Ibid., pp. 89–90.
6. Goldman, "The Child and Its Enemies," p. 9.
7. Leo Tolstoy, "Education and Culture," *Tolstoy on Education*, trans. Leo Wiener (Chicago: University of Chicago Press, 1967).
8. Francisco Ferrer, "L'Ecole; Rénovée," *Mother Earth*, Vol. IV, No. 9, (November 1909), pp. 267–275.
9. Harry Kelly, "The Modern School in Retrospect," in *The Modern School of Stelton* (Stelton, N.J., 1925), pp. 115–119.
10. Alexis Ferm, "Workers' Children and the Public Schools," The Road to Freedom, Vol. 7, No. 7 (March 1931), p. 5.
11. James H. Dick, "Radicals and Education," *The Road to Freedom*, Vol. 5, No. 8, (April 1929), pp. 1–2.
12. Ferm, "Workers' Children," p. 5.
13. A. S. Neill, *The Problem Child* (New York: Robert M. McBride, 1927), pp. 18, 114.
14. Ibid., p. 52.
15. A. S. Neill, "The Man Reich," in *Wilhelm Reich* by A. S. Neill, Paul and Jean Ritter, Myron Sharaf, Nic Wool (Nottingham, England: Ritter Press, 1949), p. 21.
16. Wilhelm Reich, *The Discovery of the Orgone: The Function of the Orgasm* (New York: Farrar, Strauss and Giroux, 1970), p. 133.
17. Wilhelm Reich, *The Mass Psychology of Fascism* (New York: Farrar, Strauss and Giroux, 1970), p. 19.
18. Ibid., 32, 55–59.
19. Wilhelm Reich, *The Sexual Revolution* (New York: Farrar, Strauss and Giroux, 1962), p. 77.

20. Reich, *Mass Psychology,* pp. 32, 55–59.
21. Ibid., p. 61.
22. Neill, "The Man Reich," pp. 24–25.
23. Neill, *The Problem Child,* p. 100.
24. Ibid., pp. 211, 231–232.
25. A. S. Neill, *The Problem Teacher* (New York: International Press, 1944), pp. 19–32.
26. Ibid., p. 27.
27. Ibid., p. 27.
28. A. S. Neill, *The Problem Family* (New York: Hermitage Press, 1949), p. 151.
29. A. S. Neill, *Hearts Not Heads in the School* (London: Herbert Jenkins Ltd., 1944), pp. 19–32.

CHAPTER 5

Free Space and No Schools

In the latter part of the twentieth century, free schools addressed new concerns about the complexity of modern technology, growth of urban centers, and the increasing linkage between educational credentials and jobs. Paul Goodman believes that individuals are losing control over their lives as they increasingly depend on complex technology. The reliance on technology, he argues, results in dependency on technical experts. In addition, as population centers become more complex, according to Goodman, it is difficult for people to participate in the political control of their own communities. Goodman concludes that free schools should exist in small, decentralized communities where it is possible for all people to share political control. In addition, he argues, there should be a revolution in the design of technology so that people do not have to depend on experts.

Ivan Illich also worries about increasing dependence on expertise. He believes this dependence is a function of the organization of the traditional school. In addition, Illich believes that the reliance on educational credentials for jobs is resulting in schools reinforcing the social class structure of society. From his perspective, schools are translating economic differences into differences in educational credentials. His solution is to change the structure of the traditional school so that people are not trained to depend on experts and schools cannot be used to maintain differences in social classes.

Also, by the latter part of the century, the word "free" in free schools is primarily used to mean the freedom for children to learn or not to learn. Freedom not to learn might be another means of enslaving people. Denying people an education is a traditional means of controlling a population. Ignorance is not a source of freedom. For free schools, the resolution of this issue is essential for making education a real contribution to human freedom. The debate about the meaning of freedom for children raises important questions about the ability of education to not plant wheels in the head.

PAUL GOODMAN: DECENTRALIZATION AND FREE PLAYGROUNDS

Paul Goodman, a founder of the Summerhill Society in the United States and a leader of the free school movement in the 1960s and 1970s, advocates decentralizing contemporary institutions as a means of equalizing power. He is concerned that technology is making it more difficult for individuals to exert control over their personal worlds. For example, as technology becomes increasingly complex, it is more difficult for people to understand and repair the products they use. For instance, an icebox is a very simple structure compared with a refrigerator. Most people can build, use, and repair an icebox without too much difficulty, whereas a refrigerator makes them dependent on other people's expertise. In other words, a refrigerator might free people from worries about food storage, but it reduces their freedom to act independently of refrigerator manufacturing and repair services.

Goodman does not want to abandon technological development, but he does want different goals for it. Most technological development, other than military technology, has the single goal of enhancing corporate profits. A corporation cares little, if at all, about whether technological development increases human happiness or gives people more power over their lives. In fact, new technologies under corporate control are not introduced into the workplace if human labor is cheaper, nor are they introduced into consumer markets unless they can reap a profit. Corporations can also increase their profits if the technology requires consumers to depend on corporate services after the purchase. Furthermore, from the standpoint of maintaining profits, a goal of corporate technological development is to make existing products appear obsolete so that consumers will continuously purchase new technologies that perform the same function.

One way Goodman believes people can gain greater control over technology and their lives is through decentralization of industry and democratic control of technological development. Decentralization of industry, as Goodman envisions it, would create small manufacturing units in which workers would share equal power in decisions about technological development. He hopes the profit motive will be replaced by a motive to develop technology that would be simple and allow for individual understanding and control. In this context, industrial decentralization would increase the power of both the worker and consumer.

Goodman applies the concept of decentralization to most aspects of contemporary life including schools.[1] He believes decentralization will result in more democratic control, as well as increasing the quality of life and level of happiness for most people. Goodman argues that large urban areas should be broken up into smaller units in which people can directly participate in the management of their communities. Large-scale bureaucracies, according to Goodman, should follow the same path of decentralization that he advocates for industry and urban living.

It is important to emphasize that Goodman is concerned both with increasing democracy by equalizing power and with improving the quality of human life. In other words, he believes that smaller units of operation will assure that industry, community services, and other organizations will be better able to serve human desires and needs, while at the same time increasing democratic control.

Goodman applies the same reasoning to education. Like other free school advocates, he believes public schools serve the interests of a ruling industrial elite, not those of students. In his most famous book on education, *Compulsory*

Mis-Education and the Community of Scholars, he contends that the real function of public schools is to grade students and to market their job skills. He writes, "This means, in effect, that a few great corporations are getting the benefit of an enormous weeding out and selective process—all children are fed into the mill and everybody pays for it."[2]

Goodman's vision for education includes decentralization of large, cumbersome school systems and the establishment of small-scale schools. These small schools would operate along the lines of Summerhill, except that they would not be boarding schools. From Goodman's perspective, small schools would make it possible for students to share power in controlling their schools and, in addition, provide a better education.

Goodman wants schools to be tied to the life of the community and the city. Small schools, he argues, would help to overcome the powerlessness and loss of community experienced in contemporary urban life. Furthermore, he suggests that small urban schools can dispense with formal classes as we know them and use other teaching methods including streets, stores, museums, movies, and factories as places of learning. These schools would replace state-certified teachers with other kinds of teachers, including neighborhood people such as druggists, storekeepers, and factory workers.

Goodman's proposals are an attempt to create environments for the equal sharing of power and for the individual expression of freedom in a world that is overly structured and rationalized. The free playground movement was founded on a similar desire to provide spaces where children can exercise freedom. One of the first free playgrounds was founded in Copenhagen in 1943. Shortly after World War II, the idea spread to Sweden, Switzerland, and the United States. In Stockholm the playground was known as "Freetown," in Minneapolis as "The Yard," and in Switzerland as a "Robinson Crusoe Playground." The basic principle of the adventure playground is that children construct their own play equipment and structures. The playground is equipped with tools, lumber, nails, junk metal, shovels, and building equipment. There is no manufactured equipment such as swings or seesaws; essentially the children are given the means to build, destroy, and rebuild their playgrounds.[3]

Goodman's proposals and the free playground movement represent attempts to find space for the exercise of power and freedom. This same concern is reflected in the work of Ivan Illich, who believes that the forces of modern technology and institutional development are destroying people's ability to act independently of the advice or control of experts, government, and corporations. Like Goodman, Illich is concerned that for people who do not have the ability to exercise independent action, freedom has little meaning.

IVAN ILLICH: DESCHOOLING SOCIETY

During the late 1960s and the 1970s, Illich headed the Center for Intercultural Documentation (CIDOC) in Cuernavaca, Mexico. CIDOC attracted radical school reformers and free school advocates from all over North and South America. At the heart of Illich's concern is creating an alternative to the traditional concept of school.[4] Illich believes that the institution of the school and the relationship it creates between student and teacher destroy the ability of people to act independently. Illich coined the term "deschooling" to represent his efforts to rid society of all traditional forms of schooling. As I discuss later in this chapter, CIDOC represented one alternative proposed by Illich to the traditional school. He also proposes other methods of deschooling society.

To appreciate Illich's advocacy of deschooling, one first must understand his criticism of schooling. Illich's initial interest in the social impact of schools began with his work as a Catholic priest among Puerto Ricans in New York and Puerto Rico. He quickly realized that public schools promised to provide equality of opportunity to Puerto Ricans, but, in reality, they were condemning Puerto Ricans to the lowest rungs of the economic ladder. The same phenomenon, Illich argues, was happening in South America with the spread of compulsory education. From Illich's perspective, education holds out the hope of equality of opportunity, but in the end it does not fulfill this hope but only provides another means of assuring that people are kept in their economic place.

Illich argues that schools serve the function of translating economic differences into differences in schooling. In the United States and South America, universal schooling was instituted with the promise that it would serve as a ladder for upward mobility for the poor. But in reality what happens, Illich argues, is that family income determines the quality and amount of education received by students. Students from rich families attend better schools and receive more years of education than children from low-income families.

In addition, schools educate people to believe they are fair and just institutions. The poor, according to Illich, are told that school provides an equal opportunity for all people to improve themselves economically. The schools convince students that they are fair and benign institutions. Consequently, when children of the poor do not advance economically and do not experience social mobility as a consequence of their education, they blame themselves for failing to achieve in school. If children believe in the goodness of schools, then they accept the social position the schools prepare them for as right and just.

For Illich, the myth that schools provide equality of opportunity serves the same function as the myth of the metals in Plato's *Republic*—both myths provide a rationale for getting people to accept their place in society. Plato's myth of the metals sorts people according to who contains more of one metal than the others. The myth of the school convinces people that some students are by nature superior to others. Both myths obscure the fact that achievement is related to external factors, not innate qualities. As a result of the myth that schools provide equality of opportunity, people tend to blame themselves, not the system, for their own personal failure or achievement in school.

The myth of schooling, Illich argues, leads the poor to accept their poverty as their right and just position in life. In the past, Illich contends, it was clear to people that social differences resulted from differences in wealth. People had power because they had more money. But with the advent of universal school-

ing, power was equated with academic success, not wealth. These e
ferences were translated into differences in schooling. Since the my
ing is that all people have equal opportunity to achieve in school
cept their lower status in society because they believe they deser
as a result of their failure to achieve in school.

One of Illich's concerns is this role of schools in maintaining social class differences. He is also concerned that schools, along with other institutions, are
teaching a dependence on expertise and technology. The traditional teacher-
student relationship, Illich argues, teaches students to depend on expertise (the
teacher) before acting. This relationship reinforces the patterns of dependency
of modern society. People are taught not to act until they are told the correct
way to act by some expert. Rather than believing in their own power to make
choices, people are taught they should make choices only after consulting and
paying experts.

Illich, like Paul Goodman, is particularly concerned about the dependence
on professional expertise that is created by modern technology. It is difficult for
the average person to understand the technology that is commonplace in every-
day life. Consequently, most of us must depend on the knowledge of experts for
servicing and repair. Illich also shares Goodman's opinion that the benefits of
technology are unevenly distributed through the population because technological development is based on the profit motive.

For instance, consider the issue of health care in poor regions in South
America. In some of these areas, Illich argues, advanced technology for heart
operations is introduced to save the lives of a few wealthy individuals, while
vast areas of the countryside suffer from multiple health problems resulting
from contaminated water supplies and poor sewage systems. Of course, it is
more profitable for the health industry to focus on expensive treatments for the
rich than on community health projects for the poor. It is thus more profitable to
develop expensive technology to save a few rich people's lives than to worry
about the conditions of the poor.

According to Illich, the poor are doomed to inaction because they are taught
to be dependent on experts and technology. Dependence on experts and technology teaches people that they are unable to act on their own to solve their own
problems. For instance, people could launch a community health program to
rectify the problems associated with water supply and sewage systems. These
projects could be aided by technology if technological development were directed at producing products that would allow poor people to take charge of
their lives. Rather than developing an expensive set of equipment to save the
lives of a few rich people, scientists could develop inexpensive equipment that
poor people could use to improve community health conditions.

Therefore, Illich's call to deschool society is based on his opposition to the use
of schools to maintain social class differences and to teach dependence on experts
and technology. The organizational structure of CIDOC reflected these two concerns. CIDOC was primarily an institution for learning. To avoid any relationship
between education and social class, and education and jobs, CIDOC kept no student records and issued no grades or certificates. This system overcame the

objections of many libertarian-anarchists that the function of traditional schools is primarily that of job training and certification.

To help break down a sense of dependence on experts, no distinction was made between teacher and student. Anyone could teach and anyone could be a student. In fact, it was possible to be a student and a teacher at the same time. This was accomplished through notices on a bulletin board in the dining room. Anyone was allowed to post a notice of a course she or he wanted to offer. At a certain time and location, anyone posting a notice would give a public lecture on the content and value of the course. After this lecture, anyone who wanted to take the course could sign up for it. People could teach one course and attend other courses.

Originally, people paid CIDOC for any courses they took and, after general operating expenses were paid, the money was then given to the teacher. Under this system, a teacher's pay would be based on the number of students attracted to the course. This system caused many complaints from those who confused the concept of a free school with that of a free education (one that doesn't cost any money). Because of these complaints, Illich adopted a more direct way of paying those who wanted to teach. People attending CIDOC as either students or teachers would pay a charge to cover the general operating costs of the institution. People who taught courses would announce to those attending what they felt they were worth. For instance, a teacher might announce a charge to each student of $10 per class meeting. The student could then decide whether or not the class was worth $10 a meeting.

CIDOC was a model for the type of learning institution that would exist in Illich's deschooled society. It was primarily an institution for bringing together people who wanted to teach and learn; it did not grade or certify people for employers and did not function to determine one's place in society. And, by not making a distinction between teachers and learners, Illich hoped CIDOC would socialize people to depend on themselves, not experts.

The CIDOC model is implicit in Illich's proposal for the general deschooling of society. Illich advocates the creation of a series of public utilities for education. An important aspect of these utilities is that one person or group cannot gain control over the educational process. This type of organization solves the problem of politicians, businesspeople, and other interest groups controlling the distribution of knowledge for their own benefit. The utilities would also be protected against use by the state to fulfill its own goals and policies.

In Illich's proposal, the traditional functions of schooling would be divided between separate and distinct units. For instance, he suggests the creation of a public utility that would serve as an information center, a kind of expanded library where books and other media would be available, as well as information on things such as opportunities to visit industrial centers or observe a variety of community activities. Of course, none of the utilities proposed by Illich is compulsory. People would be free to use or not use any of them.

Another utility would provide instruction in any subject or skill that people want to teach. Similar to CIDOC, people who want to teach could register their skills, such as typing, fishing, bricklaying, or historical research. Those who wish to learn a skill could go to the utility and select an appropriate teache this utility, as in the information center, people would be free to learn anythin they want. No one would be in a position of power to make decisions for a person or to decide what is in the person's best interests.

Separation of the information and skill utilities, Illich hopes, would make it impossible to develop an extended or graded curriculum. A curriculum might exist within a skill, such as typing, but this curriculum would not extend beyond that particular skill. In other words, general curriculum planning would be turned over to the individual. This would give everyone the opportunity to select his or her own curriculum goals while planning the learning experience.

Illich believes an important function of traditional schools is creating a community of learners. To overcome this loss with deschooling, Illich proposes a utility for linking people of common interests. People could go to this utility and request, for instance, to be put into contact with people interested in discussing a particular book. The utility would match people through computers, journals dealing with specific interests, or simple notices in which people register the interests they wished to share.

Illich's proposals do not include abandonment of government as a source of organizational and financial support. He suggests the issuance by government of educational "credit cards" at birth that would allow people to use the utilities for their entire lives. Parents would use their children's credit cards to arrange learning experiences for them, and when the children became adults they could use these cards to continue their learning.

While Illich's plan does not require complete separation of state and education, he does hope to eliminate the worst features of state control. The state would sponsor the utilities and finance the educational credit cards. But the separation of utilities and the protection of them from outside political and economic influences would ensure that learning would not be used as a means of ideological control by political rulers, for producing compliant workers for industry, or as a mechanism of maintaining social class differences.

Illich's deschooling proposal contains an important criticism of the free school movement. In the nineteenth century, libertarian-anarchists were primarily interested in protecting children from ideological control by the state. But in the twentieth century, the free school movement went beyond concern about protection to arguing that free schools could be the source of revolutionary change. A. S. Neill believed that the good society could be brought about by the spread of Summerhills.

By advocating deschooling, Illich rejects the idea that any school, including free schools, will be the source of radical social change. In fact, Illich would argue, there is the danger that free schools would create even greater dependence on experts and institutions, because free schools might teach people that they need an institution to give them freedom. Illich thus rejects the concept of a free school and argues that true autonomy can result only if individuals are free from dependence on institutions and experts.

Of course, Paul Goodman and advocates of free playgrounds might argue that children need space in which to practice freedom, especially in a society that

e tightly controlled and organized. In other words, they would
hools are necessary to teach children to be free. But this is the
e school that Illich rejected, advocating instead complete inde-
ny form of schooling. Also, the idea of providing a space in
in act freely is very different from the definition of freedom
arly free school movement. The early free schoolers defined
freedom" as freedom from ideological control by the state and freedom from
the placement of any wheels into the head. In fact, as I discuss in the next section, it is the issue of freedom for children that created the major stumbling block
for the free school movement.

WHITE LION STREET FREE SCHOOL

Founded in 1972, the White Lion Street Free School in North London is one of
Britain's best-known free schools. Supporting its establishment were a number
of famous educators, including A. S. Neill. The purpose of the school is to provide a space where children can practice freedom and democracy. The democratic aspect of the institution centers around the concept of equal sharing of
power. To accomplish this goal, there is no distinction between teachers and
other workers at the school, such as maintenance people and cooks. All school
personnel, called "workers," meet with the children to make decisions about the
school. In addition, parents participate equally in this sharing of power.
Decisions are made by democratic consensus. The majority does not rule. All
participants must agree on all decisions.

The major problems in the White Lion Free School result from the fact that
it is an oasis of freedom and democracy in a society that is highly organized and
often hostile to these ideas. For instance, one problem is gaining parental in-
volvement. While some parents participate, others do not. A basic reason for this
problem is that the demands of work and daily living do not leave many parents with the time and energy to participate in school decisions. In a world of
small, simply organized communities, one might imagine parents gathering
weekly to make decisions about their children's school. But this is not a realistic
goal in the fast-paced, complex world of modern London.

The pressures of the surrounding world also create problems for the exercise of freedom. In the first place, British law requires school attendance.
Consequently, children's attendance at any school, including the White Lion
Free School, is not a matter of personal choice. Obviously, being forced to attend
school contradicts a basic principle of noncompulsory education. Second, the
White Lion Free School is only one school in the midst of many other more traditional schools. Some parents move their children from school to school, resulting in a highly transient student population. New children require a period
of adjustment to the atmosphere of a free school. By the time many of them make
this adjustment, they are withdrawn by their parents and sent to another school.
And third, many parents see the school as a place for their problem children,
who are often very disruptive. Many of these children require psychological

help that is beyond the capabilities of the workers in the school. Even A. S. Neill warns, "One simply cannot sacrifice other children to one problem child."[5]

A transient student population and the presence of problem children create major problems for the exercise of freedom. Some children at the school are bullies who try to dominate other children; others use freedom as an opportunity for willful destruction. Nigel Wright, a teacher at the school, describes the resulting problems: "Sometimes children would go through rooms like whirlwinds, throwing everything on the floor, upsetting furniture, smashing crockery, tearing up books, breaking fittings, spilling liquids."[6] Wright worries that freedom in this situation results in a new aristocracy of children who dominate the resources of the school.

There is also dissatisfaction at the school because freedom to learn means that some children choose to learn nothing. A typical day at the school, according to Wright, begins with the workers gathering at nine o'clock in the ground-floor dining room for discussion and tea. Children begin arriving at nine with most in attendance by ten o'clock. As the children arrive, workers begin to solicit them to participate in some form of learning activity. A small number of children choose to learn something and eventually move to one of the learning rooms with a worker. The majority of students spend their time "hanging out." Most of the time spent hanging out is devoted to listening to music or wandering in and out of the school.

CONCLUSION: THE PROBLEM OF FREEDOM IN FREE SCHOOLS

When freedom to learn results in no learning, free school advocates are presented with a major dilemma. Historically, education can be used as a method of control by either denying people an education or imposing a controlling ideology. However, people who are ignorant of any learning are perhaps the most easily controlled. A. S. Neill's response to this dilemma is given in terms of the responsibility of adults to children. Neill argues that it is the responsibility of the adult to stop children from doing something harmful to themselves.[7] For instance, if a child is about to run in front of a car, it is the responsibility of the adult to stop the child. Clearly, total freedom for children, such as freedom to run in front of cars, is absurd; if they are hurt or killed, they will automatically be denied future freedoms.

The same argument can be applied to learning. Giving a child freedom not to learn can result in restricting the child's future freedom and happiness. For instance, without knowledge and understanding of the workings of government and the economic system, people can easily be oppressed and exploited. Without basic reading, writing, and mathematical skills, people do not have access to history, literature, science, and all other fields of knowledge. Without knowledge of personal health care, people's freedom to act can be restricted by chronic medical problems or early death. Without knowledge and understanding of the arts, people's happiness might be limited.

In other words, education is both a source of freedom and happiness and a source of control. In recent years confusion over this issue has caused many problems for the free school movement. Many parents scorn the free school movement because they believe their children should learn some particular body of knowledge. Socialists and others who support state intervention as a method of radical change criticize free schools for not making children consciously political; consequently, they claim, free schools prepare children to be exploited later in life.

In addition, I would argue that meaningful use of freedom of choice requires some knowledge of what choices one has. In other words, a young child does not know what it is possible to learn. For example, it is difficult for people to choose to learn sociology or art history if they do not know what these areas of learning cover or that this body of knowledge exists.

I would argue that one way out of this dilemma is to examine the various meanings of freedom used in the free school movement. The first concern of the libertarian-anarchist movement is that political rulers use education to perpetuate their own power and to control citizens. "Freedom," in this situation, means freedom from state control of education. The second concern is to avoid having wheels placed in the head. In this situation, freedom means the ability to choose one's beliefs and ideals freely. The third concern is to ensure the use of knowledge to equalize power among people and to promote the happiness of all. In this situation, freedom is the opportunity to gain knowledge that will help people to understand their lack of freedom and, thus, how to achieve freedom. In other words, education should be consciously political. The fourth concern is the repression of physical desires and needs for the benefit of political and economic rulers. In this situation, freedom is the ability to want a world that satisfies one's needs and desires as opposed to a world where people are taught to want to sacrifice themselves for the good of the state or the economy.

These various meanings of "freedom" provide a guide for organizing a free school that does not result in the loss of freedom for children because they learn nothing. First, the free school should be protected from political and economic elites who want to use education as a means of control and oppression. Second, the school should not impose morals, beliefs, or ideals. Third, instruction should be consciously political in the sense that children learn how to protect and enhance their freedom and political power. Fourth, teachers should act as guides to make children aware of what can be learned. Fifth, teachers should organize some form of curriculum so that children can make choices about what to learn. And last, as adults, teachers have the responsibility to act in a nonpunitive manner to ensure that children are learning.

In addition, any guide to free schools must consider the issues raised by Paul Goodman and Ivan Illich. As Goodman points out, size is an important factor in ensuring a sense of control over the educational environment. Small schools can create a sense of community and make it possible for students and faculty to share power. Large, complex institutions make it difficult for students and faculty to know one another. They also make it difficult for a single individual to have an impact on the control of the institution. In addition, as Illich suggests, to avoid the use of schooling as a means of reinforcing the social class structure of society, schools should not issue credentials that can be used in the labor market. The determination of a person's fitness for an occupation should be the responsibility of employers or professional associations. Realistically, this seems difficult because employers can always ask about a job applicant's educational background. Consequently, Illich's goal might not be obtainable. But it does seem reasonable to conclude that the principles of a free school stated on the previous page, work best in a small school in which teachers are aware of the potential of education to define a student's social class.

NOTES

1. See Paul Goodman, *New Reformation: Notes of a Neolithic Conservative* (New York: Random House, 1970), and *Communitas* (New York: Random House, 1965).
2. Paul Goodman, *Compulsory Mis-Education and the Community of Scholars* (New York: Vintage Books, 1966), p. 57.
3. Colin Ward, "Adventure Playground: A Parable of Anarchy," *Anarchy* 7 (1961), pp. 193–201.
4. See Ivan Illich, *De-Schooling Society* (New York: Harper & Row, 1971) and *Celebration of Awareness: A Call for Institutional Revolution* (New York: Doubleday, 1971).
5. Quoted in Nigel Wright, *Free School: The White Lion Experience* (Leicestershire, England: Libertarian Education, 1989), p. 28.
6. Ibid., pp. 28–29.
7. Ibid., pp. 67–68.

PART THREE

The Politics of Culture

CHAPTER 6

Cultural Unity and Cultural Literacy

Is an education in a particular cultural tradition necessary for the continuation of a free society? Or, is cultural education another method of authoritarian control? Authoritarian states might use the transmission of culture through schools as another method of winning the allegiance of citizens. Certainly in Nazi Germany the transmission of the culture of the fatherland was part of the process of creating a sense of nationalism and building patriotic fervor. On the other hand, a democratic state might want to pass on a cultural heritage that is supportive of democratic institutions. From the standpoint of Amy Gutmann, a democratic state should consciously transmit a cultural tradition to students that is supportive of her principle of nonrepression. On the other hand, the methodologies of John Dewey and Henry Giroux are in opposition to the transmission of a particular culture. Working from the principle of the social construction of knowledge, both methodologies assume that culture is a product of human interaction and that it should constantly be reconstructed to meet the changing needs of society.

For the democratic state, the imposition of knowledge and, consequently, culture is an issue. Should a democratic state impose on students a belief in the freedom of ideas or, in Amy Gutmann's words, nonrepression of the consideration of alternatives to the good life? In the framework of the politics of culture the question could be stated: Should a democratic state impose on students a single cultural tradition that is supportive of freedom of ideas? Of course, the problem is that a cultural tradition might be imposed that is contradictory to the beliefs of some students and their parents. One way out of this dilemma is to believe that diversity of ideas and, in this case, diversity of cultures is necessary for giving substance to the concept of freedom. Freedom of thought has little meaning if all people think and believe the same things. Therefore, from the perspective of this argument, the answer is no to the question of whether a democratic state should disseminate a single cultural tradition through the schools.

THE PROBLEM OF CULTURE IN A GLOBAL ECONOMY

While the preceding parts of the book suggest that passing on a single cultural tradition might be detrimental to the maintenance of a democratic state, the recent development of global corporations and the internationalization of the labor force have sparked debates about the transmission of culture. Corporations are faced with the problem of a multicultural work force and multicultural consumers. Global corporations are now able to move their production and information-processing facilities from nation to nation to take advantage of the cheapest labor supply. Consequently, corporations must worry about how their economic practices fit into the general cultural practices of the host country. In turn, workers move from nation to nation, seeking the highest wages. Europe and the United States are experiencing a large influx of immigrant laborers. In addition, the breakdown of the European colonial empires is resulting in large numbers of former colonials moving to the homeland of their previous rulers. For instance, Great Britain now houses numerous former colonials, such as Indians, Pakistanis, and West Indians. War and political unrest are causing other population shifts, sending scores of Vietnamese, Cambodians, Soviet Jews, Cubans, Haitians, and other immigrants in search of new lands.[1]

The internationalization of the labor force creates a dilemma for corporations. On the one hand, corporations are interested in maintaining cultural standards that are supportive of capitalism and free enterprise. On the other hand, corporations must promote multicultural tolerance so that different cultural groups will cooperate in the workplace. In addition, cultural groups that are in the minority in certain countries are interested in empowering their own cultures against the dominant ones.

These dilemmas about multicultural populations are present in various forms in the United States. First, a number of widely read books and articles appeared in the late 1980s and early 1990s defending the necessity of maintaining Western cultural traditions and cultural unity against the rise of multiculturalism. The most popular books are Allan Bloom's *The Closing of the American Mind* and E. D. Hirsch's *Cultural Literacy: What Every American Needs to Know*. Second, reflecting a concern about the multicultural composition of the U.S. labor force, the Secretary of Labor's Commission on Achieving Necessary Skills lists the following as one skill necessary for the food service industry: "Interpersonal. Participate in a staff meeting with a multicultural group of workers."[2] In this situation, multiculturalism is linked to cooperation at work. And third, the United States experienced a burst of multicultural education programs in the late 1980s and early 1990s whose goal was the empowerment of minority cultures against the dominant European culture.

These events raise a number of issues for the political philosophy of education. In this chapter, I will focus on two important and politically related arguments dealing with the protection of Western cultural traditions and cultural unity. The first is that Western culture supports the best form of government, namely, one that is representative and based on a natural rights philosophy. Second, it is argued that the continued existence of the state depends on national cultural unity. In other words, schools should teach a single culture as a means of maintaining national unity. Great Britain adopted this approach in 1988 by instituting a national curriculum. Given Britain's increasingly diverse population, the purpose of the law is to assure national cultural unity based on British cultural traditions. Because cultural minority groups in Great Britain lack significant political power, there is little pressure for a multicultural curriculum.[3]

In the United States, on the other hand, cultural minority groups have more political power than those in Great Britain. Consequently, this political power results in a great deal of pressure on public schools to teach a multicultural curriculum, which has touched off a debate in the United States over the direction of multicultural education and the nature of U.S. political culture. One side of the debate argues that schools should teach about other cultures to ensure tolerance among cultural groups. Obviously, business is interested in establishing toleration among cultural groups so that cultural friction in the workplace will be reduced. But on this side of the debate, the emphasis on toleration is accompanied by a call for national unity through the teaching of basic American political values. In other words, schools are to teach children toleration for other cultures and, at the same time, bring all cultures under the umbrella of a dominant set of political values.

The other side of the debate, originates primarily among groups that are dominated by European Americans, such as African Americans, Native Americans, Puerto Ricans, and Mexican Americans. Some members of these cultural groups argue that schools should teach a multicultural curriculum designed to empower their particular cultural traditions in the dominant European-American culture. This, it is believed, will result in greater political and economic power for these groups. This form of multiculturalism envisions a pluralistic society in which traditional political values are reshaped by the interplay of different world cultures. This approach takes a more dynamic view of political values as compared with the type of multiculturalism in which toleration and national unity are emphasized. People advocating toleration and national unity want to protect traditional values, while those advocating empowerment envision the birth of a new form of society with possibly differing political values.

This chapter focuses on the arguments for protecting Western values and maintaining national unity. In my discussion of these arguments, I will refer to previous discussions of the role of education in authoritarian and democratic states and the dissenting traditions to state education. As the reader will discover, a discussion of multiculturalism adds another dimension to the political role of education in a world economy.

ALLAN BLOOM: *THE CLOSING OF THE AMERICAN MIND*

The most articulate and thoughtful defense of preserving Western cultural traditions through education is philosopher Allan Bloom's *The Closing of the American Mind*. Bloom's arguments reflect a love of Socratic thought and of Plato's *Republic*. In fact, a large part of Bloom's scholarship and teaching focuses on *The Republic*.[4]

Central to Bloom's defense of basing education on Western cultural traditions is a concern with preserving the natural rights doctrine. The doctrine of natural rights, Bloom believes, serves as the basis for the U.S. Constitution and is superior to other political doctrines. The basic tenet of natural rights is that all humans are born with equal rights to life, liberty, and the pursuit of happiness. Included in these rights is the right to gain and retain property. In Chapter 8, I will provide a more complete analysis of the natural rights arguments as stated by John Locke and Jean-Jacques Rousseau.

Bloom believes that the maintenance of the Western cultural tradition is necessary for the preservation of these rights. Central to this cultural tradition is respect for the free exercise of reason. The free exercise of reason, Bloom argues, is both a part of the natural rights doctrine and a necessity for its protection. The right to liberty guarantees protection of the free exercise of reason. In addition, the free exercise of reason allows people to understand and make decisions that will protect their rights. Schools can preserve this tradition, according to Bloom, by protecting and nurturing a rational quest for truth.

Since Bloom believes in the political superiority of the natural rights doctrine, he rejects cultural relativity. In fact, he argues against all forms of relativity. He maintains that not all cultures and values are of equal worth. Consequently, he is opposed to multicultural curricula in schools because of the potential damage to the tradition of natural rights and the free exercise of reason. Many of the world's cultures, he argues, do not respect the free exercise of reason or recognize the existence of natural rights.

Therefore, Bloom contends, national unity should be created through teaching in schools about natural rights and the cultural traditions that support those rights. Similarly to Amy Gutmann, he believes that education should cultivate the free exercise of reason. National unity based on a culture that respects natural rights and the free exercise of reason is the foundation, he maintains, of preserving a democratic state.

Criticism that school curricula in the United States are Eurocentric, Bloom argues, does a disservice to the importance of Western political values. Most of the world's cultures, Bloom argues, are *not* tolerant of other cultures; they are ethnocentric. Cultural tolerance and the abandonment of ethnocentricism appear to be primarily a reflection of Western values. Contrary to the intentions of Western advocates of cultural tolerance, Bloom maintains, the imposition of cultural tolerance on cultures that do not value toleration might again reflect a belief in the superiority of Western values.

Current advocates of cultural relativity and tolerance, Bloom argues, distort the concept of openness that originated in Western culture with the scientific revolution of the eighteenth and nineteenth centuries. Bloom considers the values of the scientific revolution to be an essential part of the cultural tradition that supports natural rights and the free exercise of reason. In this context, openness is a virtue that permits people to exercise reason in the pursuit of truth. In other words, people are open to the consideration, through the exercise of reason, of any ideas. However, Bloom contends that openness, as current supporters of cultural relativity and tolerance define it, means *acceptance* of all ideas as being of equal worth. The difference between this meaning of openness and Bloom's can be understood in the context of studying other cultures. The concept of openness that originated in the scientific revolution and the belief in the free exercise of reason accept the use of reason to study other cultures. For instance, the exercise of reason, in this sense, might allow one to determine if other cultures are supportive of natural rights and the free exercise of reason and, thus, to make statements about the value of other cultures. On the other hand, the concept of openness, defined as acceptance and toleration, leads to the position that studies of other cultures should be free of judgments about their worth. According to this meaning of openness, one purpose of studying other cultures is to build toleration and understanding.

Bloom's rejection of the relativity of culture and values reflects his broader belief in the purposes of education in a democratic state. While he rejects the relativity of values, he does not advocate the imposition of values and beliefs. Rather, he believes that for each individual, values and beliefs should be formed through the free exercise of reason. His model is Socrates. For him, Socratic thought is at the core of the Western tradition that supports a democratic state, and the Socratic dialogue is the model for the free exercise of reason.

Therefore, Bloom's ideal of the best education, particularly higher education, which is his main concern, is the Socratic dialogue. He believes the core of education should be a reasoned dialogue about broad questions such as the meaning and purpose of life, the ideal society, and the nature of love and beauty. Of course, this reasoned dialogue would be based on the reading of philosophy and great works of literature and the exploration of science. Bloom is particularly scornful of university practices in the twentieth century that promote an emphasis on practical and job-related studies. For instance, while teaching during the Cold War era of the 1950s and 1960s, he was incensed by the emphasis on the study of engineering and science as a means of increasing the supply of engineers and scientists to win the military race with the Soviet Union. He claims that, in fact, students he met during this time really wanted to study the meaning of their lives and, in general, wanted to engage in a rational quest for meaning.

Bloom considers the scientific revolution of the eighteenth and nineteenth centuries as fulfilling the Socratic goal of creating a world in search of truth through the exercise of reason. Of course, a major difference is that this search is no longer to be limited to philosopher-kings. In the framework of natural rights, all people are born equal regarding the exercise of their natural rights, including the right to participate in a reasoned quest for truth.

Bloom compares the scientific revolution in the eighteenth and nineteenth centuries, a period that historians call the Enlightenment, to Socrates' parable of the cave discussed in Chapter 1. Bloom argues that the very term "enlightenment" suggests the image of the prisoners in the cave rushing out into the light of truth. By breaking their chains and turning from the projected images of reality that appear on the cave wall, the prisoners, according to Bloom, toss off social conventions and leave the cave. Similar to Stirner's concern with freeing people from wheels in the head, the cave's prisoners are now free to gain enlightenment through the exercise of reason. Referring to the escape from the deceptions and myths created by the shadows on the wall of the cave, Bloom writes, "The false opinions can be corrected, and their inner contradictions impel thoughtful men to seek the truth. Education is the movement from darkness to light. Reason projected onto the beings about which at first we only darkly opine produces enlightenment."[5]

During the Enlightenment, the elitist, authoritarian quality of Socrates' concept of the exercise of reason, Bloom contends, shifted to a belief that all people can be educated to exercise reason. Under the aristocratic concept that only philosopher-kings have access to truth, the reasoned quest for truth focused on questions of beauty or other broad ideals. Under the democratic concept, the focus is on enlightened self-interest, that is, the enlightened use of reason by individuals in quest of their own self-interest. Since the pursuit of self-interest inevitably includes the general problems of life and death, individuals are forced to deal with a whole range of philosophical issues. Therefore, Bloom believes, an important role for education in a democracy is helping people to move from a narrow concern with personal self-interest to a concern with broader ideals.

In addition, Bloom feels that education can help protect against majority opinion limiting the free exercise of reason. Similar to Amy Gutmann's fear of majority rule limiting the consideration of alternatives to the good life, Bloom argues that the problem for democracy is the power of public opinion to cause conformity in thinking. Bloom identifies the limitations that public opinion places on the exercise of reason as one of the contradictions of democracy. On the one hand, democracy removes impediments to the free exercise of reason, but on the other hand, it preaches that the majority should rule. Consequently, the democratic person tends, because of the emphasis on majority control, to conform to the opinion of the majority of people. "So," Bloom argues, "unless there is some strong ground for opposition to majority opinion, it inevitably prevails."[6]

Bloom maintains that education can give people the ability to resist conformity to the opinion of the majority. Universities, according to Bloom, will prepare people to withstand the pressure of public opinion and to reason independently. This is precisely the position taken by Amy Gutmann when she calls for nonrepression to be a guiding principle of education. The school becomes a haven for free thought in a society tending toward conformity to majority opinion. Education can also, Bloom argues, help people to extend the use of reason beyond its application to immediate problems of self-interest to consideration of the broader problems of the meaning of life.

In other words, in Bloom's thinking, education can help people expand the use of reason beyond the confines of narrow personal self-interest, as well as protecting the free exercise of reason from the pressures of public opinion. What this means, according to Bloom, is that a close interrelationship exists between education and the democratic state; a democratic state makes possible the existence of educational institutions that allow for the free exercise of reason. In turn, educational institutions, by emphasizing the free exercise of reason and a natural rights philosophy, pass on from generation to generation a culture that is supportive of the conditions that make democracy possible.

Changes in social conditions, Bloom believes, can undermine the role of education in passing on this cultural tradition. Bloom is particularly concerned with the decline of both community and the traditional family. These social changes, Bloom argues, result from another dilemma for the democratic state, namely, the fact that an emphasis on freedom and independence can result in people feeling separate from any community. The way this problem is overcome is through the family unit. The family stands between the individual and the state. It is the family that creates close personal relationships and other attachments for the individual to the rest of society. It is the love of one's spouse and children that can temper a pursuit of materialistic self-interest. Therefore, while independence and freedom might cause people to act autonomously, the family balances that pressure by creating strong social relationships. In addition, Bloom argues, concern about the safety of one's family will cause people to be loyal to the state.

Bloom claims that the deterioration of the traditional family through divorce is a major cause of the decline of civic culture in the twentieth century. The ideas of the Enlightenment, Bloom contends, contained the seeds of the destruction of the family. By preaching equality of rights, the Enlightenment prepared the way for women to demand equality in relationships, including marriage. Since women today are more unwilling to accept unequal relationships, Bloom concludes, there is a greater tendency for the family unit to be destroyed by divorce. Without a strong family unit, it is difficult for youths to learn how to establish close relationships with other people. Under these conditions, the family no longer serves to build the individual's commitment to the community and the state.

Bloom's arguments regarding the family are strikingly different from those of Wilhelm Reich and A. S. Neill discussed in Chapter 4. All three believe that the family is the basis of the organization of the state. In a sense, all three view the family as the state in miniature. But, whereas Reich and Neill believe that freedom from the oppression of the patriarchal family is key to the establishment of a truly free society, Bloom believes the family is essential for the stability of society because it establishes close relations between people, which, in turn, create a loyalty to society and the state.

A source of the differences in these two sets of arguments regarding the family can be found in attitudes about sexuality. For Bloom, the sexuality of modern youth has been diluted by the commercialization of sex and the lack of meaningful relationships. A high point in the commercialization of sex, he argues, can be found in rock and roll music, as represented by Rolling Stones star Mick Jagger. Bloom writes, "He [Jagger] played . . . with one eye on the mobs of children of both sexes whom he stimulated to a sensual frenzy and the other eye winking at the unerotic, commercially motivated adults who handled the money."[7] In addition, the destruction of the family through divorce makes students wary of relationships. Consequently, Bloom argues, youths have sex but it does not occur in the context of a meaningful relationship.

The commercialization of sex and lack of meaningful relationships results, according to Bloom, in destroying the power of sex in human lives. Sex is no longer, Bloom writes, using the arguments of Socrates, divine madness or Eros. The lack of divine madness, Bloom contends, can be found in the lack of romance. Youths no longer dream of playing guitars under their lover's window. They no longer dream of doing great deeds for their lovers. Sex, according to Bloom, has become lame and weak.

It is the divine madness of sex, Bloom argues, that causes people to seek to be whole by embracing others. It is this divine madness that produces poetry and art and sends people in search of the meaning of life. It supplies the energy for the rational search for truth. Divine madness causes people to desire knowledge about themselves. Without Eros, students do not quest for wholeness and meaning.

Bloom's argument is based on different assumptions than those held by Wilhelm Reich and A. S. Neill. Reich and Neill see sexual drives as central to the general quest for pleasure. They assume that sexual freedom will produce a nonauthoritarian personality who, in rejecting authoritarian governments and institutions, will demand a world that allows people to pursue pleasure. In other words, the nonauthoritarian personality will create a world in which people can truly pursue their own happiness. Bloom, on the other hand, assumes that Eros is needed to provide the energy for the rational quest for truth. But for sex to serve this purpose, he argues, it must be in the context of a close relationship. Stripped of its divine madness, according to Bloom, modern sex no longer energizes the rational quest for truth and, consequently, drives another nail into the coffin of a society that, in some golden age, was devoted to natural rights and the free exercise of reason.

Therefore, in Bloom's view, the closing of the American mind is caused by a combination of several factors: belief in the relativity of cultures and values; changes in philosophical traditions; the emphasis on practical and work-related studies in educational institutions; the collapse of the traditional family; and the destruction of Eros. The closing of the American mind, Bloom argues, is a threat to the continuation of a society committed to the principles of equality, natural rights, and freedom of thought. In this context, the only hope for the maintenance of a democratic state is to dedicate the educational system to teaching that the culture of democracy is the best culture and that natural rights and the free exercise of reason are ideal values. In addition, the educational system should practice these ideals by leading students on a rational quest for truth.

Bloom's emphasis on education as the free exercise of reason is similar to some of the libertarian-anarchist traditions discussed in Chapters 4 and 5. In fact, libertarian-anarchist thought was born during the Enlightenment—the same historical period that Bloom hails as the birthplace of natural rights. In addition, Bloom argues, as did the early libertarian-anarchists, that freedom of thought is necessary for the progress of science and, consequently, the progress of civilization.

A major difference between Bloom and the libertarian-anarchist tradition is the emphasis on the political nature of knowledge. Libertarian-anarchists locate the forces working against the free exercise of reason in the political control of education by the state and powerful economic forces. On the other hand, Bloom gives no consideration to these forces. In *The Closing of the American Mind*, he relies on changes in philosophical thought and social conditions to explain the decline of education as a rational quest for meaning. For instance, in criticizing the emphasis on scientific and work-related subjects during the Cold War, he fails to examine the political and economic reasons for educational institutions adopting those programs. People within the libertarian-anarchist tradition would, in this particular case, point to government policies that were distorting the free exercise of reason for the purpose of winning the Cold War. This distinction is important because it results in a focus on differing issues. The libertarian-anarchist tradition would identify the existence of political authority exercised through the state as limiting the free exercise of reason, while Bloom would attribute any limitation on the free exercise of reason to changes in philosophy and social conditions.

These differences in the conceptualization of the problem are related to different meanings given to the term "equality." Bloom considers political equality to mean primarily that everyone has equal rights. Included in this definition is the idea that everyone has equal rights to pursue property. In addition, Bloom believes that an important part of the rights tradition is the rational pursuit of self-interest. The right to pursue the acquisition of property and an ideology supporting the pursuit of self-interest provide a justification for inequality in wealth and the right of corporations, including global corporations, to pursue their economic self-interest.

It is for the above reasons that corporations favor a natural rights philosophy and the transmission of a culture that is supportive of that philosophy. The natural rights philosophy is not critical of inequalities in wealth because it supports the right of all people to pursue and retain property. In addition, the tradition of natural rights assumes that society is self-regulated by the rational pursuit of self-interest. Any suggestion that wealth should be equalized or corporations regulated is considered a violation of natural rights because it represents an attack on the right to property.

In contrast, the libertarian-anarchist tradition primarily defines political equality to mean equality of power. In this tradition, the existence of the state creates an opportunity for the unequal use of power. In particular, there is a concern that the concentration of wealth in the hands of individuals or corporations allows for unequal political influence on the state. The libertarian-anarchist ideal is to create a society in which power is equally distributed and not distorted by differences in wealth and social position.

Therefore, while both Bloom and libertarian-anarchists advocate an education that emphasizes the free exercise of reason, they differ in their analysis of the factors hindering that form of education. Since for Bloom this form of education is linked to a natural rights philosophy, he is primarily concerned with the conditions that undermine that philosophy. And since he believes that natural rights depend on the perpetuation of a particular culture, he is concerned about factors that undermine that culture, such as a belief in cultural relativity and the breakdown of the family. And, because he believes in the right to pursue and hold property, he does not question the political power resulting from concentrations of wealth. Consequently, Bloom does not consider, as libertarian-anarchists would, the possibility that corporations in pursuit of an inexpensive and compliant source of labor could, by exercising power through the state, force school systems to focus on job-related studies and to limit the opportunity for students to freely exercise reason. For Bloom to take this approach would be an admission of one of the basic problems in the natural rights philosophy, namely, that the right to pursue property can contribute to inequality in the exercise of power. This inequality of power can result in some groups using educational institutions for their own purposes, including the restriction of the free exercise of reason.

Ironically, within the framework of Bloom's arguments, natural rights philosophy might contain the seeds of its own destruction. For instance, it is in the self-interest of those with wealth and power to limit the free exercise of reason, because that use of reason might result in criticism of concentrations of wealth. And, of course, since natural rights philosophy protects the pursuit and retention of property, it protects concentrations of wealth. According to Bloom, if the free exercise of reason is limited, then the culture supporting a natural rights philosophy is undermined. Therefore, the right to pursue and retain property might, at least within the framework of Bloom's argument, destroy the culture necessary for maintaining natural rights.

E. D. HIRSCH JR.: *CULTURAL LITERACY*

The argument that educational institutions should transmit a culture that supports natural rights is quite different from the argument that educational institutions should teach students cultural literacy. In fact, Bloom would probably react quite negatively to cultural literacy arguments because they assume the relativity of culture.

The cultural literacy argument was popularized in E. D. Hirsch Jr.'s *Cultural Literacy: What Every American Needs to Know*, which includes a list of 5,000 names, phrases, dates, and concepts that, according to the author, Americans need to know to be culturally literate.[8] Hirsch makes a clear distinction between literacy and cultural literacy. Literacy is simply the ability to read. Cultural literacy is the ability to read with full understanding. Hirsch illustrates the difference with a quotation that refers to "the knockdown pitch, the beanball, the duster and the purpose pitch." Simple literacy would involve reading these words without necessarily comprehending their meaning. Cultural literacy would involve reading these words against a background of knowledge about baseball. In other words, to be culturally literate people must have a framework of knowledge to interpret the information that they receive from the outside world. Therefore, from Hirsch's perspective, schools should teach children the cultural information they need to understand the information they receive from reading and other sources.

Cultural literacy, Hirsch argues, includes an unconscious schema for organizing impressions from the outside. A schema allows people to take the surface elements of what they see and put them together into a whole. For instance, to understand a written description of Lee's surrender to Grant at the end of the American Civil War, one must know that there was a civil war, who fought, and who won. This cultural knowledge allows the reader to understand the surface knowledge of the description. But for the reader to integrate the description into a meaningful whole, Hirsch argues, schema with information about what a civil war is, what an army is, what surrender means, how a military functions, and other similar types of information is required. This schema could be used for integrating the description of Lee's surrender and other military conflicts. That is, according to Hirsch, a culturally literate person has the information necessary to understand surface details, such as information about the American Civil War, and also a deeper schema, information about war and armies in a more general sense, that allows integration of surface information into a larger framework.

Hirsch's concept of cultural literacy is relative to a particular period of time. The cultural knowledge required for literacy is different in the 1990s than in the 1890s. Of course, Bloom would object to this concept of cultural transmission. Bloom wants the schools to teach a specific culture that originated in the thinking of the Enlightenment. Hirsch wants the teaching of a culture that is relevant to a particular moment in time. In other words, Hirsch argues, the substance of cultural transmission should be determined by doing research about current cultural information, such as the 5,000 names, phrases, dates, and concepts listed in the appendix of his book, which are a product of the research done by Hirsch and his colleagues Joseph Kett and James Trefil at the University of Virginia.

Culture, according to Hirsch's use of the term, is relative in another sense. If the information Hirsch believes is necessary for cultural literacy were common to all people, then there would be no reason for teaching it. All people sharing the same culture would have the same cultural information. But not all Americans, according to Hirsch, share the same cultural information. The major divisions among people regarding cultural information follow social class lines. According to his argument, the group that suffers the most from a lack of cultural literacy are the poor. Obviously, as Hirsch admits, the poor do have a culture that contains cultural information. The problem is that their cultural information does not create the type of cultural literacy needed for participation in the dominant institutions of U.S. society.

Consequently, Hirsch claims, a program of cultural literacy would help to alleviate poverty in the United States. In an argument that might be challenged by people who believe that poverty is caused by economic conditions, Hirsch states that poverty is perpetuated by the lack of proper cultural literacy. Therefore, similarly to other school reformers, Hirsch claims that cultural literacy programs in public schools will help the poor gain employment and climb out of a state of poverty.

In addition to claiming that cultural literacy will help the poor, Hirsch argues that cultural literacy provides the cultural unity that is necessary for the maintenance of the state. Similarly to Bloom, Hirsch believes that all people in the United States should share the same cultural background. And, similarly to

Adam Smith, discussed in Chapter 1, Hirsch believes that modern industrialism requires a specialization of labor that tends to destroy a feeling of national unity. Consequently, Hirsch believes that public schools should play a major role in building national cultural unity. For this reason, he emphatically rejects multicultural programs in public schools that teach from the perspective of particular cultures, such as instruction based on the cultural perspective of African Americans or Mexican Americans. He believes that schools might teach tolerance of other cultures but at the same time should teach a common culture to all students.

The central problem in Hirsch's call for national unity through cultural literacy is deciding what the cultural model will be. Obviously, it is not a culture held by all Americans, since, as Hirsch claims, the poor lack the correct cultural knowledge. On the other hand, Hirsch claims that he is not advocating making the culture of the elite the standard for cultural literacy. In fact, he argues that culture develops through the free interaction of all people. In this context, he believes, the building of culture is a democratic process.

However, when cultural standards are imposed through a national system of schooling, they are not democratically created. And since the cultural standards that are imposed through the schools are not common to all people, then the process does involve a form of cultural domination. The cultural knowledge that children might receive from other sources is superseded by the cultural knowledge imposed by the school.

In defending the necessity of creating a national culture, Hirsch provides a perfect example of cultural domination. His example is a textbook on rhetoric written by Hugh Blair in 1783 that went through 130 editions by 1911. The book was a standard for the teaching of rhetoric in Great Britain and the United States for over a hundred years. It provided, according to Hirsch, the basic elements of cultural literacy in both countries. The important point about this example is that Blair's book represents an imposition of English culture onto a Scottish culture. In 1762, Blair was appointed to the first professorship in English at the University of Edinburgh in Scotland. The professorship was created, Hirsch argues, because it was believed that English national culture should be taught in Scotland. In other words, the purpose was domination of Scottish culture by English culture. Consequently, Blair's book focuses on English literary traditions and contains no references to Scottish poets. In Hirsch's words, "Blair created, in effect, a dictionary of cultural literacy for those who had not been born to English literate culture, for use by provincials like the Scots and colonials like the Americans."[9]

Hirsch does not explore the political implications of Blair's book. From the standpoint of the English, Blair's work served the purpose of promoting political stability within Great Britain. If they shared the same cultural background as the English, the Scots would be less likely to engage in a movement for political independence. The supplanting of Scottish culture by English culture was not a democratic process; it was a process of cultural domination.

In a similar way, Hirsch's call for creating cultural unity through schooling does involve a form of cultural domination. But again, this raises the question of what the model for cultural literacy will be. At one point in his book, Hirsch refers to teaching students "mainstream culture."[10] At other points, he refers to "current literate American culture" and "a high school level of literacy."[11] None of these terms have much specificity. Mainstream culture might mean the culture of television, and literate culture might mean the culture of college professors. Therefore, the most direct way of understanding what Hirsch considers the cultural basis of literacy in the United States is to examine the method he used to construct the list of "5,000 essential names, phrases, dates, and concepts."[12]

The task of creating the list of "essentials" was divided among Hirsch, Kett, and Trefil. Hirsch represented the general field of humanities, while Kett represented the discipline of history and Trefil represented the sciences. The three of them consulted magazines, reference books, dictionaries, general books, and textbooks to create lists for their particular fields. The three of them would meet to criticize each other's lists. After merging their individual lists into one, they submitted it to "more than a hundred consultants outside the academic world."[13] In addition, they began working on definitions of the items on the list. Hirsch writes that the definitions "consist of the associations that each item tends to call forth in the minds of *literate persons* [emphasis is mine]."[14] The work on definitions, Hirsch claims, will "reproduce the shared cultural schemata that underlie literate communications of the present day."[15]

I carefully quoted parts of Hirsch's description of the construction of the list because the quotes reveal an astonishing process for defining what the national culture of the United States should be. This process can simply be described as three college professors deciding what all U.S. citizens should know. They never describe the hundred people they consulted. Did these hundred people represent a statistically significant number of U.S. citizens? Were they randomly selected? If they weren't randomly selected, what criteria were used? Who are the "literate people" providing the definitions that are to serve as a national cultural schemata? Hirsch's book provides no answers to these questions.

One could simply dismiss Hirsch's list as a pompous hoax, but that would be missing the important point that any construction of a list of what people should know would raise similar questions. And these questions lead back to an issue raised in Chapter 2: In a democratic state, who should decide what all people should know? Hirsch's list highlights another important fact: Any attempt to teach cultural literacy through public schools involves cultural imposition unless that culture is already shared by all students. But, paradoxically, if the culture is common to all students, then it is not necessary to teach it.

Hirsch specifically rejects John Dewey's solution to the role of the public school in a democratic state. As I discussed in Chapter 2, Dewey argued that a particular method of instruction would serve to educate people to be critical, active, democratic citizens. The method could be applied to any subject matter. Hirsch attacks Dewey for emphasizing methods of instruction over subject matter. In fact, Hirsch blames Dewey's ideas for causing public schools to neglect the teaching of cultural literacy. In attacking Dewey, Hirsch offers no solutions to the political problem of who should determine what knowledge should be taught in government-operated schools in a democratic state. The only solution he really suggests is that national culture should be determined by "literate persons."

Hirsch makes it clear that his intention is not to be undemocratic in the sense of forcing his list of cultural items onto public schools. In fact, he disavows any support for a national curriculum. But he does argue that his goal can be achieved indirectly by influencing textbook and test publishers. Quite rightly, he argues that controlling the content of textbooks is the most effective means of controlling the cultural content of schooling. Control of culture through text-books avoids any political problems that might occur when dealing with state and local school officials. The same thing is true of nationally distributed stan-dardized tests. Teachers, Hirsch maintains, tend to teach to the test.

Hirsch's reliance on indirect means of controlling the content of instruction allows him to avoid discussing issues of democratic control. Consequently, his desire to impose cultural literacy seems more appropriate to an authoritarian state. Even Allan Bloom would probably view Hirsch's scheme for building na-tional unity as undemocratic. After all, Bloom believes there are certain cultural traditions that all people must share to maintain a democratic society, as op-posed to sharing arbitrary cultural items gleaned by three professors from cur-rent books and magazines.

Thus, Hirsch's proposals seem more appropriate for an authoritarian state in which one person or one group of people claims to have knowledge of truth and, therefore, believes that this truth should be imposed on all people. Another reason Hirsch's ideas seem more appropriate to an authoritarian state is the de-gree of control necessary to transmit "what every American needs to know." Hirsch proposes not only controlling the cultural information going into stu-dents' minds, but also, by forming their schema, controlling how they process incoming information. Max Stirner would certainly consider this an attempt to put wheels into the head.

CONCLUSION: NATIONAL OR WORLD CULTURES?

Are the progress of civilization and the maintenance of a free society dependent on schools educating students in a particular cultural tradition? The supporters of building national unity through educating all students in the cultural tradi-tion of natural rights face the same criticism as that leveled at Amy Gutmann's proposal to make nonrepression the guiding principal of a democratic educa-tion. Should a cultural tradition be imposed on students and parents that might be contradictory to their beliefs and needs? As I discuss in Chapter 7, dominated groups in the United States object to the imposition of Western cultural tradi-tions. African Americans, in particular, object because it was the Western liberal tradition, with its emphases on the protection of property, which provided the justification for the protection of slaves as property during the years of slavery.

For advocates of cultural literacy, the problem is who will define literate cul-ture. Should it be defined by three college professors or by a majority of the peo-ple? In either case, the culture prescribed for instruction in schools will not be the culture of all people. Consequently, cultural literacy as Hirsch uses the term involves the imposition of culture. This creates a particular problem for dominated groups, such as African Americans, Native Americans, Mexican Americans, and Puerto Ricans, who might view this cultural imposition as an attempt to destroy their own cultures. Thus, it would seem that Hirsch's advocacy of cultural literacy is more appropriate to an authoritarian state than a democratic one.

The next chapter will consider these issues in an entirely different framework. In this chapter I discussed solving the problem of multicultural populations by the imposition of some form of national culture; the next chapter will examine solutions focusing on building world cultures. These world cultures would leap across national boundaries and unite people with similar cultural backgrounds. For instance, the culture of African Americans would be united with the culture of other Africans. This form of multicultural education breaks down national boundaries.

NOTES

1. For a discussion of the development of a global economy and work force, see Robert Reich, *The Work of Nations: Preparing Ourselves for 21st-Century Capitalism* (New York: Knopf, 1991).
2. Lonnie Harp, "Schools Urged to Revamp Instruction to Stress Workforce Skills," *Education Week*, Vol. X, No. 40, (July 31, 1991), p. 11.
3. Susan Chire, "A National Curriculum: Seeking Fairness for All," *New York Times* (January 8, 1992), pp. 1, 87.
4. See Allan Bloom, *The Republic of Plato: Translated, with Notes and an Interpretative Essay* (New York: Basic Books, Inc., 1968).
5. Ibid., p. 265.
6. Ibid., p. 247.
7. Ibid., p. 78.
8. E. D. Hirsch, Jr., *Cultural Literacy: What Every American Needs to Know* (New York: Vintage Books, 1988).
9. Ibid., p. 85.
10. Ibid., p. 28.
11. Ibid., p. 136.
12. Quoted from copy included on cover of ibid.
13. Ibid., p. 135.
14. Ibid., p. 135.
15. Ibid., pp. 135–136.

CHAPTER 7

National or
World Cultures?

Using schools as a vehicle for passing on a single culture based on either Western traditions (Bloom's argument) or a set of standards for cultural literacy (Hirsch's argument) creates problems for cultures that have been subjected to domination by outsiders or whose members are immigrants in nations where they make up only a small part of the population. Throughout history, conquerors have tried to force weaker native cultures to adopt their ways. For example, European colonialism and imperialism caused local Indians in North and South America to be suddenly engulfed by the culture of Europeans. Other examples, among many, include British colonization of India, parts of Africa, and numerous Caribbean islands, and French, Spanish, Dutch, and Portuguese domination of colonies around the world.

History is also full of forced migrations of peoples fleeing from their homelands to escape persecution, domination, or poverty. The Diaspora, for example, sent Jews to many parts of the world. Other populations emigrated for other reasons, such as the Chinese and Indian merchants, who left their homelands to follow trade routes; the Italian, Irish, and Eastern European immigrants in the nineteenth and early twentieth centuries, who left their native lands to escape poverty, or—more recently—the South and Central American, Asian, East European, and Caribbean peoples, who have emigrated for economic reasons or to avoid political persecution. The slave trade of the eighteenth and nineteenth centuries is yet another example of displacement—one of the worst; in this case, large numbers of Africans were captured and removed by force from their homelands to be dispersed against their wills as slaves in North and South America.

Whatever the reason for their displacement, each of these cultural groups faces the same dilemma: loyalty to their native culture versus accommodation to the culture of the nation to which they have immigrated or by which they have been dominated. The choice a particular cultural group makes varies with its circumstances. Many Jews, for instance, preserved their culture and religion in their new homelands against an often hostile government and national culture, and they demonstrated their loyalty to their own culture by emigrating to Israel when that nation was formed as a Jewish homeland. Chinese and Indian merchants established communities in their new homelands in which they carried on their native cultures and ways of life as well as possible. However, for other immigrant groups who are minorities in their lands, the conflict is harder to resolve. Today, the internationalization of corporations and the labor force, the breakdown of colonial empires, and the speed of modern transportation and communication heighten the dilemma these displaced people face.

Perhaps the most difficult conflicts between loyalty to a native culture and to the culture of a conquering group or nation occur among dominated cultures. By dominated cultures, I mean those groups that are exploited in some fashion by another nation or cultural group that has more power. For instance, in the United States, a number of groups were forced to become U.S. citizens, such as American Indians, Africans, Puerto Ricans, and Mexican Americans. For American Indians, the conquest by European Americans resulted in varying responses. Currently, the American Indian Movement (AIM) is attempting to unite all American Indians with the claim that all tribes share certain cultural characteristics. Africans brought to the United States as slaves, Puerto Ricans conquered by the United States in the Spanish-American War, and Mexicans living on lands taken over by the United States all face the same dilemma[1]

Youths of these minority cultures, in particular, often feel without a homeland or identity as they are pulled between the culture of their parents and the majority culture of the nation in which they live. For instance, in his novel *Tea in the Harem*, Mehdi Charef eloquently describes the plight of Algerian immigrants to France, who confront the dilemma of assimilating into a hostile French culture or retaining ties to the culture of Algeria. For Algerian youth in France, assimilation into the French culture holds out the promise of jobs and a higher standard of living. But, as Charef describes, these hopes are constantly dashed as these young people encounter hostility and discrimination in schools and government services. Living in a hostile society and adrift between the culture of their parents and that of France, these youths, according to Charef, erupt in rage against society. Their rage leads to random violence, theft, and a strong resistance to the education provided by French schools.[2]

The inferior economic and social status, in relation to European Americans, of conquered or formerly enslaved peoples presents them with a variety of options for resolving this dilemma. One option, mentioned above, is to abandon their own cultural traditions and adopt the traditions of the dominant European-American culture, in order to gain—they hope—equal political and economic power. The second option is to gain respect for and acceptance of their cultural traditions by the dominant power structure. It is hoped that by gaining respect for and acceptance of their cultures, these groups will gain equal economic and political power.

These two options are especially difficult for members of minority cultures facing racial discrimination because even if members of these cultures choose to assimilate to the majority culture or gain respect for their native cultures, they still face discrimination on the basis of race. Some of these cultural groups therefore choose a third option, loyalty to their native culture versus accommodation to the dominant culture. The third option is premised on a belief that neither abandoning one's culture nor gaining respect and acceptance will do anything to change the basic political and economic relations in society. Thus, this option involves either seeking a power base outside the dominant power structure of society or building a power base through linkages with other people in the world who share the same culture. For instance, some African-American leaders, such as Malcolm X, believe that the only hope for real economic advancement of African Americans is building black economic enterprises and establishing ties with other African cultures.

To be able to judge the economic and political importance of these different options, one must understand the role of power in cultural relationships.

POWER AND CULTURE

There are two dimensions to the relationship between power and culture. The first is social class. There are cultural differences between social classes within a particular culture. The second is the relationship between two distinct cultures. Cultural differences between social classes serve as an important source of political and economic power. These cultural differences are usually nested within a common culture. A common culture might be built on the sharing of a common language, historical traditions, religion, literature, and art. Nested within this common culture, there are usually differences in what I will call personal cultural characteristics, which include behavior, manners, dress, accents, and patterns of speech. Often, these personal cultural characteristics distinguish one social class from another.

Consequently, people from lower social class backgrounds might find it difficult to enter positions of power because they lack the personal cultural characteristics of the upper class. People might feel inferior because they do not act and speak like the social elite. Education can contribute to cultural differences between social classes. Historically, the collegiate education of "gentlemen" was often used to distinguish one social class from another. In the eighteenth and nineteenth centuries, the liberal education provided by elite schools such as Harvard, Yale, and Princeton was rooted in the study of Greek, Latin, and classical literature. Except for certain professions, such as theology and law, the study of classical languages and literature was of little practical value. But knowledge of these subjects did serve an important social function by dividing social classes. Those possessing an elite college education, no matter how impractical, were considered "gentlemen" and socially superior to those who did not possess this body of knowledge. On the other side, those receiving a collegiate education might internalize a belief in their own inferiority. Consider this issue in the framework of the previous discussion about the study of Greek and Latin in the eighteenth and nineteenth centuries. If a person is taught that a collegiate education produces a superior human and she or he is never able to achieve that level of learning, then she or he would tend to believe that she or he were inferior to the college educated.

The same feelings of superiority and inferiority can be caused by differences in manners, accents, dress, and patterns of speech. A working-class person who is invited to a dinner attended by very rich people might feel uncomfortable because of a lack of knowledge about what is considered proper dress and table manners. This lack of knowledge can easily slip into a feeling of social inferiority. In addition, our working-class person might worry about carrying on a dinner conversation. She or he might not share the same set of experiences as more affluent dinner companions. These shared experiences often serve as reference points in conversations. A person could feel inferior by not understanding references to these shared experiences. In addition, a working-class person might feel inferior because of his or her accent and speech patterns.

In the United States, the children of the very wealthy share a similar set of educational experiences that provides them with common manners, conversational points of reference, accents, and speech patterns. An important part of this shared educational experience is attendance at secondary boarding schools. The most prestigious of these schools are located in New England and affiliated with the Episcopal Church. At the top of the list of secondary boarding schools are Saint Paul's, Saint Mark's, Groton, Middlesex, Saint George's, Phillips Exeter, and Phillip Academy. A major emphasis in these schools is on building character through a shared set of experiences. The focus on character training results in graduates sharing a common set of cultural attributes. Sociologist William Domhoff quotes one upper-class woman: "Where I went to boarding school, there were girls from all over the country, so I know people from all over. It's helpful when you move to a new city and want to get invited into the local social clubs."[3]

Graduates of these elite boarding schools usually attend prestigious private universities and colleges such as Harvard, Princeton, Yale, and smaller Ivy League schools. At these institutions, graduates of boarding schools tend to create their own social world that is separate from that of other students. Sociologist C. Wright Mills writes, "That is why in the upper social classes, it does not by itself mean much merely to have a degree from an Ivy League college. That is assumed: the point is not Harvard, but which Harvard? By Harvard, one means Porcelain, Fly, or A.D.: by Yale, one means Zeta Psi or Fence or Delta Kappa Epsilon: by Princeton, Cottage, Tifer, Cap and Gown or Ivy."[4]

These shared cultural characteristics of the American elite play an important role in maintaining its economic and political power. For instance, employment in the upper echelons of leading banking, investment, legal, and corporate firms is made much easier for those with the correct cultural background and personal friends. Of course, one might argue that a person might be able to gain the cultural trappings of the elite and enter their world by receiving a scholarship to an elite preparatory school, attending the right college, and, while attending these institutions, cultivating friends among the children of the elite. Of course, this process is not without a certain level of emotional strain, because a person in the process of adopting a new culture must abandon the ways of his or her parents. Certainly, the personal-psychological cost of adopting a new culture is higher than retaining the culture of one's birth.

Personal-psychological costs are heightened when cultural differences also include differences in race. In European countries and the United States, belief in cultural and racial inferiority is often used to justify political and economic exploitation. For instance, colonialism was usually accompanied by a belief on the part of Europeans that people of color were racially inferior. In addition, Europeans believed that Asian and African cultures were inferior. Europeans who conquered American Indians were convinced of the cultural and racial inferiority of their opponents. In the United States, the sale and purchase of slaves were justified by theories of racial and cultural inferiority.

While beliefs in cultural and racial inferiority gave Europeans a justification for conquering other people, the practice of cultural domination helped to solidify their power over colonies. For instance, each European nation made its language the official language of its colonies and attendance in its schools the only route to government positions. The colonized were expected to be grateful for the right to participate in and learn from a superior culture. These policies had several effects. First, the colonized were taught that their culture was inferior to that of European nations. Second, access to political power depended on absorbing the culture of the Europeans.[5]

In summary, there is a complex relationship between culture and power. On the one hand, beliefs in racial and cultural inferiority can be used to justify the exploitation of other races and cultures. In turn, particularly if these beliefs are institutionalized in an educational system, dominated people might internalize a belief in their own inferiority that might result in them accepting their own exploitation. In addition, governments and economic institutions will be organized around the culture of the dominant group. This makes it difficult for other cultural groups, including other social classes, to gain entrance to these institutions and, therefore, helps to solidify the power of the dominant group. Of course, the dominant group will resist any cultural changes that might threaten its control of political and economic institutions.

POWER, CULTURE, AND EDUCATIONAL OPTIONS

The relationship between power and culture is a factor in considering educational options for dominated groups. One option is abandoning one's culture for the culture of the dominant group. Educationally, this means that schools should actively try to transform minority cultures into the culture of the dominant group. The second option, which I previously discussed, is building tolerance and acceptance of minority cultures among members of the dominant culture. This approach results in schools emphasizing education for cultural tolerance. And in the latter option, dominated cultures try to build a power base outside the dominant power structure of society. This option can include building linkages to other people in the world who share the same culture. With this option, schools would teach from the cultural perspective of the children; for instance, one could create African- or Hispanic-centered schools.

The first option needs to be considered in the context of racism. For instance, American Indians could abandon their cultural traditions and embrace the culture of European Americans. One epithet for this type of Indian is "apple"—red on the outside, white on the inside. A similar term is used to describe African Americans who embrace European-American culture: "Oreo"—black on the outside, white on the inside. While these terms are meant to be derogatory of this type of cultural change, they do convey an important point. The adoption of a European-American culture does nothing about racism. Just because an African American or American Indian changes culture, the end of racism and entrance into the halls of power are not guaranteed.

If a dominated people chooses the path of assimilation into the culture of the ruling elite, then, for that choice to be effective, strong political activity to ensure that racism does not remain as a factor in blocking access to equal power is required. But for a dominated group to maintain a strong political movement, there has to be some sense of a collective need. In other words, an American Indian or an African American might choose the path of assimilation, but he or she will still have to retain an identity with other American Indians or African Americans in order to sustain a fight against racism.

The fact that dominated groups will have to retain some cultural identity to fight racism creates a problem for those seeking assimilation to the dominant culture. For dominated groups to protect against racism and ensure equal power, they can never completely assimilate into the dominant culture. They must now hang between two worlds. For instance, an African American might choose the route of education for assimilation. This form of education might give African Americans the cultural characteristics that are compatible with those of the ruling elite. On the other hand, in order to gain protection against racism the African American would still have to support civil rights organizations, such as the National Association for the Advancement of Colored People, which represent the collective interests of African Americans in the battle against racism. In joining a civil rights organization, the African American exhibits a collective identity with other African Americans. Consequently, the route of assimilation into the dominant culture creates two psychological burdens. First, the dominated group must strip itself of its previous culture in order to be assimilated. For an American Indian to adopt the culture of European Americans, a belief that European culture is superior to Indian culture and, to a certain extent, that Europeans were justified in conquering Indians is required. Second, the assimilated person must still be stretched between two cultural identities to sustain the battle against racism. It is difficult to measure the psychological burden of maintaining these two identities.

The second option, using education to build cultural tolerance, might reduce the problem of racism. Schools could focus on eliminating intolerance between cultures and, in the process, eliminating racism. Of course, building tolerance and eliminating racism do not solve the problem of attaining equal political power. A dominant culture would still exist. Tolerance does not mean that all cultures will be of equal political and economic worth. One way out of this problem is to add cultural empowerment to the educational goal of tolerance. In other words, the educational goal would be to build tolerance between cultural groups and to empower each culture. In this context, empowerment means people becoming aware that they can exercise political power to change social and economic conditions. For instance, a mixed school of American Indians and European Americans would try to reduce prejudice and racism between American Indians and European Americans while at the same time giving the

American Indian students the knowledge and skills required to exercise their political power. In this scenario, American Indian students, after graduation, would enter a world free of racial and cultural prejudice. While maintaining allegiance to their cultural heritage, these former students would use political power to ensure that they could retain their culture and, at the same time, improve their economic conditions.

One might wonder if this scenario is realistic. As I discussed in Chapter 3, Max Stirner warned that school people confuse the thinkable with the doable. It is certainly thinkable that schools might create cultural equality. But can schools really use these methods to achieve equality of power for all cultures? Would an American Indian growing up on a reservation in the West have an equal chance with an upper-class European American in gaining employment at a Wall Street banking or legal office if cultural and racial prejudice were eliminated from society? Possibly—if political pressure is placed on these firms to hire American Indians.

The last option is completely different from the assimilation model or the cultural tolerance model. In fact, in this option there is little concern with assimilation or tolerance. The major concern is building economic institutions and political movements that will serve each dominated group. For instance, in this option, American Indians and African Americans would abandon any hope of achieving equal power in a society dominated by European Americans. In the context of this option, the only hope is for each dominated group to create its own economic institutions and political allegiance. For instance, American Indians might decide to establish their own businesses. Goods might be sold to non-Indians, but the purpose of the Indian-owned enterprises would be to make Indian communities self-supporting. In this scenario, American Indians would owe their primary allegiance to other Indian groups, including those in other countries. For instance, North American Indians would be more concerned with allegiance to all North American Indians as opposed to allegiance to the governments of Canada, the United States, and Mexico.

The interesting thing is that this last option might be the one most closely attuned to the political and economic issues arising from the internationalization of corporations and the labor force. Allegiances that jump over the boundaries of nations might be more politically and economically effective than those contained within a single nation. I will explore this last option in more detail in the next section, on Afrocentric education. In a global economy, will an Afrocentric education provide greater equality of power for African Americans and other Africans than the other two options? Is the model of Afrocentric education applicable to other dominated groups?

AFROCENTRICITY

In the United States, Afrocentric education developed out of a desire to reconstruct the consciousness of African Americans and to find a method of helping African-American youth who were failing in public schools. The reconstruction of consciousness will, it is argued, solve the problem of the resistance of African-American youths to receiving an education. Proponents of Afrocentric education argue that African-American youths resist education because most U.S. public schools teach from the cultural perspective of European Americans. In addition, many African-American youths believe that doing well in school requires "acting white." These same arguments can be extended to other dominated groups, such as American Indians, Puerto Ricans, and Mexican Americans.

The basic assumption of Afrocentricity is that all Africans share elements of a common culture. In the words of Molefi Asante, chairperson of the Department of African Studies at Temple University: "We have one African Cultural System manifested in diversities. . . . We respond to the same rhythms of the universe, the same cosmological sensibilities, the same general historical reality."[6] Part of the common heritage is rooted in the diaspora that spread Africans throughout North and South America. With the end of slavery and colonialism, these Africans are now transformed into new cultural groups, such as African Brazilians, African Jamaicans, etc. The African culture of these groups has been reshaped by particular historical and national experiences, but the original roots in Africa still remain.

One goal of the Afrocentricity movement is to help reconstruct the African culture of these groups and build ties with a world African culture. The goal is not to recreate a past African culture or to go back to some point in history. The goal is to create and reconstruct African values and genius in the context of a postcolonial world. In the future, it is believed, Africans will play a central role in the world. From this perspective, Afrocentricity is a preparation for assuming a leadership role in world politics and economics.

Of course, reconstructing African culture among African Americans or African Brazilians involves separating European influences from African roots. The very term "African American" suggests a split between two cultures. The "American" part of the term "African American" is primarily European in origin. The hope of advocates of Afrocentricity is to go beyond just understanding what is African and what is European in African-American culture. Of central importance is showing how the very thought processes of African Americans are dominated by European culture.

Afrocentric school lessons reflect this concern with European-American domination of thought processes. For instance, Jawanza Kunjufu, in his textbook *Lessons from History: A Celebration in Blackness*, presents elementary school students with a picture of an African woman with her hair done in cornrows. In reference to the picture, Kunjufu instructs students: "Some African-Americans want their hair to look like that of Whites. Cornrows are a special braid design once worn only by African queens."[7] In this passage, the instructional goal is twofold. First, the elementary student learns that whites can dominate African-American thinking about dress and hairstyling. As students mature, they are made aware of other forms of European-American domination of thought processes. Second, students are shown another aspect of African culture. In the junior and senior high school edition of his textbook,

Kunjufu instructs students: "White people and the media choose our leaders, provide more favorable information about those leaders with whom Whites are more comfortable, and then we make ill-informed decisions about messengers rather than critically looking at the messages."[8] In this passage, African-American students are made aware of how European-American culture can manipulate thinking about their own leadership. This manipulation results, this passage suggests, in African Americans making decisions that are in the interests of European Americans, not of African Americans.

Therefore, a goal of Afrocentricity is reconstruction of thought processes by helping African Americans see the world through the eyes of a world African culture. Asante writes about becoming Afrocentric: "a new perspective . . . a new consciousness invades our behavior . . . with Afrocentricity you see the movies differently, you see other people differently, you read books differently, you see politicians differently . . . nothing is as it was before."[9]

This transformation of consciousness can be illustrated by using the Socratic image of the cave that was discussed in Chapter 1. A person can imagine African Americans being chained together to watch the shadows on the wall of the cave. Behind them walk European Americans, casting shadows of the thoughts and objects of their world, including attitudes about Africans and justifications for racism. Unable to look behind them, the African Americans think that what they see is reality and, consequently, they internalize the beliefs and thoughts represented by the passing shadows. By removing the chains, Afrocentricity allows the former prisoners to turn around and to see that they had mistaken white thoughts and actions for their reality. Taken out of the cave, they gain the ability to see the world through African eyes.

Advocates of Afrocentricity believe that this new consciousness and perspective will break down the resistance of many African-American youths to acquiring an education. For instance, Kunjufu uses the concept of resistance as developed by anthropologist John Ogbu to explain the attitudes of African-American youths regarding public schools. Kunjufu has played a major role in the development of Afrocentric education. Besides writing textbooks, he has also written and distributed an Afrocentric curriculum. Using Ogbu's arguments, Kunjufu believes that African-American students resist complying with schooling because it requires them to "act white."

Ogbu argues that African Americans face several collective problems resulting from their domination by European Americans. These collective problems include white prejudice, relegation to menial jobs, and segregation. Ogbu claims that African Americans have learned to cope with these problems by developing a collective distrust of whites and white-controlled institutions. In addition, African Americans have developed their own survival strategies to cope with racial barriers. And, most important for youth, African Americans have developed their own cultural style, which in some cases is in opposition to European-American culture.

These collective ways of coping, Ogbu argues, are carried by youths to the schoolhouse door. First, African-American youths view public schools as primarily white institutions. Therefore, they feel distrust of the institution of schooling and white teachers. This hostility feeds a cultural style that is in opposition to the requirements of schools. This results in a paradoxical situation. African-American students do not reject schooling, but their behavior is oppositional to the work of the school. For instance, Ogbu writes, "they [African-American youths] tend to be excessively tardy, lack a serious attitude toward their schoolwork, and not to persevere in doing their schoolwork."[10] In addition, black hostility toward whites can erupt into open aggression, which can be directed at white students or teachers.

Compounding these feelings, many African-American youths have little faith that doing well in school will lead to success. In fact, according to Ogbu, African Americans with educational levels similar to those of European Americans earn, on average, less money than whites. The existence of racial barriers to employment and the historical exploitation of the black community by the white community contribute to a general disillusionment with the idea that success can be achieved through education. Therefore, the combination of distrust of white institutions, the development of an oppositional cultural style, a feeling of hostility toward whites, and disillusionment with the idea that education can lead to success can, according to Ogbu, contribute to low academic achievement.[11]

Using Ogbu's analysis, Kunjufu investigates black teenage life in a book with the title *To Be Popular or Smart: The Black Peer Group*.[12] Illustrating the dilemma for African-American youth, he recalls his own ostracism from his black peer group when he joined a college debating society. The debating society was considered by his peer group to be an organization that required one to act white. Kunjufu describes his college days as hanging between two worlds. He argues that he was able to avoid total rejection "because I was an athlete, liked to dance, and could 'talk the talk.' I learned how to roller skate, because this was the most important weekend activity in local Black culture."[13] Of the group of approximately 1,000 African Americans who entered college with him, Kunjufu states, only 254 graduated. Those who failed, he claims, spent their college years roller-skating, partying, hanging out in the cafeteria and dormitory, playing records, and getting high.

What Kunjufu experienced with black college students is typical, he feels, of black youth around the country. These youth described "blackness" as including a pattern of speech, music, and outside school activities. In Kunjufu's words, "If a student spoke standard English, listened to rock or classical music, and went to museums—they were White. If a student spoke Black English, listened to rap or rhythm and blues, and went to parties—they were Black."[14]

Of course, Kunjufu argues, the rejection of studying and schooling is not typical of African culture. African civilizations pioneered in science and mathematics. Scholarship is not an exclusively white phenomenon. What has happened in the United States, according to Kunjufu, is that black youth have lost this tradition of scholarship because of the need to cope with traditional white hostility and domination. This coping process has resulted in a culture based on a rejection of what are perceived to be cultural characteristics of whites. As a result of confusion about what is characteristic of whites, black youths end up rejecting part of their own African tradition of scholarship.

Just as Afrocentric education will show African Americans how whites have controlled the shadows on the wall of the cave, it will also show African-American youths how their reaction to white domination results in a rejection of a cultural tradition of scholarship. Consequently, by emphasizing African scholarship and the effect of white domination on African-American culture, Afrocentric education will break the cycle of failure in school by many African-American youths.

CONCLUSION: GLOBAL CORPORATIONS AND WORLD CULTURES

In comparison to the options of assimilation and toleration, educational plans modeled on Afrocentricity offer a meaningful alternative for dominated groups. This approach certainly avoids the psychological costs of assimilation, which requires dominated groups to reject their own culture but still hang on to former cultural ties in order to fight racism. It also avoids what may be the false hope of education creating racial and cultural tolerance. After all, prejudice is often built on economic exploitation. Simply to think that a school program on cultural and racial tolerance will eliminate economic differences may be naive.

Schools modeled on Afrocentric education, on the other hand, may be a more realistic approach for dominated groups. It is difficult to avoid economic exploitation in a world of international business and an international work force. Corporations can move from country to country to avoid paying high wages and complying with safety and other labor laws. Consequently, little can be achieved against economic exploitation by a dominated group within one nation.

In fact, I would argue, allegiance to a nation opens the door to economic exploitation for most of the world's workers. Just as corporations now leap across national borders to increase profits, workers must make the same leap to improve wages and working conditions. This is particularly true of dominated groups. In general, Africans, Hispanics, Indians, and many Asians are exploited by world economic powers. For instance, African Americans are economically exploited in the United States, while Africans in general are exploited in other parts of the world. Dominated groups that build allegiance to a world culture might have more political and economic power in the global economy than if they remain within the limits of a single nation.

Therefore, a yes must be given to my original question: Will an Afrocentric education provide greater equality of power in a global economy for African Americans? And, in answer to my second question, the Afrocentric model is applicable to other dominated groups. American Indians, like other dominated groups, can also be viewed as the prisoners in the cave whose chains must be broken so that they can turn and see how their minds have been controlled by images created by a dominant European culture. Each dominated culture can find its own traditions of scholarship so that learning is no longer considered "acting white."

Therefore, Afrocentric education provides the best model for the education of children of dominated groups in a world of global corporations and international labor. Focusing education on Western traditions or cultural literacy does little to help dominated peoples. In both cases, the goal is to build national unity, which is contradictory to the need to build international unity among workers to counter the power of international corporations. In addition, creating national unity by teaching the Western traditions of natural rights does little to reduce the inequality of power created by inequalities of wealth. Dominated people subjected to this type of curriculum will never be able to free themselves from the yoke of domination. The same thing is true of arguments for cultural literacy. Neither of these positions does anything about the wheels of domination spinning in the heads of Africans, American Indians, and Hispanics.

Schools modeled on an Afrocentric education might be effective in attempts to equalize power in a global economy. Their chances will be improved by adopting some of the principles of free schools discussed at the end of Chapter 5. Obviously, I do not mean that part of the free school movement that advocated freedom for children not to learn, as the historic problem for many dominated peoples has been the denial of an education, which allowed for continued exploitation. What I do mean is that part of the free school movement that urged freedom from political rulers using education to control citizens and perpetuate power. For these forms of education, such as the Afrocentric, sustaining an international movement requires separation from existing national governments.

Obviously, education based on the Afrocentric model is in agreement with free school efforts to protect against wheels in the head. In this case, the concern would be with wheels in the head placed there by the dominant group. There would also be agreement on the free school idea that education should be consciously political. Certainly, the whole purpose of an Afrocentric education is political and designed to increase the power of Africans throughout the world.

And finally, advocates of Afrocentric schools would agree that children should not be taught to sacrifice their physical desires and needs for political rulers. After all, dominated people, particularly those who suffered slavery, have traditionally had their desires and physical needs sacrificed for the benefit of their rulers and owners. Therefore, I would argue that schools for dominated groups modeled on an Afrocentric education should teach children to want a world that satisfies their needs and desires as opposed to wanting to sacrifice themselves for the good of the nation or of a dominant group.

In addition, dominated people must share the concern of Ivan Illich that schools can be used as a means of reinforcing the class structure of a society. When racial discrimination is a factor, schools, as Illich suggests, can be used to ensure that a racial group remains at the bottom of the economic ladder. Also, Paul Goodman's proposal for decentralized, small schools is important because of the historic problem of dominant groups using schools to maintain their power. For instance, it is easier for American Indians to exercise control over a small school that is not managed by the government than over a school system dominated by a huge government bureaucracy. As Kenneth J. Meier, Joseph

Stewart Jr., and Robert England have demonstrated in two important books, the key factor in reducing discrimination and segregation in education is the exercise of political power by minority cultures over the schools serving their children.[15]

Finally, I believe that all forms of culturally-based education must include an education in human rights. However, this proposition raises a whole series of questions. Is human rights instruction based on Allan Bloom's concept of Western culture? Is human rights education a form of cultural imposition? Are human rights doctrines compatible with multiculturalism? Does human rights become another wheel in the head? I will answer these questions in the final chapter.

NOTES

1. Many in my own tribe, the Choctaws, made an effort to assimilate to European culture. Therefore, my grandfather, who lived and died in Indian territory, was a banker and dressed and acted like European Americans. In the 1970s, I worked with Russell Means, at the time leader of AIM, in organizing schools for American Indian children. Means argued that all Indians shared certain cultural characteristics and, consequently, they should form a united movement.
2. Mehdi Charef, *Tea in the Harem* (London: Serpent's Tail, 1989).
3. G. William Domhoff, *Who Rules America Now?: A View from the '80s* (New York: Simon and Schuster, 1983), p. 25.
4. C. Wright Mills, *The Power Elite* (New York: Oxford University Press, 1956), p. 67.
5. Martin Carnoy, *Education as Cultural Imperialism* (White Plains, N.Y.: Longman, 1974).
6. Molefi Kete Asante, *Afrocentricity* (Trenton, N.J.: Africa World Press, Inc., 1988).
7. Jawanza Kunjufu, *Lessons from History: A Celebration in Blackness Elementary Edition* (Chicago: African-American Images, 1987) p. 83.
8. Jawanza Kunjufu, *Lessons from History: A Celebration in Blackness Jr.-Sr. High Edition* (Chicago: African-American Images, 1987), p. 37.
9. Asante, *Afrocentricity*, p. 6.
10. John U. Ogbu, "Class Stratification, Racial Stratification, and Schooling," in *Class, Race, & Gender in American Education*, ed. Lois Weis (Albany: State University of New York Press, 1988), p. 170.
11. Ibid., pp. 174–175.
12. Jawanza Kunjufu, *To Be Popular or Smart: The Black Peer Group* (Chicago: African-American Images, 1988).
13. Ibid., p. 22.
14. Ibid., pp. 14–15.
15. See Kenneth J. Meier, Joseph Stewart Jr., and Robert England, *Race, Class, and Education: The Politics of Second-Generation Discrimination* (Madison: University of Wisconsin Press, 1989); and Kenneth J. Meier and Joseph Stewart Jr., *The Politics of Hispanic Education* (Albany: State University of New York Press, 1991).

PART FOUR

The Politics of Gender

CHAPTER 8

Classical Liberalism and the Politics of Gender

In Western society, the unequal political power of women is rooted in the liberal political tradition of the seventeenth and eighteenth centuries. The denial of equal political power to women can be found in the educational and political writings of two prominent members of the liberal tradition—John Locke (1632–1704) and Jean-Jacques Rousseau (1712–1778). Besides making important intellectual contributions to classical liberalism, Locke and Rousseau wrote influential books on pedagogy that shaped the educational traditions of the Western world.

Of fundamental importance in discussing the writings of Locke and Rousseau is the nature of the family. In contrast to A. S. Neill's advocacy of the free family based on equality between husband and wife, Locke gave power to the husband in family matters. Rousseau not only gave the power to the husband, he also made the family the central institution for developing human attachments in a society driven by the pursuit of self-interest. Rousseau believed that women should be educated to assume a subservient role to their husbands'. In fact, Rousseau's political philosophy depends on women remaining in the home and expressing their citizenship through their husbands. The family and mother love, according to Rousseau, are the keys to holding society together. It is not an exaggeration to say that classical liberalism was built on the denial of equal political power to women.

Also, similar to A. S. Neill, sexuality is of central importance to the educational philosophy of Rousseau. Rousseau believes sexual drives are responsible for turning self-interest into compassion for other people. In his educational writings, Rousseau refers to the awakening of sexual drives as a new birth that produces the social person. In contrast to the advocacy of sexual freedom by A. S. Neill and Wilhelm Reich, Rousseau proposes *shaping* sexual drives as a means of developing both compassion and a person who is free from vanity.

Both Locke and Rousseau related their political ideals to educational methodologies. Locke's *Some Thoughts Concerning Education* (1693) and Rousseau's *Emile* (1762) contain lengthy discussions of methods of instructing children that are reflections of their political philosophies. In fact, these philosophers begin a tradition extending from Locke to the contemporary work of Paulo Freire of searching for instructional methods that would prepare students to carry out their particular political agendas.

The denial of equal power to women is an inherent problem in the liberal tradition of the seventeenth and eighteenth centuries. For some contemporary philosophers such as Allan Bloom, Rousseau was correct in his insistence on the importance of the family for curbing the economic excesses of modern society. These economic excesses can be linked to Locke's stress on the importance of protecting property and his belief that people are born with minds that are blank slates that can be molded by rewards and punishments. It is the individual pursuit of rewards and avoidance of punishment that becomes the basis for Western economic systems.

By teaching the importance of human relationships, the family, according to Bloom and Rousseau, can curb the worst excesses of a society based on individual pursuit of wealth. Of course, Bloom argues that classical liberalism contained the possible seeds of its own destruction by its emphasis on equal rights. The later extension of these rights to women, according to Bloom, contributed to the undermining of the family structure. In this debate, Bloom can be considered a latter-day representative of the natural rights doctrines of Rousseau.

JOHN LOCKE: PROTECTING PROPERTY AND CONTROLLING WOMEN

John Locke's *Some Thoughts Concerning Education* appeared three years after the completion of his masterpiece, *An Essay Concerning Human Understanding* (1690). In *Some Thoughts Concerning Education*, Locke applies his theories of human nature and government to pedagogy. Locke's life spanned a period of intellectual ferment resulting from the development of scientific methods.[1] The intellectual developments of this period served as a background for the eighteenth-century Commonwealthmen who, as I discussed in Chapter 3, were concerned with the development of political structures that did not interfere with the free exercise of reason. In fact, Molesworth's study of the relationship between government-operated schools and authoritarianism in Denmark was published in 1692, just one year before the publication of Locke's book on education.

Central to Locke's political philosophy and to the debates over government in the seventeenth century was the question of "indifferency." Simply stated, the question of indifferency is concerned with those human actions and institutions that are not dealt with by the laws of God. The Bible, which Locke considered the word of God, contains many prescriptions for human action, such as that a person should not commit murder or adultery. But the Bible does not provide a basis, according to many Protestants of the seventeenth century, for judging many other human actions, such as whether a man should be clean-shaven or bearded. These are areas of human action to which God—since there is no discussion in the Bible—is indifferent. Therefore, the Bible provides the laws of God to govern human action, while governance of those things to which God is indifferent is determined by human laws.[2]

Locke's arguments on religious toleration and the nature of government develop out of his concern with indifferency. In fact, his major contribution to liberal political thought is his defense of tolerance and the social contract theory of government. Similar to those of all philosophers, Locke's ideas were tempered by the times. His concern with toleration reflected a society torn apart by religious strife as Protestant sects battled over such issues as whether or not one should wear a hat in church. His concern with the origins of government reflects a period of political change in England during which the king was executed, Cromwell was made ruler, and later the monarchy was restored.[3]

In his early writings, Locke argues that a magistrate should govern those things to which God is indifferent. This magistrate could be a king or some other form of ruler. For Locke, there were two possible origins of government. One is the family modeled on the scriptural depiction of Adam and Eve. In this model, government is a father (Adam) ruling over a dependent population (Eve). The other possible origin of government is a contract created by the consent of the governed. In Locke's early work, the primary reason for people to consent to a contract for government was the assurance of order. Later, he made the protection of property and the public good the primary reason for people consenting to a government.[4]

The family model of government clearly places women in a subservient role to men. In this model, which Locke used in his discussion of education, the ruler of the family is the father. In addition, both models for the origin of government are authoritarian. In the first, the magistrate-as-father exercises paternal control over citizens. In the second, people give up their power to rule themselves when they consent to a government. Locke did not advocate self-government or democratic control. He argued that if a government does not protect property or the public good, then citizens have the right to break their contract and enter into a contract for a new government.[5]

Therefore, in Locke, and later in Rousseau, the social contract theory of government supports the existence of an authoritarian government as long as that government works for the public good. In fact, Locke argues that, with the creation of a social contract, people must submit themselves to the will of the state. This is a theory of popular consent without popular control. Since the ruler is bound by the original contract to maintain the public good, people cannot be allowed to violate the public good by breaking the law. If the ruler does not maintain the public good and protect property, people have the right to a new government. In this concept of the social contract, individual political control is limited to making and breaking the contract. Otherwise, the ruler has the right to demand obedience in the name of the public good.

While people must remain obedient to their rulers, there is still the question of the extent to which rulers can interfere with individual freedom. In Locke's argument, earthly rulers are concerned with those things to which God appears to be indifferent. Does this mean that rulers should exercise control over all the things not mentioned in the Bible? This question leads to Locke's arguments regarding toleration.

Locke argues that God's indifference to aspects of religious ceremonies and dress indicates that the state can also treat them indifferently. unless they cause a public disturbance. In this argument, he makes a distinction between objective and subjective knowledge. Objective knowledge is achieved by the use of human reason to discover the laws of nature. Objective knowledge might find nature, and therefore God, to have no laws governing the nature of religious ceremonies, the dress of the minister, or the place of worship. On the other hand, subjective knowledge imparts moral value to these issues. Individuals treat these issues as if there were some objective law that determined whether they were moral or immoral. The result is religious strife and attempts by rulers to outlaw religious practices. But, Locke argues, since there is no objective knowledge that declares these indifferences to be immoral, rulers should allow citizens to make their own individual decisions. In other words, rulers should tolerate the existence of a variety of religious groups as long as that tolerance does not injure the public good.[6]

Locke's position on indifferency and toleration partially opens the door to arguments supporting freedom of speech and conscience, as well as the free exercise of reason. Within the framework of his argument, rulers should not interfere with freedom of speech and conscience unless there is a violation of God's laws or the public good. But the emphasis on the disruption of the public good places a severe limitation on freedom of speech and conscience. For instance, Locke denies toleration to some opinions and beliefs, including Roman Catholicism and atheism, that he considers destructive of government.[7] And, since rulers have the authority to decide what the public good is, they have the right to limit free speech and conscience.

Despite the authoritarian power Locke gives to rulers, he did place restraints on their actions. In his mind, rulers should be limited by the laws of God and the original social contract, which requires them to protect property and the public good. In his *Two Treatises on Government*, Locke writes, "The great and chief end . . . of men's uniting into commonwealths, and putting themselves under government, is the preservation of their property."[8] Along with the protection of property, Locke included protection from foreign enemies. Constrained by the laws of God and the requirement to protect the public good, rulers, according to Locke, cannot act arbitrarily to limit freedom.

Locke's educational proposals reflect these general arguments regarding indifferency, the social contract, and toleration. Families, of course, have the responsibility to educate their children. Locke argues that the family is the first society formed by humans before the social contract. Locke argues that disputes do occur in the family and, therefore, "being necessary that the last determination, i.e. the rule, should be placed somewhere; it naturally falls to the man's share, as the abler and the stronger."[9] While Locke places the husband in the position of ruler of the family, he limits the husband's power to things that are of common interest to both the husband and wife. The woman is free to act on all things that do not touch upon their common interests and are not a violation of the laws of God or the government.

The idea of the father as ruler of the family is carried over into Locke's educational proposals. Locke informs parents that one of the first things they should do is "Be sure then to establish the authority of a father, as soon as he [the child] is capable of submission, and can understand in whose power he is."[10] The power of the father over the child, according to Locke, should continue until the age of twenty-one. Locke argued that while children are born free and with reason, they still must remain subservient to their parents until they have the capacity to know the law. Until they are able to know and to reason about the laws of the state, the father functions as "a temporary government."[11]

The unequal power of women is reflected not only in the idea of the father as ruler of the family, but also in Locke's educational proposals. In the first place, his educational plans are intended for the education of young boys, specifically for "a gentleman's son."[12] Second, whenever there is a discussion of women in his educational writings—and this does not occur very frequently—it is clearly indicated that their education should be limited. For instance, Locke describes two levels of the learning of languages. At one level, language can be learned by rote without learning grammar, which Locke states is suitable for common affairs and for "the softer sex . . . [who] show us, that . . . without the least study or knowledge of grammar, [they] can . . . [demonstrate] a great degree of elegancy and politeness in their language."[13] On the other hand, men who do business in the world, according to Locke, need to learn the proper rules of grammar.

In addition to Locke's educational proposals reflecting the unequal political power of women, they also reflect unequal power based on wealth. His primary concern is the education of gentlemen and members of the aristocracy. He is not concerned with the education of the masses of humanity. This adds an interesting element to his concept of the social contract. As I will discuss later in this section, one of Locke's educational goals is to teach boys the value of protection of property, which, of course, is the reason Locke gives for humanity entering into a social contract. It is precisely this protection of property that allows for the continued existence of wealthy gentlemen and the aristocracy and the unequal distribution of education.

The issue of wealth is directly related to Locke's proposal that children should be educated at home by tutors. Locke warns parents not to send their children to school because schools function as colleges of vice, where children pass on their bad habits to other children. For the same reason, Locke expresses concern about family servants passing on bad habits to children. Therefore, he recommends that children be educated at home by the father or a tutor and that great care should be taken to avoid contamination by the household servants. Obviously, this is not an educational plan for children of the poor.[14]

The authoritarian qualities of Locke's concept of the state and family are also evident in his concept of education. For him, the child is similar to "wax, to be moulded and fashioned as one pleases."[15] The image of the child as wax gives almost complete authority to the father or tutor to shape the future character of the child. This authoritarian power over the child is based on Locke's concept of the human mind, which he described in *An Essay Concerning Human Understanding*. In contrast to Socrates, who believed that human reason should be used to find the truth that is within all of us, Locke rejects the whole concept of innate ideas.[16] While humans have innate desires and capacities, such as reason, their minds at birth are blank slates. It is interaction with people and the environment that fills up the blank slate of the mind. Locke argues that there are two sources of ideas. The first is our senses. "This great source, of most of the ideas we have, depending wholly upon our sense, and derived by them to the understanding, I call sensation."[17] The second source of ideas is the operation of our minds on the ideas that are supplied by our senses.

Therefore, education involves putting knowledge into the human mind as opposed to the Socratic ideal of turning the eyes to the truth within each human. As Locke states in *Some Thoughts Concerning Education*, "I may say, that, of all the men we meet with, nine parts of ten are what they are, good or evil, useful or not, by their education."[18] This image of the child gives a great deal of power to the educator. Essentially, Locke believes the child can be molded in any direction. Locke states, "I imagine the minds of children as easily turned this or that way as water itself."[19]

Molding the child, Locke argues, can be accomplished through a system of rewards and punishments. In general, Locke rejects the idea of physical punishment as a method of education. In fact, he strongly objects to the use of corporal punishment. He also objects to physical rewards, such as candy or gifts. Instead, he chooses psychological controls, such as love and shame. "Esteem and disgrace are, of all other," Locke writes, "the most powerful incentives of the mind."[20] Through the withholding or giving of love and praise, Locke hoped to educate the rational child.

These psychological controls are to be used to overcome what Locke calls one of the first desires of childhood—love of power and domination. The wishes for power and domination, he feels, are natural and are the most vicious of human desires. In childhood, these desires are sometimes achieved through displays of crying, temper, and peevishness. It is through these actions that children get adults to comply with their demands. Later in life, these desires become major sources of injustice as humans try to gain domination over others. Controlling these desires in childhood, according to Locke, will reduce their occurrence in adulthood and, therefore, contribute to the public good.

Locke applies the concept of indifference to the problem of controlling the desire for power and domination. Parents, like rulers, have an obligation to conform to the laws of God or, in this case, the laws of God as reflected in the laws of nature. Therefore parents, in confronting attempts by children to exercise power and control, must make a distinction between those things required by the laws of nature and those things about which nature is indifferent. Therefore, children, like the population of a state, have the right to declare their natural wants for food, drink, shelter, and avoidance of pain. Parents, like rulers, have an obligation to meet these natural needs. On the other hand, it is the decision of the parents and the rulers as to how these natural needs should be met. For instance, the demand for food can be met by supplying dark bread or white bread. However, the child might want a particular type of bread. The desire for a particular type of bread Locke classifies as "wants of fancy" in contrast to wants that originate in nature.[21]

Where children learn to exercise power and domination is in the realm of wants of fancy. The same thing is true of civil society. People, according to Locke, have a right to expect their rulers to meet their natural needs. People consent to a social contract to obey their rulers, and their rulers consent to rule for the public good. Struggles for power begin to occur when people begin to make demands based on their wants of fancy: for instance, when people begin to demand and seek gold and other forms of riches.

To curb this early drive for power and domination, Locke argues that parents should never meet the wants of fancy. In fact, he states that the very speaking of a want of fancy by a child should result in the child experiencing some loss. For instance, Locke writes, "Clothes when they need, they must have; but if they speak for this stuff, or that colour, they should be sure to go without."[22] These lessons will destroy the confidence in people that they can change wishes into demands and that they ought to obtain these demands. Consequently, people will set aside demands based on fancy and will believe that they should obtain only those things required by the laws of nature.

The issue of property, the basis of the social contract, Locke considered part of the reason for curbing children's desire for power and domination. Central to Locke's concept of justice and the social contract is the protection of property. While God gave the earth to all humans to be held in common, Locke argues, humans, prior to forming a social contract, still owned things. For instance, when a person picks an apple from a tree, that apple becomes that person's property. This form of property is a result of humans mixing their labor with the common property given by God. In addition, Locke argues, people possess the property of their own being. The purpose of entering into a social contract is to protect the property of the person and the property acquired through that person's labor.[23]

Part of the natural desire for power and domination in children, according to Locke, is the desire for property or domination over things. It is through the idea of property that children gain a notion of justice. Therefore, Locke argues, children must be taught the concept of property at a young age, even before they learn language. The early sources of property for children are gifts. At this age, children are to be taught not to take or keep anything that is not given to them as a gift. As the child matures, Locke suggests, the father or tutor might take something that the child feels is his or her property. This action will supposedly teach the child how unwise it is to take other people's property because there will always be someone stronger who could take the child's property. Therefore, children will learn to want a society that protects their property from possession by others.[24]

While boys are learning to respect property, the basis for the organization of the state, they are also developing their ability to reason, which is the means for them to understand the laws of nature and God. Similarly to Socrates, Locke believes that there is a basic conflict between reason and desires. The great principle of all virtue, he argues, is when individuals can deny their desires and follow the dictates of reason. One method of instilling this concept in children, Locke argues, is to teach them that they will get only those things that reason dictates are fit for them, as opposed to getting those things that they desire.

In addition, Locke argues that the father and tutor can serve as models of rationality. Of course, this does not mean talking to young children about philosophical issues. What it does mean is that the father and tutor should act rationally and treat children as "rational creatures."[25] Treated as rational creatures, children's ability to reason will increase as they study arithmetic, languages, history, sciences, and the laws of the state. And, once having achieved the ability to understand and reason about the law, children are freed from the authority of their fathers.

In general, Locke's concepts of the state and education reflect what I would call "liberal authoritarianism." His concepts of the state and education contain important elements of humaneness and toleration. He envisions a state in which people are free to act as long as they do not interfere with the right to property or the public good. On the other hand, people are without power to participate in the governing of this liberal state. While he advocates treating children kindly and without physical punishment, he does believe that they should be molded by a system of rewards and punishments. The father is the authority over the child until the child is able to understand the authority of the laws of the state.

While Locke's concept of the state does place limits on the power of the ruler, it does little to enhance equality of power. His concept of the family does not provide equal power for women. His concept of property does not assure equal power between men. In fact, his theory that the state originated to protect property primarily serves to justify the protection of the property of the middle class and aristocracy. His method of instruction is also designed to instill in children the idea that property is the basis of the state. In addition, the method of instruction reflects an authoritarian attitude toward children. Children are treated as "wax" to be molded in any direction.

JEAN-JACQUES ROUSSEAU: NATURE IS GOOD

"Man is born free; and everywhere he is in chains," writes Jean-Jacques Rousseau at the beginning of *The Social Contract* (1762).[26] *Emile*, Rousseau's companion volume to *The Social Contract*, presents an educational plan that he hopes will break the chains of political enslavement. Similarly to Locke's, Rousseau's ideas on education were a direct extension of his political philosophy. His ideas had a profound impact on educational thinking from the eighteenth to the twentieth century, when it is reflected in the work of psychologist Jean Piaget.

In contrast to Locke, Rousseau argues that the state originates from the mutual interdependence of people. This gives a different meaning to the purpose of the social contract and the authority of the state. Locke's argument that the state originated from the desire to protect property is based on a concept of economic individualism: The state exists to protect individual property. In contrast, Rousseau's argument is based on the concept of the social person. The state exists to protect collective interests and should be governed, according to Rousseau, by a collective will.

Rousseau's description of the evolution of the state is intended to show the descent of humanity from freedom to slavery. His overall goal is to recapture, through new political forms and education, the freedom he believes humanity had in a state of nature. And, as I will demonstrate in my discussion of *Emile*, Rousseau's ideas on the evolution of the state parallel the developmental stages of the child and adolescent in *Emile*.

In the first stage of the development of society, all people, including women, are free. Humans gather food and mate but do not form families or any type of social organization. This is the stage Rousseau refers to in his opening line: "Man is born free." At the second stage, families begin to form and there are scattered settlements, but there is still no concept of private property. During these first two stages, humans are naturally sympathetic and protective of one another. This natural sympathy begins to disappear in the third stage, when the advantages of mutual aid lead to the creation of nations. At this stage there appears what Rousseau refers to as the "artificial person," as opposed to the "natural person." Part of Rousseau's educational plan is designed to avoid the creation of this artificial person. In the fourth stage, people begin to hoard property and personal ownership of property is declared a personal right. In the fifth stage, struggles over property between the rich and poor lead to the creation of representative government, which, according to Rousseau, primarily protects the property of the rich. It is in this final stage that Rousseau declares people to be in chains.[27]

Rousseau's proposals to break the chains binding humanity in *The Social Contract* and *Emile* do not include an equal distribution of power to women. First, women, as I will show in my discussion of *Emile*, are disqualified by Rousseau from participation in civic life except through their husbands. In fact, Rousseau's proposals for the education of women are centered on preparing them to be extensions of their husbands' intellectual and political lives. Second, individual power, according to Rousseau, should be governed by what he calls the general will. As I will discuss later, the general will plays an authoritarian role in Rousseau's ideal society.

These limitations on the equal distribution of power are clearly evidenced in Rousseau's educational writings. For instance, *Emile* is an educational plan for a wealthy male child. In *Emile*, Rousseau provides an alternative and decidedly inferior educational plan for Emile's future wife. While Rousseau expresses concern about the differences between the rich and the poor, his educational proposals for the masses of children in Poland are strikingly different from the one proposed for Emile. Emile's education is designed to make him free, while the plan for Poland is designed to prepare citizens to submit to the authority of what Rousseau called the general will. It is possible, as I will discuss later, to argue that the freedom achieved by Emile includes obedience to the general will.

In addition, Rousseau writes that Emile "is rich, since it is only the rich who have the need of the natural education that would fit them to live under all conditions."[28]

Since Emile is portrayed as the son of a rich family, it is possible for Rousseau to suggest that, as a means of getting Emile closer to nature, he be placed in a small country home under the guidance of a tutor. Emile's education for freedom begins in infancy and continues through to early youth. One of the striking features of Emile's education, and one of Rousseau's major contributions to educational thinking, is that it parallels the stages of human development. In fact, one could argue that Emile is the first modern psychological text on human development. Also, Rousseau's stages of human development parallel his stages in the development of civilization. For instance, infancy parallels the first stage of civilization, when humans were free to act without concern for society.

The stage of human development that Rousseau believes is crucial for the evolution of society is adolescence, which parallels the third and fourth stages of civilization. An important factor of adolescence, according to Rousseau, is the birth of reason. This represents an important distinction between Locke and Rousseau. Locke believed the child was born with the capacity for reason, while Rousseau believed it appeared with the onset of the sexual drive. In addition, Rousseau made a very specific distinction between two types of reason. For instance, a child can reason about physical things, such as deciding how to avoid getting wet when it rains. On the other hand, it is only with the onset of adolescence, Rousseau argues, that an individual can reason about social issues and morality. Therefore, Rousseau wants to protect Emile from society and moral instruction until the age of reason, or adolescence.

Within the context of these ideas about human development and reason, Rousseau outlines a carefully crafted plan to educate the freeman. Near the beginning of *Emile*, Rousseau gives a specific definition of freedom that serves as a guide to understanding his educational proposals: "The true freeman wants only what he can get, and does only what pleases him. This is the fundamental maxim. Apply it to childhood and all the rules of education follow."[29]

This definition of freedom contains two important elements. First, freedom is defined as wanting only what you can get. Or, to reverse the idea, one feels one lacks freedom only when one cannot get what one wants. To achieve this goal, Rousseau insists on the teaching of the law of necessity during the early stages of childhood. Learning what is necessary in life, according to Rousseau, helps to avoid wanting things that are contrary to necessity. For instance, it is necessary to eat in order to survive. Therefore, wanting not to eat can be attained only by dying. Because of the impossibility of avoiding eating, the desire not to eat makes people feel a lack of freedom.

In the context of the law of necessity, Emile gains freedom when he accepts the necessity of dying. During the final stages of Emile's education, his tutor tells him, "Extend the law of necessity into the sphere of morals and learn to lose whatever can be taken from you, and to rise above the chances of life. Then you will be happy."[30] One of the things that Emile must come to terms with is the loss of his own life. The law of necessity dictates acceptance of one's own death. "When you no longer attach an undue importance to life," the tutor advises Emile, "you will pass your own life untroubled and come to the end of it without fear."[31]

The law of necessity also serves as an important motivator in Emile's education. For instance, Rousseau proposes teaching reading only when Emile asks to learn it. In order to achieve this goal, the tutor proposes that Emile receive a number of invitations which, since he can't read, he must find someone to read to him. By the time this occurs, the event will have already passed. From this situation, Emile learns that it is necessary to learn how to read in order to participate in enjoyable social situations.

The second part of Rousseau's definition of freedom is that people should do only what pleases them. This idea is very similar to Max Stirner's concern with wheels in the head. For Rousseau, it is the principle of negative education. What hinders the pursuit of pleasure, according to Rousseau, is the fixing of moral ideas in the child before the age of reason.

With the birth of reason during adolescence, an individual gains the ability to reason about moral issues and, therefore, is able to accept moral principles by choice. Therefore, Rousseau proposed that words like "duty," "obey," "command," and "obligation" should be banished from the early stages of education. An adult, such as the tutor, should not confront a child with any claim of authority or duty, but with the simple reality that the adult is stronger and older. In other words, the child obeys the tutor not because of a moral imperative, such as "duty," but because of the law of necessity.

The second part of negative education is the avoidance of verbal learning. Learning during the early stages of development, according to Rousseau, should be based on experience. Education through experience is an aspect of Rousseau's proposals, the other being instruction paralleling human development, that is a lasting contribution to educational discussions. Rousseau felt that books were one of the great plagues of childhood. It was for this reason that the tutor postponed teaching reading until Emile expressed a desire to learn.

Therefore, the law of necessity and the idea of negative education served as guiding principles of Emile's education prior to adolescence. The boy, at this stage of education, is primarily motivated by self-love, which Rousseau calls the "only passion natural to man."[32] All human impulses are related to self-preservation and self-love. Rousseau argues that appeals to self-love as opposed to appeals to duty should be the method of motivating Emile to learn.

Similar to Locke, Rousseau believes that the "first idea a child should have given him is not that of liberty but of property."[33] Again, similar to Locke, Rousseau argues that the first feelings of justice arise over issues of property. And, since the boy's primary motivation is self-love, the appeal to justice must be based on what others owe the boy as opposed to what the boy owes others. For instance, Rousseau suggests that the boy plant and tend beans in the garden so that he develops a feeling that the plants belong to him. After the beans begin to mature, the gardener should dig up the plants. According to Rousseau, the boy in this situation learns that the ground belongs to the gardener and that he has to make arrangements with the gardener before planting. In an example of a destructive boy who breaks the windows in his room, Rousseau suggests that you let the boy suffer from the cold air. If the boy continues to break windows, he should be shut up in a windowless room. "The time will come," Rousseau writes, "when he has learned what property means and he is willing to respect other people's belongings."[34]

In addition to learning about the meaning of property, Rousseau argues, these early years should be devoted to training the physical senses in preparation for further education. For instance, he suggests many night games to develop a sense of touch. With regard to sight, he argues that this is the most unreliable of the senses. Sight provides only inaccurate estimates of length, height, and depth. Therefore, the boy is asked to constantly check the accuracy of what he sees. For example, the tutor is to show the boy a tall cherry tree and ask the boy if the ladder in the barn is high enough to pick cherries ripening on the tree. Or the boy is asked to estimate the length of line needed to fish in a moat. The training of sight also involves the learning of basic geometry. For instance, the tutor makes a circle by drawing it with a pencil attached to a length of thread that turns around the center. The boy is then asked to compare the radii of the circle. Of course, Emile responds that all the radii have to be equal. In addition, hearing, taste, and smell are all to be developed using similar methods.

At the age of twelve, Emile is introduced to the law of utility. At this age, Rousseau states, a boy's mental and physical powers are growing much more rapidly than his needs. This is just before the awakening of sexual passions and the dawning of the age of reason. With his growing energy, the boy is now ready to begin exploring the world and learning the law of utility. Similarly to the law of necessity, the law of utility helps the boy to be free. In discussing the role of the law of necessity by the age of twelve, Rousseau writes, "The law of necessity, always operative, soon teaches man to do what he does not like, in order to avoid evils he would like still less."[35]

The law of utility teaches Emile that certain things in life are useful. Combined with the law of necessity, Emile will be free, according to Rousseau's definition, because he will want those things that are necessary for living. Some of Rousseau's finest examples of teaching by experience are incorporated into Emile's lessons on the law of utility. For instance, Emile asks his tutor why it is useful to know the position of a forest north of the local village. The tutor responds by getting lost during a morning walk with Emile. After a series of questions from the tutor, Emile determines their location by shadows cast by the sun and with the knowledge that the forest is north of the village. Another method of teaching Emile what is useful is the game of Robinson Crusoe. Rousseau writes that the book *Robinson Crusoe* is the finest example of a natural education and it is to be the first book read by Emile. Rousseau wants Emile to use his imagination to consider all the problems of a man alone on an island.

As part of learning what is useful, Emile is taught that people are useful to one another. Of course, since Emile has not reached the age of reason, his introduction to the interdependence of humans is not accompanied by moral issues or abstract ideas of social relations. Emile's introduction to the value of mutual aid roughly parallels Rousseau's third stage of civilization, when humans begin to form nations because of the advantages of working together. Emile's lessons on mutual aid include visiting a variety of workshops, where, following the principles of learning through experience, he tries his hand at a number of different trades. These work experiences are supposed to teach Emile why particular tools and trades are useful and how organized society can be useful.

By the time Emile reaches the age of reason, he has learned several things that will contribute to his future freedom. Learning to want those things that are necessary and useful, and being free of moral strictures, Emile begins to take on the characteristics of Rousseau's "True freeman [who] wants only what he can get, and does only what pleases him."[36] But the age of reason creates the possibility of Emile losing his freedom by becoming an artificial man.

In Rousseau's scheme, adolescence roughly parallels the third and fourth stages of civilization, when, according to Rousseau, the natural man becomes the artificial man. As humans come together for purposes of mutual aid, they begin to compare themselves with others. This results in what Rousseau considers the major problem for modern civilization, the development of vanity. Vanity creates the artificial person. Prior to the birth of vanity, humans are co-operative, peaceful members of families. The development of vanity causes people to want to accumulate more property than others, to be praised, and to gain power over others. Rivalry, vengeance, jealousy, and aggression characterize the actions of the artificial person. It is vanity, Rousseau argues, that destroys the peaceful calm of the natural person. And, of course, it is vanity that threatens Emile's freedom as he enters adolescence.[37]

Rousseau refers to the sexual awakenings of adolescence as a second birth that will push Emile out of the narrow world of self into the social world. These new passions are directly linked, according to Rousseau, to the original sentiment of self-love. One effect of self-love is pitying other people's misfortunes because of the possibility that those misfortunes might strike oneself. In addition, self-love leads to love of others who appear to want to help. This love can eventually extend itself to a love of humanity. Love of humanity continues when a person believes that the rest of humanity is willing to help him or her.

The problem, Rousseau argues, is that self-love can turn into vanity, which could turn Emile into an artificial man. To avoid this possibility, the tutor exposes Emile to cardsharps who through flattery swindle him of his money. The tutor has Emile read fables that demonstrate the foolishness of listening to flattery and biographies that are to serve as models of human action. And, to assure that self-love does not become vanity instead of love of humanity, the tutor has Emile work among the poor and sick.

As Emile approaches the final stage of youth, his tutor begins to worry about a suitable mate. It is at this point in the story that Rousseau describes the ideal education for women through the character of Sophie. As I stated earlier in this chapter, Rousseau wants women to participate in civic life through their husbands. Consequently, Rousseau wants Sophie's education to prepare her to accept the ideas and will of her husband. In a passage reflecting Rousseau's feelings about women, he describes the intended results of Sophie's education: "Her mind is still vacant but has been trained to learn: it is well-tilled land only waiting for the grain. What a pleasing ignorance! Happy is the man destined to instruct her. She will be her husband's disciple, not his teacher. Far from wanting to impose her tastes on him, she will share his."[38]

Sophie's education centers on dressing dolls, worrying about personal dress, drawing, counting, reading, and writing. In striking contrast to Emile's education, Sophie is kept under constant control and kept busy from an early age. Rousseau calls the enforced industry and control placed on Sophie a necessary hardship for a future life as a woman. Women, Rousseau writes, "must be disciplined to endure them [constraints] till they come to take them as a matter of course and learn to overcome caprice and bow to authority."[39]

The marriage of Emile and Sophie symbolizes the importance Rousseau gives to the role of the family in maintaining the state. In this idealized marriage, Sophie bows to the authority of Emile and participates in civic life through his actions. Rousseau believes that the emotional attachments of the family are the basis of emotional attachments to neighbors and the state. The heart, Rousseau writes, "is linked with the great fatherland through the little fatherland of the home; that it is the good son, the good husband, the good father, that makes the good citizen."[40]

Prior to their marriage, the tutor takes Emile on a tour of foreign countries so that Emile can study other governments. Rousseau argues that everyone is born with the right to break the social contract with his or her country. Emile rejects this opportunity because he believes that true freedom cannot be found in any government, it can be found only in the heart of the freeman. And, for women, freedom is found through the heart of a husband who is a freeman.

Emile is now free because he understands the laws of necessity and utility and because he is not an artificial man driven by vanity. He can feel free in his heart, while others are constrained by the pursuit of wealth, power, and other worldly desires. He never feels a lack of freedom, because he wants only what it is possible to achieve. The mistake others make, Rousseau writes, is to think that freedom can be attained under the protection of law. But it is not government that provides true freedom, Rousseau argues; it is individuals who must provide their own freedom.

For philosopher Allan Bloom, whose work I discussed in Chapter 6, Emile and Rousseau's other works are concerned with saving civilization from the new middle class that was developing in Europe. The new middle class, according to Bloom, was motivated by fear of violent death and by vanity. This is the artificial person, who, driven by vanity, is primarily concerned with making a good impression on others through dress and ostentatious displays of wealth. Trapped by vanity, the artificial person shows little concern about those suffering from misfortune. In addition, artificial people seek their own self-preservation outside the boundaries of the common good.[41]

In a broader perspective, Rousseau is attempting to overcome the type of economic individualism that was being created by the emerging doctrines of capitalism and the liberal tradition inaugurated by John Locke. These doctrines envisioned a society in which the common good would be a product of the economic competition caused by citizens pursuing their own economic interests. It is certainly questionable whether or not individual economic competition will produce the common good. And it is certainly legitimate to ask the question, as Rousseau did, how human relationships and a sense of community can be maintained in a world driven by economic competition.

Rousseau hoped that his natural man, Emile, would resolve these questions. Emile, similarly to the economic individualist, was driven by the desire for self-preservation. But for Emile, self-preservation did not result in a loss of compassion for the rest of humanity. Saved from vanity, Emile learns empathy and compassion for the poor and unfortunate by appeals to his own sense of self-preservation. In addition, Rousseau attempts to resolve the problem of community by arguing for the importance of the family and participation in the general will.

It is from Rousseau's discussion of the importance of the family that Allan Bloom develops his arguments for the collapse of the culture of Western liberalism in the twentieth century. Rousseau, according to Bloom, predicted that egalitarianism and rationalism would inevitably lead to equality between the sexes and this equality would cause the destruction of the family. Commenting on Rousseau's prediction, Bloom states, "The unaltered fragment of nature remaining [after the disappearance of the natural family] . . . would be the selfish . . . individual, striving for self-preservation, comfort, and power after power. Marriage and the family would decay and the sexes be assimilated. Children would be burdens and not fulfillments."[42]

Therefore, one cannot simply dismiss Sophie's education as a simple reflection of the status of women during the period of time in which Rousseau was writing. In fact, Rousseau's political philosophy depends on the continued inequality of political power of women and their continued domestication. The only hope in a world splintered by economic competition, according to Rousseau, is the sense of human relations developed in the family. In this model, it is the role of women to exist as symbols of virtue and models of domestic relationships. In Rousseau's vision, husbands should act for wives in the affairs of the world, while wives focus on the concerns of the family.

Not only is the political power of women limited in Rousseau's philosophy, but men must give up power to the general will. Simply stated, the general will is an expression of the collective interests of the citizens of a state. Rousseau's discussion of the general will highlights the fact that Emile's education is a model for the rich and not for the masses. The major goal in educating the masses, according to Rousseau, is the submergence of individual wills in the general will. In a 1755 article, "Political Economy," Rousseau discusses the role of education in preparing citizens to participate in the collective interests of the state. He states: "If . . . we train them [citizens] early in life never to think of their individual interests except in relation to those of the state as a whole, and never to regard their own existence as having any meaning apart from the state, they will come in course of time to identify themselves in some fashion with this grand Whole and be conscious of their membership in their fatherland."[43]

Of course, it is the human relationships learned in the family, according to Rousseau, that prepare people to be emotionally attached to the collective interests of the state. Love of family leads to love of country. In fact, Rousseau compares the love of nation with the love fostered by a tender mother. If children are to be citizens, Rousseau writes, they must be "imbued with the Laws of the state and the maxims of the general will" and "surrounded by objects that unceasingly remind them of the tender mother that fosters them . . . they will learn to cherish each other as brothers and wish only what the community wishes."[44]

The sublimation of individual interests to the general will is central to Rousseau's proposals for an educational system in Poland. In these proposals, he affirms his conviction that the family is the central institution for building emotional ties to the general will and that mothers play the key role in that process. He writes, "A child ought to look upon his fatherland as soon as his eyes open to the light, and should continue to do so till the day of his death. Every patriot sucks in the love of country with his mother's milk. This love is his whole existence."[45]

To reinforce the love learned in the home, Rousseau proposed that the Polish educational system focus on group activities in developing a sense of mutual interests among the children. For example, he proposed that all games be conducted in public "so that there may always be a common end to which they aspire, and by which they are moved to rivalry and emulation."[46]

The creation of "a common end" is key to understanding how Rousseau's attempt to achieve freedom through the general will results in the establishment of an authoritarian state. As I previously mentioned, Rousseau rejects representative government. He believes that an individual will cannot be represented by another person. Citizens, like Emile, must be free to exercise their individual wills. But, of course, people following their own individual wills can result in a society filled with conflict. Rousseau's solution is to make individual wills inseparable from the general will. The education planned for Poland, Rousseau hoped, would accomplish exactly that goal. Children were to be taught that their interests are the same as the group's interests. As Allan Bloom points out, this means replacing "I want" by "we want. . . . The man who wills only what all could will makes a community of shared, harmonious wills possible. . . . General will is the common good."[47]

The concept of gaining freedom through the general will parallels the concept of freedom in *Emile*. Emile learns that freedom is wanting only what one can get. Freedom through the general will is gained when one wants only those things that are in the common interest of all people. This reasoning opens the door to authoritarianism, where a single ruler, a political party, or a philosopher-king can claim to know the general will and that all individual wills must be the same as the general will. In the twentieth century, both the Communist and Nazi parties declared that they knew the common good and that all children should be educated so that their personal interests would be the same as the common interest. Therefore, while Rousseau hoped that his method of education and political philosophy would counter what he perceived to be the negative aspects of economic individualism, the result was a new form of authoritarianism dependent on a subservient role for women, a family structure dedicated to preparing the child to love the state, and the subjugation of individual wills to the general will.

CONCLUSION: MAINTAINING CIVILIZATION THROUGH THE SUBMISSION OF WOMEN

The writings of Locke and Rousseau demonstrate how differences in the treatment of children are related to concepts of childhood. Locke's image of the infant born with a blank slate of a mind and as wax to be molded by adults turns the child into an object to be manipulated by adult authority. Locke's method is to use psychological controls to shape the child according to the desires of the adult. In addition, Locke's model of childhood is the type of economic person who was at the center of Rousseau's critique of the new middle class. Similarly to the economic person of the developing capitalism of the seventeenth and eighteenth centuries, the child in Locke's educational writings is controlled by rewards and punishment. In the marketplace of capitalism, the behaviors of the economic person are shaped by profits and losses or, in other words, by rewards and punishments. In addition, reflecting Locke's liberalism, an important part of Locke's educational program focuses on teaching the importance and value of property. This is the classic economic person who values property and who acts in a rational manner to increase economic rewards.

Rousseau's concept of childhood gives more importance to the inner nature of the child. Consequently, the child is not simply a piece of wax to be molded. The tutor must plan lessons according to the child's desire and natural development. While Emile is taught the value of property, he also learns that the value of property must be weighed against the reality of death. Faced with the knowledge of death, Emile realizes the foolishness of putting too much emphasis on accumulating property. Saved from vanity, Emile becomes the opposite of Locke's economic person. After learning the laws of necessity and utility and after being protected from developing vanity, Emile is interested not in economic reward but in the social relationships of the family and the feeling of freedom he finds in his heart.

In the end, both philosophers succumb to the idea of the authoritarian state. Women are denied equal power with men. In Locke's arguments, the husband is given the power to make decisions over the common interests of the household.

Locke did declare that women should have freedom to act on matters outside the common interests of the household and on matters that are not threatening to the common good. Of course, in Locke's ideal state, the ruler has the right to limit the power of both men and women when their actions are in conflict with the common good. While Locke does not support self-governance, Rousseau advocates self-governance by making individual wills the same as the general will. And, for Rousseau, it is the family, with the subservient wife, that will teach the human relations necessary for tying the individual to the collective interest. With both philosophers, the individual gives up political power to the common good or the general will. As represented by these two philosophers, classical liberalism opens the door to greater government toleration of human behavior but closes the door on equality of political power for women.

In the next chapter, I will analyze responses to the political and educational theories of classical liberalism. While arguing that women should not be denied equal rights and political power, these responses contain complex and conflicting arguments about nature, the family, sexuality, and the possible differences in the use of reason by men and women.

NOTES

1. Peter Gay, "Introduction" in *John Locke on Education*, ed. Peter Gay (New York: Teachers College Press, 1964), p. 1.
2. Philip Abrams, "Introduction" in *John Locke, Two Tracts on Government*, ed. Philip Abrams (Cambridge, England: Cambridge University Press, 1967), pp. 3–115.
3. Ibid., pp. 30–63.
4. Ibid., pp. 63–84.
5. John Yolton, *The Locke Reader: Selections from the Works of John Locke with a General Introduction and Commentary* (London: Cambridge University Press), pp. 237–330.
6. Abrams, "Introduction," pp. 84–112.
7. Ibid., p. 105.
8. Yolton, *The Locke Reader*, p. 285.
9. Ibid., p. 242.
10. Ibid., p. 29.
11. Yolton, *The Locke Reader*, p. 236.
12. Locke, *Some Thoughts Concerning Education* in Gay, *John Locke on Education*, p. 176.
13. Ibid., p. 129.
14. Ibid., pp. 46–54.
15. Ibid., p. 176.
16. John Locke, *An Essay Concerning Human Understanding*, ed. Peter Nidditch (Oxford, England: Clarendon Press, 1975), pp. 104–118.
17. Ibid., p. 105.
18. John Locke, *Some Thoughts Concerning Education* in Gay, *John Locke on Education*, p. 20.
19. Ibid., p. 20.
20. Ibid., p. 36.
21. Ibid., p. 77.
22. Ibid., p. 78.
23. Yolton, *The Locke Reader*, pp. 287–295.

24. Locke, *Some Thoughts Concerning Education* in Gay, *John Locke on Education*, pp. 84–85.
25. Ibid., p. 65.
26. Jean-Jacques Rousseau, *The Social Contract and Discourses* (New York: E. P. Dutton and Company, Inc., 1950), p. 3.
27. Stephen Ellenburg, *Rousseau's Political Philosophy: An Interpretation from Within* (Ithaca: Cornell University Press, 1976), pp. 71–80.
28. *The Emile of Jean-Jacques Rousseau* trans. and ed. William Boyd (New York: Teachers College Press, 1956), p. 20.
29. Ibid., p. 35.
30. Ibid., p. 159.
31. Ibid., p. 160
32. Ibid., p. 40.
33. Ibid., p. 44.
34. Ibid., p. 45.
35. Ibid., p. 80.
36. Ibid., p. 35.
37. Ellenburg, *Rousseau's Political Philosophy*, pp. 73–76.
38. *The Emile of Jean-Jacques Rousseau*, p. 153.
39. Ibid., p. 139.
40. Ibid., p. 133.
41. *Allan Bloom, Giants and Dwarfs: Essays 1960–1990* (New York: Simon & Schuster, 1990), pp. 179–181.
42. Ibid., p. 202.
43. Jean-Jacques Rousseau, "Political Economy" in *The Minor Educational Writings of Jean-Jacques Rousseau*, ed. William Boyd (London: Blackies and Son, 1910), pp. 42–43.
44. Ibid., p. 45.
45. Jean-Jacques Rousseau, "Considerations on the Government of Poland," in ibid., pp. 141–142.
46. Ibid., pp. 145–146.
47. Bloom, *Giants and Dwarfs*, p. 223.

CHAPTER 9

Reason and Motherhood

John Locke and Jean-Jacques Rousseau rely on women and the family to temper the economic isolation and greed resulting from a society based on economic individualism. Modern psychologists, such as Carol Gilligan, argue that a male vision of society caused Locke to see the social contract as being based on a desire to protect property. In addition, a male view of society is embedded in Rousseau's belief that the proper functioning of the family depends on male domination of women. It can be argued that classical liberalism is built on the subjugation of women and reflects a peculiarly male vision of morality and the proper organization of society.

Responding to Rousseau, Mary Wollstonecraft argued that female reasoning is the same as that of men. Consequently, she dismissed Rousseau's plan to educate women as companions to men and have them gain citizenship through their husbands. Wollstonecraft argued that women, like men, should be educated to exercise their reason and should have the same rights as men.

The debate over differences in male and female reasoning continues despite Wollstonecraft's arguments. In the nineteenth century, Swiss educator Johann Pestalozzi argued that mother love is the basis of all morality. Pestalozzi believed that females were distinctly different from males with regard to moral reasoning. The morality of women, Pestalozzi believed, is the basis for social reform. This concept of women received support in the 1980s by Carol Gilligan, who, in her psychological research, found striking differences between male and female moral reasoning. Moral reasoning in women, Gilligan argues, reflects a concern with caring for others and social relationships, while men think in terms of hierarchy and rules. In addition, contemporary social critic Camille Paglia rejects Rousseau's belief that nature is basically good and links differences in moral reasoning to sexual conflict between men and women.

MARY WOLLSTONECRAFT: REASON AND VANITY

Mary Wollstonecraft's *A Vindication of the Rights of Woman* (1792) appeared thirty years after the publication of Rousseau's *Emile*. Though critical of Rousseau, Wollstonecraft shared many of his assumptions about humans and society. To a certain degree, one could argue that Wollstonecraft stood Rousseau on his head by accepting the central importance of the family in building human relations while rejecting the argument that the existence of the family depends on women being educated for domination. Wollstonecraft maintains, in sharp contrast to Rousseau, that the proper functioning of the family depends on women receiving an education equal to that of men. The development of women's reason, she maintains, will strengthen family ties.

Similarly to Rousseau, Wollstonecraft was concerned with the nature of the family because of a fear that economic individualism was destroying the fabric of society. Rousseau believed the family structure will teach its members the value and meaning of human relationships. This counters, according to Rousseau, the tendency for the pursuit of self-interest to cause alienation between humans. The key concept for understanding this argument is vanity. Both Rousseau and Wollstonecraft give a broad meaning to the term "vanity." For instance, according to their use of the term, vanity results in people wanting to accumulate wealth beyond their needs. In the framework of this definition of vanity, people pursue the accumulation of unnecessary wealth for the purpose of public display and comparison to other people. Wealth also serves other forms of vanity, such as a concern with personal appearance.

For Rousseau and Wollstonecraft, vanity is the central problem in a society based on the pursuit of individual self-interest. The problem is not that people pursue their own self-interests by accumulating property, but that people accumulate more than they need. The pursuit of unnecessary wealth leads to extreme divisions between the rich and poor. As I discussed in Chapter 8, Rousseau believes that self-interest, which he considers a basic human instinct, can lead in two directions during adolescence. In one direction, self-interest leads to vanity. In the other direction, self-interest leads to the development of compassion by the relating of others' misfortunes to oneself. Rousseau educated Emile away from vanity and in the direction of compassion.

Therefore, the issue of vanity is central to the problem of economic individualism resulting in extremes of wealth. Without vanity, people would still pursue their own economic self-interest, but they would not be concerned about accumulating excess wealth as a means of proving themselves better than their neighbors. Ideally, compassion would temper the pursuit of economic self-interest.

Wollstonecraft links the idea of vanity to the accumulation of wealth and the subjugation of women. Under male domination, women's self-interest leads in the direction of vanity. To gain male favors, women are concerned with developing a personal appearance and manners that are pleasing to men. Lacking equal power, she argues, women attempt to exert power over men by being sexually attractive. In turn, men try to be pleasing to women in order to gain sexual pleasure.

It is precisely the development of vanity in Rousseau's plan for the education of Emile's future mate, Sophie, that Wollstonecraft finds most reprehensible. She writes, "Rousseau declares that a woman should never . . . feel herself independent, that she should be . . . made a coquettish slave in order to render her a more alluring object of desire."[1] In order to be sexually appealing to men, Wollstonecraft argues, women become artificial creatures. The concept of being an artificial person, as opposed to a natural person, is similar in both Rousseau and Wollstonecraft. Artificiality is a result of vanity.

Wollstonecraft rejects Rousseau's argument that the development of vanity in women is necessary for the maintenance of family. In fact, she argues, it destroys meaningful relations. The sexual passion that women try to arouse in their husbands is not healthy for the maintenance of the family. Ideally, she argues, the passion between husband and wife should turn into friendship. But this becomes impossible, she states, when women are educated merely to please men. In addition, the cultivation of vanity prevents the development of compassion between husband and wife. The lack of friendship and compassion between husbands and wives seriously compromises the ability of the family to develop the sense of human relationships necessary to correct the errors of a society in pursuit of economic gain. "Why must the female mind," Wollstonecraft asks, "be tainted by coquettish arts to gratify the sensualist, and prevent love from subsiding into friendship, or compassionate tenderness?"[2]

In addition to the destruction of friendship and compassion between husband and wife, the focus on developing the arts of pleasing men undercuts the ability of women to properly regulate their families and educate their children. Therefore, according to Wollstonecraft, Rousseau's proposals for the education of women rather than strengthening the family destroy its proper functioning. "Mankind," she writes, "seems to agree that children should be left under the management of women during their childhood. Now . . . women of sensibility are the most unfit for this task."[3] In this sentence, "sensibility" refers to the education of women's senses as opposed to their reason. It is the development of reason in women, she argues, that is necessary to the well-functioning family.

Even in a situation where a woman is married to a good man, Wollstonecraft feels, there is still the problem of her governing the family if her husband dies. "But alas!" Wollstonecraft declares, "she has never thought, much less acted for herself. She has learned to please men, to depend gracefully on them."[4] Not having the ability to act independently and never having been educated in the exercise of reason, a widow, according to Wollstonecraft, becomes an easy victim for a fortune hunter, who strips the family of its property. Without property, the widow is unable to provide her children with an adequate education. Therefore, the widow's lack of an education in the use of reason results in the destruction of the family unit.

Therefore, Wollstonecraft believes, vanity has the same effect on the family as it does on society. She often compares the values of the wealthy to those of subjugated women. "In short, women, in general," she declares, "as well as the rich of both sexes, have acquired all the follies and vices of civilization, and missed the useful fruit."[5] She casts as much scorn on the accumulation of wealth as she does on the subjugation of women. She writes, "From the respect paid to property flow, as from a poisoned fountain, most of the evils and vices which render this world such a dreary scene to the contemplative mind."[6] The pursuit of property, she argues, results in one class of people pressing for advantage over another. To correct this malaise, Wollstonecraft proposed a national system of education to cultivate the exercise of reason in women and men, in the poor and the rich. She recognized that the call for an education to improve the reasoning of women ran counter to the existing attitude that women did not have the ability to fully reason. In fact, this was one of the arguments used to deny women full citizenship. It was argued that since women were incapable of reason, they were incapable of carrying on the duties of citizenship. Consequently, they could exercise their citizenship only through their husbands. Without a husband, women were without any rights. By emphasizing the rationality of women, Wollstonecraft was making a claim to equal citizenship with men.

Similar to the Commonwealthmen discussed in Chapter 3, Wollstonecraft believed that the free use of reason was necessary for the progress of civilization. "Reason is," she writes, "the simple power of improvement; or, more properly, of discerning truth."[7] Reasoning, she argued, leads to understanding, which she defines as the ability to generalize ideas. Women are denied understanding when they are educated in only the use of their senses. With a narrow education, women merely observe nature and society without any exercise of understanding.

In proposing a national education, Wollstonecraft gave added importance to the role of the family. First, she rejected the idea of boarding schools because they were "hot-beds of vice and folly" and cultivated selfishness.[8] Second, she rejected the idea of the child being educated at home by a tutor because that form of education, she believed, cultivated vanity because of the attention given to the child by the tutor and servants. In place of the boarding school and the home tutor, she advocated the establishment of day schools. The advantage of this arrangement, she argued, was that children still retained the structure of the family while avoiding the development of vanity caused by the influence of tutors and servants.

In her mind, the family and the day school would play an important role in the development of the citizen. "The domestic affections," she writes, "that first open the heart to the various modifications of humanity, would be cultivated, whilst the children were nevertheless allowed to spend great part of their time, on terms of equality, with other children."[9] Living within the bosom of the family, the child would develop feelings for others that would bind society together. While attending school, the child would be exposed to the feelings and attitudes of a cross section of peers.

Key elements in what she referred to as attending school "on terms of equality" were the mixing of rich and poor children and coeducation. She proposed that the government establish day schools for girls and boys from five to nine years of age that would be free of cost and open to all social classes. She argued that the mixing of sexes and social classes would extend the affections of the home to all people. In other words, within the family children would develop warm feelings for their mother and father, their brothers and sisters. While attending day schools, Wollstonecraft maintained, the affections of the family would be extended to other children. In this context, the affections learned in the family would be the basis of binding society together. "Few," she writes, "I believe, have had much affection for mankind, who did not first love their parents, their brothers, sisters, and even the domestic brutes, whom they first played with."[10]

The development of vanity, Wollstonecraft argued, would be inhibited in an egalitarian day school. As a means of avoiding the growth of vanity in children, she proposed that all children dress alike and receive the same discipline. No distinctions would be made in the day school between boys and girls or between the rich and poor. In addition, an intermingling of sexes and social classes would occur in the school's playground.

Unlike Rousseau, Wollstonecraft proposed that these young children would be exposed to a wide variety of book work. Rather than being free and learning by experience, the children in Wollstonecraft's day school were to study reading, writing, arithmetic, science, religion, history, and politics. In addition, she proposed that these subjects be taught in a Socratic form. In Chapter 1, I explained that the Socratic method involves asking questions that help the child to use reason to arrive at a correct answer. The use of the Socratic method reflected Wollstonecraft's commitment to make all people active citizens. The development of reason in girls was particularly important because it was the key to equal citizenship. Denied citizenship except through their husbands, women were to gain equal citizenship by learning reason and avoiding vanity. In addition, the children of the poor were to be empowered by the development of their ability to reason.

The egalitarianism of Wollstonecraft's plan ended at the age of nine, when children were to be divided according to their future employment. This meant a division according to social class and gender. Children destined for domestic work or the trades were to be placed in a separate school, where in the morning boys and girls would receive common lessons but in the afternoon would be educated separately for their future employment. Boys and girls with talent or money would attend a separate school from that attended by the poor, where they would continue their study of language, history, politics, and science.

While Wollstonecraft's egalitarianism regarding social classes breaks down after the age of nine, coeducation continues into later years. Of course, coeducation was not essential to the development of women's reason, which could be done in gender-segregated schools. But coeducation was essential for equalizing relationships between males and females. Stripped of vanity, Wollstonecraft believed, women and men would learn to relate to one another as friends. Women would no longer focus on sexual allure as a means of establishing a relationship with a man.

Therefore, according to Wollstonecraft, coeducation would strengthen marital bonds and the family. "Marriage," she writes, "will never be held sacred till women, by being brought up with men, are prepared to be their companions rather than their mistresses."[11] In addition, she believed that coeducation would cause early marriages, which, according to her beliefs, would have a beneficial effect on society. Marriage, she argues, helps to broaden the narrow selfishness of the individual who lives alone. "What a different character," she exclaims, "does a married citizen assume from the selfish coxcomb, who lives but for himself."[12]

In summary, Wollstonecraft's arguments interrelate a broad range of issues affecting the organization of society. Women were to gain full citizenship through the development of reason in government-operated coeducational schools. Coeducation and the mixing of children from different social classes in a national school would help break down differences between social classes and increase social harmony. The mixing of students would also eliminate vanity, which, according to Wollstonecraft, enslaves women to men and causes people to pursue wealth beyond their needs. Women educated in reason and free of vanity would be better able to carry out the responsibilities of spouses and mothers. In addition, the marriage bonds would be strengthened by being based on companionship as opposed to subjugation. A family structure built on equality between husband and wife would result in a broadening of individual self-interest. Husbands, wives, and children would learn in the family to be considerate of others, and their emotional world would expand to include other family members. In a national school, the feelings developed in the family would be extended to other members of society. Wollstonecraft provides the following summary of the reasons for a national education:

> My observations on national education are obviously hints; but I principally wish to enforce the necessity of educating the sexes together to perfect both, and of making children sleep at home that they may learn to love home; yet to make private support, instead of smothering, public affections, they should be sent to school to mix with a number of equals, for only by the jostlings of equality can we form a just opinion of ourselves.[13]

In comparison to John Locke and Jean-Jacques Rousseau, Wollstonecraft's arguments are more supportive of a democratic society, where there is an equal sharing of political power. Of course, both Locke and Rousseau denied equal citizenship and, consequently, equal power to women. In addition, Locke stressed the importance of the protection of property and the importance of human action being controlled by rewards. This argument opened the door to inequality of power based on inequalities in wealth. Wollstonecraft recognized that inequalities in wealth were harming society. Her ideal for the family is very much like that of A. S. Neill, discussed in Chapter 4. Neill called for the free family, in which the husband and wife would share equal power. This, he believed, would stop the repression of children. On the other hand, Neill did not see the family as the key element in building public attachments. For Wollstonecraft, families formed around the sharing of equal power would contribute to social harmony. She accepted Rousseau's arguments on the importance of the family but rejected the idea that family life should be built on the subjugation of women.

JOHANN PESTALOZZI: MOTHER LOVE

Influenced by Jean-Jacques Rousseau, Swiss educator Johann Pestalozzi (1746-1827) based his educational method on the love a mother gives her children. Similar to Rousseau and Wollstonecraft, he believed that the affection felt for other family members is the basis for affection felt for other members of society. The moral world of the home is the foundation, Pestalozzi believed, of the general morality of society.

Pestalozzi's influence was widespread. Pestalozzian schools appeared in Switzerland and Prussia. Many American visitors to Prussia in the early nineteenth century were impressed by the use of Pestalozzian methods and spread his ideas throughout the United States. The English Home and Colonial Institution, organized in 1836, became a forum for the dissemination of Pestalozzian ideas in England, the United States, and Canada.

Following in the steps of Rousseau, Pestalozzi's model of womanhood is that of the loving mother who through her emotional relations with family members teaches morality and goodness. Pestalozzi's model of motherhood is in striking contrast to Wollstonecraft's. Wollstonecraft's model of motherhood was centered around the exercise of reason. In her ideal family, the mother would exercise reason to learn the best methods of child rearing and education and to manage domestic affairs. Her exercise of reason would be equal to that of her husband. While family members would learn human affection, Wollstonecraft gave no special emotional qualities or moral virtues to women.

In contrast, Pestalozzi's model of motherhood is morally superior to her husband. Emotions rather than reason are the hallmark of motherly virtue in Pestalozzi's writings. Pestalozzi's major work, *Leonard and Gertrude* (1781), is the story of how motherly emotions result in morality being extended from the home to the public sphere. The book is set in the small village of Bonnal with the main characters being Leonard, an alcoholic husband, and Gertrude, a brave and pious wife. The story is a moral struggle between the forces of evil and idleness and the forces of maternal love and nurturing. The opening lines of the tale describe the social conditions that can be improved with the help of maternal emotions. Pestalozzi writes, "his [Leonard's] trade would have enabled him to support his family of a wife and seven children, if he could have resisted the temptation to frequent the tavern, where there were always idle loafers to entice him in, and induce the good-natured, easygoing man to squander his earnings in drink and gambling."[14]

In Pestalozzi's story, Leonard is saved from his evil ways by the virtue of his wife. Indeed, the entire village is saved by Gertrude's motherly virtues becoming a public model. To symbolize the connection between the domestic role of women and the public sphere, Pestalozzi has three male village leaders study her system of household management. Pestalozzi uses their analysis of Gertrude's actions to explain his pedagogical methods.

In the story, the visit by the three village leaders occurs just as the family is completing breakfast. After the children wash the dishes, they immediately engage in a variety of tasks, including spinning and gardening. What is most impressive for the visitors is Gertrude's ability to integrate instruction into the activities of the household. A trademark of the Pestalozzian method is the use of common objects in instruction and the development of the child's powers of observation, as opposed to abstract teaching that has little connection to the realities of life. For instance, Gertrude gives instruction in arithmetic by having her children "count the number of steps from one end of the room to the other, and two of the rows of five panes each, in one of the windows, gave her an opportunity to unfold the decimal relations of numbers. She also made them count their threads while spinning, and the number of turns of the reel, when they wound the yarn into skeins."[15]

Later adaptations of Pestalozzian methods emphasize learning through the senses, the use of objects, the importance of active learning, and, following in the footsteps of Rousseau, learning by discovery. For instance, the following list of Pestalozzian principles was copied by Edward Sheldon in 1861, while attending a class taught by the English Pestalozzian Margaret Jones at the Oswego State Normal and Training School in New York State.

1. Begin with the senses.
2. Never tell a child what he can discover for himself.
3. Activity is a law of childhood. Train the child not merely to listen, but to do. Educate the hand.
4. Love of variety is a law of childhood—change is rest.
5. Cultivate the faculties in their natural order. First, form the mind, then furnish it.
6. Reduce every subject to its elements, and present one difficulty at a time.[16]

Shortly after witnessing Pestalozzian methods as embodied in Gertrude's instruction of her children, one of the visitors dashed back to her house and proclaimed that he would be the schoolmaster of Bonnal. The next day, after returning to observe Gertrude's family further, the village leaders asked Gertrude to help the newly self-appointed schoolmaster. "Then they explained to her that they regarded the proper education of the youthful population as the only means of elevating the condition of the corrupt village; and full of emotion, Gertrude promised them she would do anything in her power to forward the good cause."[17]

In a later work, Pestalozzi declares, "maternal love is the first agent in education."[18] In *How Gertrude Teaches Her Children*, Pestalozzi drew a direct connection between maternal love and individual moral development. He argued that people must love and trust other people before they are able to love and trust God. The beginnings of the love of both people and God develop during the mother's nurturing of the child. The mother's lack of response to the irregular desires of the infant teaches the first lessons in obedience; in addition, the infant learns to be grateful for the mother's actions. This combination of trust, gratitude, love, and obedience forms the early beginnings of a conscience.

What virtues the child learns from the mother, according to Pestalozzi, must be nurtured through a proper method of education. Similar to Rousseau's, Pestalozzi's instructional methods focus on the education of the senses. Pestalozzi contends, "The first instruction of the child should never be the business of the head or of reason; it should always be the business of the senses, or the heart, of the mother."[19] What he declares as the second law of instruction is to move slowly from the exercise of the senses to the exercise of reason.

Reflecting Rousseau's attitudes, Pestalozzi associates senses and emotions with women and reason with men. "It [education] is for a long time the business of the heart," Pestalozzi states, "before it is the business of the reason. It is for a long time the business of the woman before it begins to be the business of man."[20] In contrast to Wollstonecraft, the virtues of womanhood are a product of feelings and emotions. It is motherly love that tempers the evil ways of men. It is womanly emotions that temper the exercise of reason by men. It is motherly love that maintains the morality of the family, which in turn maintains the morality of society.

Therefore, two models of womanhood emerge from the classical liberal tradition. One model, as exemplified by Rousseau and Pestalozzi, stresses the importance of the emotional life of women to maintaining the family and the harmony and morality of society. The other model, as exemplified by Wollstonecraft, emphasizes the importance of female reason to maintaining the family and society. As I will discuss in the next section, these two views of womanhood reappear in the work of twentieth-century psychologist Carol Gilligan.

CAROL GILLIGAN: LET'S HAVE A LITTLE REASON

There is an important parallel between the debates by eighteenth-century liberals over the nature of women and Carol Gilligan's innovative study *In a Different Voice: Psychological Theory and Women's Development* (1982). Before exploring this parallel, it is important to note that Gilligan's work was done after women had gained equal rights under the law in the United States. Therefore, unlike Mary Wollstonecraft, Gilligan did not have to worry about whether or not her study supported the granting of equal rights to women. Wollstonecraft's argument for the granting of equal rights depended on showing that women's reasoning was equal to that of men. Without the burden of having to prove that male and female reasoning is the same in order to call for equal rights for women, Gilligan could explore the differences in reasoning between men and women.

Gilligan's basic argument is that women's moral reasoning is different from that of men. Interestingly, the attributes she finds in the moral reasoning of women are similar to those ascribed to women by Rousseau and his follower Pestalozzi. In addition, the moral reasoning she ascribes to men is similar to the type of reasoning Rousseau felt was characteristic of men—the ability to reason about natural rights. The difference between Gilligan and Rousseau, of course, is that Gilligan does not use these differences to justify the subjugation of women by men.

The differences in moral reasoning that Gilligan finds are best exemplified by her study of male and female responses to the story of Heinz. In this story, Heinz's wife is sick and the druggist refuses to lower the price on the drug needed to save her life. Heinz must decide whether or not to steal the drug. In presenting the story to males and females, Gilligan found that men approach this moral dilemma by the application of logic to natural rights issues. Women, on the other hand, worry about the implications of the situation for social relationships.

For instance, in one interview a boy named Jake balances the right to life with the right to property. Stealing from the druggist violates the druggist's right to property, while denying the drug to the wife denies her right to life. Viewing it as "a math problem for humans," Jake decides that the right to life outweighs the right to property in importance and therefore Heinz should steal the drug."[21]

On the other hand, an interview with a girl named Amy elicits an entirely different approach to the dilemma. Amy rejects the idea of stealing the drug because of the possible effect on the ability of Heinz to take care of his wife in the future. If Heinz is thrown into jail, what happens to his wife? If Heinz alienates the druggist, what happens if he needs more drugs for his wife? Instead, Amy suggests that Heinz try to borrow the money from other people or talk the issue out with the druggist.

These two responses to Heinz's dilemma exemplify, according to Gilligan, the differences in moral reasoning between men and women. Amy sees "a world compromised of relationships rather than of people standing alone, a world that coheres through human connection rather than through systems of rules."[22] In contrast, Jake sees the world in terms of logic and law. He believes that you solve moral problems by using logic within the framework of legal rules.

The two images that Gilligan uses to describe these differences are the web and hierarchy. Women's image of relationships is that of a web. The image of the web contains an implicit desire to be at the center of a web of human relationships. Men's image is that of a hierarchy in which the man wants to be at the top. Contained within this image is men's fear of intimacy. Men want to be alone at the top and fear anyone coming close to their position. Women, on the other hand, fear being isolated. Women want to be at the center of social relationships and fear being placed on the edge of the web. These images are reflected in attitudes about morality. For men, morality involves a concern with a hierarchy of rights, while, for women, morality involves the maintenance of social relations.

For Gilligan, women's concern with relationships results in a different approach to the rules of justice. Women, she argues, try to change the rules to maintain social relationships, while men try to abide by the rules and consider relationships easily replaced. In this context, men think of society as being composed of isolated individuals following a prescribed set of rules.

In addition, Gilligan argues that female concern with a web of social relationships involves caring for others. This, according to her, is the guiding principal of female morality. But this morality involves a dilemma for women. In agreement with Locke and Rousseau, Gilligan argues that women's first instinct is for self-preservation. Of course, concern about self-preservation creates a conflict with concern about others. Just as Rousseau thought that self-interest could be turned into compassion, Gilligan argues that women turn concern about self and others into caring. Caring about others and self becomes the hallmark of female morality. Gilligan writes, "The sequence of women's moral judgment proceeds from an initial concern with survival to a focus on goodness and finally to a reflective understanding of care as the most adequate guide to the resolution of conflicts in human relationships."[23]

Gilligan explains the historic struggle of women for equal rights as representing the tension between concern about self and concern about human relationships. Unfortunately, in her brief analysis of Mary Wollstonecraft, Gilligan does not recognize that Wollstonecraft was claiming equal rights for women on the basis that men and women shared the same moral reasoning.[24] If Gilligan had more closely analyzed Wollstonecraft and natural rights arguments, she might have concluded that these arguments reflected a male sense of morality, something not shared by women. The protection of property and the image of the independent economic person reflect, at least in Gilligan's framework, a male concern with hierarchy, rules, and isolation.

In her discussion of the nineteenth-century women's movement, Gilligan does produce evidence to support her contention that the resolution of the tension between concern with self and others is found in caring. To illustrate her point, she quotes women's rights advocate Elizabeth Cady Stanton's comments to a reporter: "put it down in capital letters: SELF-DEVELOPMENT IS A HIGHER DUTY THAN SELF-SACRIFICE. THE THING WHICH MOST RETARDS AND MILITATES AGAINST WOMEN'S SELF-DEVELOPMENT IS SELF-SACRIFICE."[25] In claiming their rights, Gilligan argues, women are taking responsibility for themselves. On the other hand, their moral reason leads them to care about others. Thus, the women's rights movement is entangled with general social reforms, such as public health, temperance, education, and poverty.

Interestingly, caring about human relations is precisely the quality that Rousseau hoped would emanate from the family. It is the mother love that Pestalozzi believed was the basis for morality. It is the morality of Gertrude that saves Leonard from alcoholism and unites the village in a caring relationship. It is the woman united to the male in the family who teaches husband and children the arts of loving and caring and provides the basis for holding together a society spinning apart because of the pursuit of money.

Gilligan might argue that it is futile for Rousseau to try to teach Emile compassion. Male social reasoning will inevitably lead to concern with hierarchy and rules and isolation from others. The real hope for Emile, Gilligan might argue, is giving equal status to his bride, Sophie, and providing an education that fully develops her powers of reason. In this context, Rousseau's proposal that Sophie's mind be cultivated so that her husband can plant the seeds of knowledge is self-defeating. If Rousseau wanted to accomplish his goals based on Gilligan's findings, then he would have demanded equal status for Sophie in her relationship with Emile and considered her moral reasoning as essential for neutralizing the negative effects of Emile's moral reasoning.

While there is no absolute proof that Gilligan's findings are true, they do suggest some interesting ways of interpreting the natural rights doctrines of Locke and Rousseau. First, as I suggested in Chapter 8, it is possible to argue that natural rights doctrines were built on the backs of women. In addition, Gilligan's findings suggest that natural rights doctrines might reflect male moral reasoning and not female moral reasoning. From this perspective, natural rights doctrines might produce a society based on hierarchical relationships in which there is a breakdown in the sense of community. At a glance, this might not be far from the truth with regard to the evolution of Western society since the eighteenth century.

Second, it could be argued that female moral reasoning is superior to male moral reasoning when considering the survival of the human species. Caring, rather than protection of property, seems a more reasonable basis for the formation of a social contract. In the framework of Gilligan's arguments, it would have to be a male mind—which of course it was—that conceived the origin of the social contract in the protection of property. A female mind might argue that people formed social contracts because of a desire to be socially related and as an expression of caring for others.

CAMILLE PAGLIA: A LITTLE SADISM IN US ALL

One thing missing from Carol Gilligan's work and the writings of Wollstonecraft, Rousseau, and Pestalozzi is the possibility that the human psyche might contain elements of sadism, aggression, and a quest for power. Rousseau assumed that nature is good and that improving the human condition only requires bringing out the natural good within us all. But, of course, nature does not necessarily appear good to the human eye when one considers that species survive by eating other species. In addition, floods, tornados, earthquakes, and countless other acts of nature lead to destruction and mayhem.

Camille Paglia rejects Rousseau's view of a benevolent nature, and she characterizes the differences between males and females as products of the demonic struggles of nature. "Pitting benign Romantic nature against corrupt society," she argues in her monumental work *Sexual Personae*, "Rousseau produced the progressivist strain in nineteenth-century culture, for which social reform was the means to achieve paradise on earth."[26] Paglia believes that Rousseau's faith in the innate goodness of humans paved the way for the nineteenth-century belief that a paradise on earth was possible through the manipulation of the social environment. The development of public schools, prison reforms, social work movements, and the evolution of the welfare state, Paglia argues, are a product of the belief that evil and disorder can be eradicated from the world by manipulating the social environment.

The correct response to Rousseau, according to Paglia, was made by the Marquis de Sade (1740–1814), who satirized the Rousseauian idea of a benevolent nature. In one of her many powerfully worded statements, Paglia makes the following contrast between Rousseau and de Sade: "Rousseau's mother nature is Christian Madonna, lovingly enfolding her infant son. Sade's mother nature is pagan cannibal, her dragon jaws dripping sperm and spittle."[27] Unlike Rousseau, who believed that the sexual drives born during adolescence could be transformed into compassion, de Sade believed that sexuality is inherently violent. In addition, de Sade believed that violence is the authentic spirit of nature. For de Sade, the basic spirit of nature erupts in the cruelty of the serial murderer and the torture of human beings. Violence, cruelty, and sadism are irrepressible parts of human nature. No matter how much civilization tries to rid itself of these aspects of nature, they continue to find expression through war and other forms of human violence. For de Sade, a return to nature would mean giving free reign to violence and lust.

Agreeing with the Marquis de Sade, Paglia argues that the function of society is to keep violence under control. Without the social controls of modern society, humanity's innate cruelty will burst through the surface. Rapists, for instance, are not created by society; they exist because of a failure to control the inner nature of men. Just as all relationships among species living in a state of nature are exploitative, she argues, so are all relations in Western society.

Modern feminism, she argues, is misguided by some of the basic contradictions of modern liberalism. These contradictions are the desire for individualism and freedom and the desire for the state to provide for the material welfare of its citizens. The provision of material welfare results in the growth of government, which, in turn, limits individualism and freedom. This contradiction in liberalism is reflected in the feminist distrust of hierarchy and the feeling that any negative statement about women is a product of male lies. Similarly to liberalism, Paglia argues, feminists have not come to terms with the limitations placed on human actions by nature. For instance, Carol Gilligan portrays the development of a society based on hierarchy as a product of male moral reasoning. But, if we look at nature, Paglia argues, we see nothing but hierarchy. Brute force and survival of the fittest are the operating principles of nature. One species eats another.

In addition, she argues, what are considered negative attitudes about women might in reality reflect women's true nature. This is particularly evidenced in the modern feminist rejection of the concept of woman as "femme fatale." Femme fatale is the aspect of womanhood Mary Wollstonecraft claimed was a product of the denial of reason in women. The family pattern, as Wollstonecraft envisioned it, was for women to use sexual attraction to gain power over men and for men to respond to that power by being nice to women. This, of course, is the issue of vanity. Vanity is what Wollstonecraft believed she could eliminate by teaching women to exercise reason. Vanity, or the femme fatale, is what Paglia considers to be an expression of the nature of women and therefore impossible to eliminate through education.

Paglia sees the femme fatale as a product of the struggle between men and women and between humans and nature. Men, she argues, struggle against the power of nature as embodied in the mother. In this struggle, men try to resist nature by creating order and objectivity. Objectivity, of course, is not possible because all thoughts and perceptions of the world are laden with emotional meaning. The quest for order and objectivity results, according to Paglia, in the development of modern organized societies, science, and technology. It is in this attempt to create an orderly world that men hoped to find freedom. But, because of the inescapable demonic power of nature, this quest for freedom is a quest for an illusion.

On the other hand, women initially allow men to exert power over them because of the ability of male strength to provide protection. But, similarly to men trying to escape the power of the mother, women try to escape male domination. To gain independence, women try to exercise power over men through sexual attraction. The femme fatale is the symbol of women's struggle against male domination.

Paglia, in agreement with de Sade, believes that sex is combat. The femme fatale is women's basic weapon in this combat. As the term implies, the femme fatale is the woman who is fatal to men. The more men attempt to control nature, the more the femme fatale reappears. The pregnant woman threatens men by her completeness and imperviousness. Using the image of the web and the womb, Paglia describes the pregnant woman: "She turns a gob of refuse into a spreading web of sentient being, floating on the snaky umbilical by which she leashes every man."[28]

Rather than dismissing the male drive for hierarchy and order as being destructive, Paglia applauds the results of male endeavors. In fact, she argues, the development of modern technology and medicine has been very beneficial to women. But she recognizes that these advances can never erase the basic aggression of male character. Technology did not result in utopia because the demonic drives are uncontrollable. Technology produces not only the means for lengthening and improving the quality of life, but also the military hardware that can be used for the destruction of life. This is, Paglia maintains, the inescapable result of the demonic quality of nature.

Men, therefore, in their combat with women for independence, express both a desire for life and freedom and a desire for destruction and death. On the other hand, women, in their quest for freedom, use the power of the femme fatale to gain control over men. Women, because they are rooted in nature by their reproductive functions and because they do not try to escape nature, show little desire to bring nature under control with science and technology. Women's quest for power is actualized by power over men. For men, the problem in their quest for control over nature is the inevitable eruption of violence. In illustrating the differences between the sexes and the contradictory nature of men, Paglia writes, "There is no female Mozart because there is no female Jack the Ripper."[29]

CONCLUSION: REASON AND THE DEMONIC

The ideas of Rousseau, Pestalozzi, Gilligan, and Paglia are related by a basic belief in the differences in mental functioning between men and women. They agree that female reasoning is characterized by a focus on a web of social relationships and caring and that male reasoning is characterized by a focus on hierarchy and individualism. But absent from the writings of Rousseau, Pestalozzi, and Gilligan is any sense that these differences might also contain elements of violence and sadism. Pestalozzi assumes that mother love will reform the world. On the other hand, Paglia sees the history of male actions as an attempt to escape the controlling power of the femme fatale. From this perspective, the ultimate consequence of attempted reforms through mother love might be a stronger male drive for independence and aggression. With regard to Pestalozzi's *Leonard and Gertrude*, Paglia might argue that Gertrude's attempt to use mother love to end Leonard's alcoholism will result in Leonard either turning into a violent drunk or fleeing the home.

In her desire to justify equal rights for women, Wollstonecraft rejected the idea of any basic differences in reasoning between men and women. Also, she accepted Rousseau's vision of nature being basically good. In contrast, both Gilligan and Paglia maintain that there is a difference in intellectual qualities, but they do not use these differences as a basis for arguing, as Rousseau did, that women should be denied equal power and rights.

One of the more interesting ideas to emerge from this analysis of classical liberalism and the arguments of Gilligan and Paglia is that classical liberalism reflects the type of moral reasoning that they think is peculiar to men. From the standpoint of Gilligan, the individualism and hierarchy that are characteristic of male thinking and classical liberalism could be tempered by the concern with caring and social relationships that are characteristic of female reasoning. Paglia would agree that the tenets of classical liberalism reflect a male orientation, but the attempt to create a good society on the principles of classical liberalism is not a reasonable goal because of the basic demonic qualities of human nature.

In the end, equal rights and equal power for women do not depend on the outcome of the debate over differences in male and female moral reasoning. In fact, Gilligan's findings could be used to strengthen demands for equal power for women because female concern with moral caring might be preferable to the male reliance on logic and rules.

The denial of equal power to women continues as a global political problem. Even in countries where equal rights have been gained by women, there is still the problem of gaining equal political power. Consequently, women's education should, in part, be focused on building a political consciousness. This can be accomplished by following some of the educational principles discussed at the conclusion of Chapter 5. Women's education should be protected from exploitative control by the state and by political and economic elites. Currently, most world governments and economic elites are dominated by men. At this point in time, it can be assumed that male-dominated governments and elites have an interest in continuing male domination of females. The only thing that would change this situation would be for women to gain equal representation in world governments and in the control of global corporations.

In addition, following the principles given in Chapter 5, education should avoid the placing of wheels into the head that convince women that they are inferior to men and that they should be obedient to men. To prepare women to overcome the historic denial of rights and power, women's education should be consciously political. Also, women should not be told to deny their own physical needs and desires for the good of men or the state. As Carol Gilligan points out, one of the traditional dilemmas for women is reconciling self-interest with caring for others. While caring might be an important attribute, women should not sacrifice themselves for some greater good. For the benefit of humanity, if caring as a part of moral reasoning is exclusive to women, women need power in order to ensure that this quality becomes a guiding principle of society.

Allan Bloom's argument that Western cultural traditions should form the core curriculum of schools creates a dilemma for women interested in equal political power. On the one hand, in its original form, this tradition denied equal power and rights to women. On the other hand, the liberal tradition resulted in women achieving equal rights. But, as I suggested at the end of Chapter 7, in a global economy dominated groups will gain more power if they form an international movement. Women's education might stress the international plight of women and the importance of an international organization.

NOTES

1. Mary Wollstonecraft, *A Vindication of the Rights of Woman: An Authoritative Text*, ed. Carol Poston (New York: W. W. Norton & Company, 1988), p. 25.
2. Ibid., p. 31.
3. Ibid., p. 68.
4. Ibid., p. 48.
5. Ibid., p. 60.
6. Ibid., p. 140.
7. Ibid., p. 53.
8. Ibid., p. 158.
9. Ibid., pp. 158–159.
10. Ibid., p. 162.
11. Ibid., p. 165.
12. Ibid., p. 169.
13. Ibid., p. 173.
14. Johann Pestalozzi, *Leonard and Gertrude*, trans. Eva Channing (Lexington, Mass.: Heath, 1901), p. 11.
15. Ibid., pp. 130–131.
16. Quoted in Ned Dearborn, *The Oswego Movement in American Education* (New York: Teachers College Press, 1925), p. 69.
17. Pestalozzi, *Leonard and Gertrude*, p. 135.
18. Johann Pestalozzi, "How a Child Is Led to God through Maternal Love" in *Pestalozzi's Educational Writings*, ed. J. A. Green (London: Edward Arnold, 1916), p. 266.
19. Johann Pestalozzi, *How Gertrude Teaches Her Children: An Attempt to Help Mothers to Teach Their Own Children and an Account of the Method*, trans. Lucy Holland and Francis Turner (Syracuse, N.Y.: Bardeen, 1898), p. 294.
20. Ibid.
21. Carol Gilligan, *In a Different Voice: Psychological Theory and Women's Development* (Cambridge, Mass.: Harvard University Press, 1982), pp. 25–26.
22. Ibid., p. 29.
23. Ibid., p. 105.
24. Ibid., p. 129.
25. Ibid., p. 129.
26. Camille Paglia, *Sexual Personae: Art and Decadence from Nefertiti to Emily Dickinson* (New York: Vintage Books, 1991), p. 2.
27. Ibid., p. 237.
28. Ibid., p. 12.
29. Ibid., p. 247.

PART FIVE

Education and Human Rights

CHAPTER 10

Pedagogy of the Oppressed

In Parts Four and Five, I dealt with the educational problems confronting dominated groups and women in achieving equality of political power. This chapter will extend those arguments to include all people who are economically exploited and politically powerless. These are the oppressed, who, according to Brazilian educator Paulo Freire, live in a "culture of silence." This chapter will focus on the work of Paulo Freire, who is the most important contemporary philosopher to develop instructional methods designed to end oppression.

Many of the topics discussed in this volume are included in Freire's educational philosophy. Freire deals with issues of sexuality and aggression similar to those appearing in the works of A. S. Neill, Wilhelm Reich, Allan Bloom, and Camille Paglia. In addition, Freire, similarly to Reich, is concerned with the development of an authoritarian personality. His instructional methods are designed to raise the level of human consciousness so that those living in a culture of silence can escape what Max Stirner called the wheels in the head. In part, he develops his instructional methods in response to what he calls the "banking method" of education used by the authoritarian state to subjugate its population. He answers the question of how the democratic state can avoid imposition of knowledge by stressing the expansion of human consciousness and the creation of a more human-loving personality. And, he accepts the tenet of the free school movement that all education should be consciously political.

Freire's educational philosophy was developed while conducting adult literacy programs in Brazil. Freire first set forth his educational method in his doctoral dissertation at the University of Recife in 1959. While working as Professor of History and Philosophy of Education at the same university, his teaching methods were implemented throughout the northeastern part of Brazil. After the military coup of 1964, Freire was jailed by the government for his educational activities. He was "invited" to leave the country, and he did not return from exile until more than two decades later.

When I first met Freire at Ivan Illich's Center for Intercultural Documentation in Cuernavaca, Mexico, in 1971, he said that his method of instruction could be followed like a cookbook and that a true application of his methods and an understanding of his educational philosophy depended on knowing his concept of what it is to be human. Consequently, his lectures focused on his concept of human nature. His linkages between instructional methodologies and political action are derived from his particular concept of the human psyche.

Based on Freire's personal view of how his material should be approached, I will begin my analysis of his ideas by discussing first his concept of human nature and then his pedagogy and concept of social change.

PAULO FREIRE: PASSION AND CONSCIOUSNESS

Freire's concept of love is directly related to his explanation of why some people accept oppression and why some people desire to overthrow it. His concept of love also provides an explanation of why certain people become revolutionary leaders and struggle for the freedom of all people and why some people want to dominate others. In the context of his argument, the revolutionary is the lover who, because of love, tries to free all people. In addition, his concept of love is directly related to his idea of human consciousness. People whose consciousness is poorly developed—I will explain what Freire means by this later in this chapter—are characterized by stilted, misdirected sexual lives, while those attaining revolutionary consciousness, according to Freire, can freely express their sexual potential.

Similarly to A. S. Neill and Wilhelm Reich, Paul Freire believes the authoritarian home shapes the child's personality so that the child later in life accepts domination by authority and wants to dominate other people. Using the language of psychoanalyst Erich Fromm, Freire distinguishes between the "necrophilic" and "biophilic" personality. In general, the oppressed of the world are characterized by a necrophilic character, which is driven by a desire to control and to be controlled. In Freire's words, "Oppression—overwhelming control—is necrophilic; it is nourished by love of death, not life."[1] On the other hand, the biophilic personality is characterized by a love of life and a desire to be free and to see all people free. One goal of Freire's educational program is to make the necrophilic personality biophilic.

While Wilhelm Reich characterized the authoritarian personality as having a fear of pleasure, Freire argues that the necrophilic person has a fear of freedom. This fear of freedom is translated into all aspects of life. In sexual terms, the primary concern of necrophilics is to control their lovers and make them dependent on them. From the perspective of the traditional family, a necrophilic husband is driven by a desire to control his wife and his children. For instance, as necrophilic parents beat or restrain their children, they might say, "I am doing this only because I love you." On the other hand, biophilic parents, because they love their children, strive to make their children independent. In addition, the necrophilic personality approaches life in a mechanical manner and treats people like things as opposed to living beings. The mechanical aspect of the necrophilic personality results in a desire to establish and work within bureaucracies and other tightly controlled authoritarian institutions.

Freire sees the necrophilic personality developing through the interaction among the child, family, and society. If the social structure surrounding the family is authoritarian, Freire argues, then the home will be oppressive and the parents will develop an authoritarian relationship with their children. The result is the increasing internalization in children of parental authority. Similar to Reich and Neill, Freire believes that interaction in the authoritarian family develops a love of authority and oppression within the child. As they grow into adolescence and adulthood, children from authoritarian families, according to Freire, either become alienated from reality or engage in destructive behavior.[2]

The traditional method of education, Freire argues, reinforces the development of necrophilic personalities. Freire refers to traditional education as "banking." As the term "banking" suggests, knowledge is deposited into the child's mind. The characteristics of banking education are recording the comments of the teacher, memorization of lessons, and repetition. An important part of banking education is the assumption by the teacher that students are without knowledge. "The students," Freire writes, "alienated like the slave . . . accept their ignorance as justifying the teacher's existence—but, unlike the slave, they never discover that they educate the teacher."[3]

Banking education, Freire argues, mirrors oppressive societies. In a banking education, the teacher is the primary actor while the students are the recipients. In banking education, teachers act as if they know everything and the students know nothing. Teachers do the talking, while students are passive. And, reflecting his general views on the necrophilic personality, the teacher in banking education is the actor, while the students are the objects. To be treated as an object is, according to Freire, to be treated as if one were without life. The necrophilic teacher treats students as inanimate objects, which, in turn, prepares the students to view other humans as objects.

In contrast to the necrophilic personality, the biophilic personality is nurtured in a family and school that desire the independence of children. Rather than knowledge being deposited in the child's mind through the dictates of the teacher and rote learning, the biophilic personality is nurtured in a school where learning is a product of interaction between the student and teacher. The teacher does not treat the child as an inanimate object into which knowledge is poured. In a school fostering biophilic personalities, children are treated as living beings with their interests and knowledge utilized as a source of learning for both students and teachers.

Having internalized parental authority, necrophilic personalities, Freire states, repeat the rigid patterns of their education. Part of that rigid pattern is not to listen to the desires and needs of others. The necrophilic who claims to help others, Freire states, most often just tells others what is best for them. This repeats the pattern learned in the family and schools. The necrophilic does not recognize that others might have a point of view about changes in society. Similar to teachers who do not consult students in the banking method of education, necrophilics impose their view of the world on others. Consequently, humans raised in authoritarian families and schools love death and oppression and hate life and freedom.

Necrophilic personalities express their sexuality through sadistic forms of love. They gain pleasure through the domination of others. This domination takes the form of trying to destroy independence and creativity in lovers. Lovers become objects. In the fully developed state, the necrophilic lover gains pleasure through torture and brutality. In the context of government, the necrophilic ruler gains pleasure by manipulating, controlling, terrorizing, and torturing the population. Necrophilic personalities love to rule or to be ruled by a police state.

For Freire, sexuality has a determining effect on the development of consciousness and reason. The necrophilic personality is open to cultural invasion by the forces of oppression. Since necrophilics love oppression, they willingly accept the domination of their consciousness by outside forces. Freire refers to this domination of consciousness as "cultural invasion."[4] In broad terms, cultural invasion is a form of economic and political domination. The invader, similar to the teacher in banking education, does not respect the creativity, the potentialities, and the world view of the invaded consciousness. The invaded consciousness is treated as an object to be penetrated by the consciousness of the invader.

The result of this invasion is that the consciousness of the invaded, according to Freire, begins to act in terms of the values, standards, and goals of the oppressors. The invaded begin to see the world through the eyes of the invader. In addition, Freire argues, for the invasion to be completely successful the invaded must be convinced of their own inferiority and the superiority of the invaders. Reflecting a necrophilic personality, the invaded consciousness loves and accepts domination by the invader. Invaded people want to become like the oppressors.

Therefore, in Freire's framework, human consciousness is motivated by necrophilic or biophilic desires that are a product of child-rearing patterns in the family and school. These desires determine what Freire calls the humanization or dehumanization of consciousness. By humanization, Freire means a consciousness that desires to think about the world and transform it. In the context of a biophilic personality, humanization includes a desire for freedom, justice, and the end of alienation and economic exploitation. By dehumanization, he means a person who supports injustice, oppression, and exploitation. Dehumanized people do not reflect on the consequences of their actions; they just act according to the prompting of their dominated consciousness.

It is the quality of consciousness, according to Freire, that distinguishes humans from animals. In fully humanized people, consciousness allows them to think about the consequences of their actions before they make choices. In addition, consciousness allows people to reflect on why they commit certain actions. Consciousness also gives people the ability to understand how institutions and ideas are created by human beings or—in the language I used in describing John Dewey in Chapter 2—consciousness helps people understand the social construction of knowledge.

A fully developed consciousness, Freire argues, allows people to understand that humans make history and that, as participants in history, they also can make history. In other words, humans with a fully developed consciousness understand that they can change social, political, and economic conditions. Freire refers to this as being a "subject" of history. A subject of history is a conscious maker of history. In contrast, dehumanized people are characterized by a consciousness that does not understand that history determines human actions and that they can contribute to history. Dehumanized people are "objects" of history. As objects of history, their actions are determined by history, but they do not make history. Dehumanized people do not consciously attempt to transform the world.

By never engaging children in discussions about what they think, authoritarian parents and teachers prepare children to be unthinking objects of history. Children are simply told what they should do. In the same manner, the authoritarian state tells its citizens what to do. Therefore, dehumanized people never learn to be a subject of history. They never learn that they have the ability to transform the world.

When an oppressor penetrates a person's consciousness, the oppressor becomes the determiner of that person's actions. Oppressed and dehumanized people act according to the will of the oppressor. In fact, they are unable to distinguish their own wills from those of their masters. In this condition, oppressed people do not make conscious choices and do not reflect on the consequences of their actions. Oppressed people act like machines whose motions are predetermined by the oppressors.

In this context, freedom has two related meanings. First, there is freedom from political constraints on actions. Second, there is freedom of consciousness. Freedom of consciousness means having the ability to reflect on the past and present before acting. Freedom of consciousness can be limited by the family, school, and oppressive state. The biophilic personality loves freedom, while the necrophilic personality hates freedom.

CONSCIOUSNESS AND SOCIAL CHANGE

The major goals of Freire's educational method is to free the consciousness of all people and to change necrophilic personalities into biophilic ones. This goal is linked to his beliefs about revolutionary change. Ideally, from his perspective, revolution will result in the transformation of consciousness and personality of all people.

Freire distinguishes between revolutions of the left and of the right. For instance, he calls the communist revolution in Russia a revolution of the right because it simply changed the palace guards from one set of authoritarian figures to another. From his perspective, there was no revolution in the consciousness of the people. The difference between revolutions of the right and left is illustrated in the following two columns:

Revolution of the Left	Revolution of the Right
1. People are subjects of history	1 Leadership knows the future
2. Leadership and people work together to develop utopian vision	2. People are domesticated.
3. Biophilic	3. Necrophilic
4. Love as liberation	4. Love as possession
5. Dialogue	5. Mutism
6. Reflective—problematizing	6. Slogans
7. People who organize	7. Organization people
8. Revolution continuous	8. Bureaucracy

The contrast between the columns on the previous page, reflects Freire's definition of the two forms of consciousness. Items 1 and 2 indicate the differences between people consciously working together to decide how the world should be transformed and self-proclaimed leaders deciding what the future should be. For instance, Freire's criticism of the communist revolution is that the Communist Party declared what the future should be as opposed to people working together to make the future. As indicated in item 5, people are engaged in a dialogue about the future in the revolution of the left, while in the revolution of the right people are kept silent. From this standpoint, the Communist revolution was a revolution of the right.

Item 6 is also about participation in revolutionary efforts. On the right, according to Freire, revolutionary leaders hurl slogans at the masses, who are viewed as objects. On the left, the leadership presents people with problems to be solved through conscious reflection and dialogue. As indicated by item 7, on the left people are involved in organizing for social change, while on the right people join organizations established by the leadership. For Freire, the right, as indicated by item 8, creates bureaucracies to protect the newly won power of revolutionary leaders against further change, while on the left, according to Freire, social change remains continuous as people engage in a search for a better world.

These two forms of revolution reflect a biophilic and a necrophilic personality. The biophilic personality wants all people to be free and to participate in social change. The biophilic personality desires to work with others in transforming social conditions. In contrast, the necrophilic personality wants to control citizens and to decide their future personality. Necrophilic personalities do not desire to work with others but want all people to work for them.

To educate people for a revolution of the left, Freire argues, requires raising levels of consciousness. As I will describe in the next section of this chapter, Freire's educational method takes people through several stages before they become completely humanized. The process of raising the levels of consciousness of the masses requires a revolutionary leadership. This revolutionary leadership emerges, according to Freire, from artists and intellectuals, who are already humanized. As biophilic personalities, these revolutionary leaders want to free all people. They love the people. As an act of love, they want to help people raise their consciousness so that they can free themselves from oppression. From this perspective, Freire's revolution is an act of love, wherein teachers love students so that they can be free.

Freire solves the problem of finding teachers and initiating social change by linking the biophilic personality with revolutionary consciousness or, as it is more frequently called, critical consciousness. In this context, Freire's teachers are lovers who desire to free human consciousness and transform the world so that all people will be free of oppression. Freire's teachers find pleasure in changing people so that they will adopt the characteristics of the revolution of the left as opposed to that of the right. Therefore, motivated by love, Freire's teachers engage in an educational process designed to raise levels of consciousness, change personalities, and transform the world.

THE PEDAGOGY OF LOVE

The central goal of Freire's pedagogical method is to teach reading and, at the same time, to raise the student's level of consciousness. Reading has an important function in the operation of consciousness because, according to Freire, learning to read is a process of learning how to name the world. Language provides the tools by which people can think about the world and see the world as a place that they can change.

As I mentioned earlier in this chapter, Freire considers his pedagogical methods to be as easy to follow as a cookbook, but their implementation requires an understanding of his definition of human nature. The central feature of his method is dialogue. Freire's concept of dialogue is quite different from that of Socrates, whom I discussed in Chapter 1. The Socratic dialogue is supposed to result in the discovery of truth as it exists within each individual. The questions asked by the teacher in the Socratic dialogue help students use their reason to arrive at knowledge about ideas and ideals ranging from arithmetic to the nature of justice.

In the Freirean method, the purpose of the dialogue is to help both the teacher and student understand the political, economic, and social forces that have shaped their lives. While teachers might have a critical consciousness, they do not necessarily understand the lives of their students. The dialogue is supposed to heighten the understanding of both teacher and learner. In this sense, the biophilic teacher believes students have their own knowledge and understanding that can be used in the learning process.

An important role for the teacher is that of "problem posing." Problem posing is directly related to the lives of students. Teachers pose problems about aspects of their students' lives. Students and teachers then engage in a dialogue about these problems, and from this dialogue there emerge words that are frequently used by the students to describe their lives. These words become the basis of the teaching of reading. In this manner, there is a direct connection between learning how to read and learning how to think about one's world.

To begin this educational process, teachers must investigate the lives of their students. During Freire's early work in adult literacy, teachers would first explain their purpose and then spend time observing the lives of their students. The purpose of this observation is to discover themes in students' lives that can be used in a problem-posing dialogue. For instance, teachers in a small village or urban barrio, Freire states, should take notes on the way people talk, their behavior at church and work, and the general social life of the community. In the initial stages of this process, teachers gather frequently to compare their observations. It is assumed that their initial observations are distorted by their own personal beliefs and knowledge.

The dialogue among the teachers helps to raise their consciousness about the social conditions being investigated and about the way in which they perceive the world. As in all Freirean-type dialogues, learning takes place on several levels. On one level, the teachers learn about their surrounding world. On another level, they learn how they themselves think about the world.

And, finally, they learn why they think about the world the way they do. Freire refers to this last process as "reflection."

Reflection involves thinking about the consequences of one's actions and the causes of one's thinking. For instance, a person can make a choice to act in a certain manner. That action will have an effect on the world. In turn, the person can reflect on the impact of that choice and why she or he made the choice in the first place. This process then affects future choices, which, in turn, become objects of reflection.

As teachers go through this process of reflection on their observations, they identify contradictions in the lives of their students that can be used in dialogues. These contradictions are then developed into what Freire calls codifications, such as sketches, photographs, dramatizations, and tape recordings. These codifications must reflect the real lives of the participants so that they can recognize the situations depicted within them. Also, they should not be overly explicit or too obscure. Ideally, the codification will spark a dialogue that will lead to the revelation of other themes in the lives of the students.

The purpose of the codification is to present students with a representation of their lives for the purpose of dialogue. For instance, a codification presented to tenement residents living in Santiago depicted a drunk staggering down the street and men conversing on the street corner.[5] In this situation, many of the tenement dwellers live in a culture of silence. Living in a culture of silence, people do not make their lives an object of reflection. They just act without reflecting on the reasons for their actions. In Freire's terminology, they are dehumanized. They are objects of history as opposed to being subjects of history. They do not make history; history makes them.

Many people living in a culture of silence, according to Freire, have never considered their lives as objects to be discussed. In presenting these codifications, Freire warns, the teacher must not assume that they know reality. For instance, in the codification depicting the drunk, an educator might assume that the person is drunk because of unemployment or lack of virtue. In the actual dialogue, the investigator, who had selected the codification because he had identified alcoholism as a problem in the community, learned that the drunk was considered by the tenement dwellers to be a productive worker who had turned to drink because of worries about low wages and supporting his family.

Freire argues that presentation of codifications causes participants to make explicit their consciousness of the world. The participants see how they act while analyzing a situation they have experienced. For instance, the tenement dwellers in Santiago see how they act when they are drunk and at the same time analyze the reasons for getting drunk. The process of analysis forces the participants to change their perception of their actions while drinking. This creates new perceptions and the development of new knowledge in the participants.

For example, originally the participants might have gotten drunk without any thought being given to the reasons and consequences. After the process of engaging in a dialogue about the codification of their behavior, the participants might now perceive their actions to be a result of their economic conditions. This perception would fundamentally alter their consciousness with regard to their own actions and the causes of alcoholism. The participants might then engage in reflection on their past perceptions and knowledge. Freire describes this process as "perception of the previous perception" and "knowledge of the previous knowledge."[6] In other words, the participants reflect on why they originally gave little thought to the causes of their own drinking.

Out of the process of codification and dialogue emerge generative words to be used in teaching reading. These generative words must have pragmatic value in helping participants to break with their culture of silence. The generative words are words that participants use in describing their own reality. Of course, some consideration must be given to phonetic difficulty in selection of the initial generative words. Ideally, each new word added to the vocabulary would be of increasing phonetic difficulty and would reflect an increasing level of consciousness. In the dialogue about the drunk walking up the street, the teachers might choose for reading instruction words such as drunk, street, walk, work, wages, and family. As the dialogue progresses, the participants might be introduced to words such as alcoholism, exploitation, economics, tenement, employment, and unemployment.

The process of learning these words also aids in heightening students' consciousness. These words stand as objects of a person's actions. To read or write about one's own actions is a process of objectification. In this process of objectification, a person reflects on the action embodied in the word. This process of reflection can transform a person's future actions. For instance, if a person learns the words "drunk," "low wages," and "family" and that person is engaged in a dialogue about the reasons for drinking, then in the future he or she might consciously think of his/her desire for alcohol as resulting from low wages and poor living conditions. With these thoughts affecting their future actions, they might—at least Freire hopes—decide to engage in political actions that will eliminate the social causes of alcoholism. In other words, they will consciously engage in transformation of the world.

One goal of reflection is expulsion of the oppressor from the consciousness of the participants. This reflective process begins with the question: Why did I think the way I did? In the case of the tenement dwellers, the question might be: Why did I simply accept a life of low wages and seek escape from my misery through alcohol? In reflecting on this question, participants would have to seek the reasons for their previous lack of awareness of how economic and social conditions caused drinking and why they never acted to change these conditions.

This process of reflection, according to Freire, can result in the expulsion of the oppressor. People become aware of how the family, the school, and the economic elite affected their consciousness so that they never realized they had the ability to change the world. This awareness leads to an understanding of how they were made a part of a culture of silence. As their understanding increases, the power of the oppressor over their consciousness decreases.

In summary, Freire identifies five stages in a dialogue about a codification. In the first stage, the participants simply describe what they see in the theme. In stage two, the teacher poses problems regarding the codified presentation. In the example on the previous page, the teacher might ask why the person is drunk and why other men linger on street corners. The problem-posing stage helps participants see their way of life as an object that can be discussed and changed. In the third stage, the participants reflect on their previous state of silence regarding their culture. For instance, they might wonder why they had never questioned the heavy drinking of so many in their community and why they never considered low wages and family problems a cause of drinking. In the fourth stage, participants go through increasing levels of critical awareness as they come to understand how their lives and thinking were shaped by political and economic circumstances. And in the fifth stage, they eject the controlling influence of the oppressor from their minds or, in the language of Stirner, they eject "the wheels in the head."

The expulsion of the oppressor, according to Freire, results in a transformation of personality. As the oppressor is replaced in consciousness by a critical awareness of reality, biophilic love replaces necrophilic love. Energized by biophilic love, the fully humanized person is driven by a desire to free all people. It is this passion for freedom that, according to Freire, causes a revolution of the left. This revolution is primarily a cultural revolution in which Freirean teachers, driven by a love of life, help people to understand and transform their lives.

CONCLUSION: EROS, CONSCIOUSNESS, AND EDUCATION

Throughout this book, I have discussed philosophers who, in various ways, consider sexual drives to be an important source of motivation in learning. In part, this is an attempt to understand why knowing, thinking, and creating are pleasurable to humans. Why do writers and painters often pursue their art without consideration for their physical conditions or the accumulation of money? Why do some people sacrifice their lives for the pursuit of truth? Why will scientists sometimes disregard their physical needs for the sake of completing an experiment? In answer to these questions, it is fair to say that people do gain pleasure from the exercise of their intellectual and creative capacities. For educational philosophers such as Paulo Freire, intellectual pleasure and consciousness have their roots in human sexuality.

In Western society, Freire is one part of a long chain of educational philosophers, extending back to Socrates, who link some form of consciousness to conditions of sexuality. In making these connections, philosophers have considered sexuality as a generalized state of energy and pleasure that can be directed at purely physical pleasure and also at the creation of great works of art and a revolutionary desire to free people. This generalized state of sexuality is called "Eros."* In Western culture, it is Eros, according to these arguments, that drives people to conquer nations for the love of another person, write poetry, or devote their lives to learning.

*Eros was the Greek god of erotic love. Eros is also an aggregate of basic instincts and needs, sublimated impulses caused by instincts and needs, and impulses to protect the body and mind.

The philosophers I have discussed in this book have taken several approaches to the issue of Eros. Socrates believed that when Eros was directed at purely physical needs, tyranny resulted. The tyrannical person is characterized by Socrates as being dominated by the desire for sexual pleasure. This domination by the physical side of Eros makes it impossible, according to Socrates, to focus on the pursuit of knowledge and the good. On the other hand, in the philosopher-king the physical drives are controlled by wisdom. The repression of physical sexuality, according to Socrates, results in the energy of Eros being utilized in the quest for truth and beauty.

In modern times, Allan Bloom argues that the commercialization of sex and the promiscuity of modern society have destroyed the power of Eros to motivate learning and scholarship. In discussing the commercialization of sex in rock music, Bloom writes, "it ruins the imagination of young people and makes it very difficult for them to have a passionate relationship to the art and thought that are the substance of liberal education."[7] It is sublimated sexuality, Bloom argues, that motivates the student to learn about philosophy, great literature, and art. Without this passion for learning, Bloom argues, a true liberal education is not possible.

Both Socrates and Bloom represent a tradition that considers the repression of sexuality as essential for allying Eros with learning. On the other hand, Jean-Jacques Rousseau sees Eros as a driving force that creates the social person. The birth of sexual drives at adolescence, he argues, can lead a person to a life of vanity or one of compassion. In this case, the issue is not repression but the channeling of Eros through education. In Rousseau's educational plan, Eros provides the psychological force for directing self-love to an understanding that an injury to another can also be an injury to oneself. This creates compassion, which leads to helping others. Without this education, Rousseau believes, Eros turns self-love into vanity, which results in people spending their lives devoted to their personal appearance and the accumulation of wealth.

America's first psychologist of adolescence, G. Stanley Hall (1844–1924), followed the same line of reasoning as Rousseau. In his classic work *Adolescence* (1904), Hall writes in reference to the birth of sexual drives, "The whole future of life depends on how the new powers [of adolescence] now given suddenly and in profusion are husbanded."[8] Hall argues that sexual drives can lead youth to a life of degradation or to a life of poetry and social service. The role of education, according to Hall, is to properly channel adolescent sexuality into a life of concern about others or, in Rousseau's terms, compassion. The role of the high school and other organizations such as the YWCA, the YMCA, the Boy Scouts, and the Girl Scouts, Hall argues, should be directing Eros to social service and learning.

In contrast to the arguments of Socrates and Bloom that control of physical sexuality turns Eros in the direction of learning and truth, Wilhelm Reich and A. S. Neill, whom I discussed in Chapter 4, argue that repression of sexuality leads to aggression and authority in society. In their view, sexual freedom results in the freeing of Eros to permeate all aspects of life. With sexual freedom, according to Reich and Neill, people seek pleasure in all aspects of their lives, including learning. Eros becomes the motivation for the creation of a world that is satisfying to all people.

Freire's work is more in the tradition of that of Reich and Neill than that of Socrates and Bloom. Similarly to Reich and Neill, Freire links the repression of Eros to authority and aggression. And, similarly to Rousseau and Hall, Freire believes that Eros can motivate people to a state of compassion for fellow humans, which, in this case, means a desire to free all people. By linking the state of consciousness to Eros, Freire continues the Western tradition of locating the desire to know truth and to be free in the interplay between sexuality and society.

The consideration of the role of Eros in the development of consciousness is what distinguishes Paulo Freire from John Dewey and Henry Giroux. Dewey and Giroux share Freire's belief in the social construction of knowledge and his desire to have all people participate in the transformation of society. While Dewey does not deal directly with the issue of different levels of consciousness or the use of dialogue, he does advocate basing learning on children's needs and experiences. Through this process children learn that they have the power to transform the world. Giroux derives his work directly from Freire but neglects the issue of necrophilic and biophilic personalities. Similarly to Freire, Giroux advocates the education of transformative teachers, who would have the same role in schools as the leaders of Freire's dialogues.[9] The major difference is the issue of motivation. Giroux's transformative teacher is one-dimensional and lifeless compared to Freire's Eros-driven teacher. Giroux does not suggest why a teacher would be motivated to be transformative and would want to raise the level of consciousness of her or his students.

Similar to Camille Paglia, Freire recognizes the possibility of evil in the world. Freire's necrophilic personality has qualities that are similar to the sadistic tendencies that Paglia argues are inherent in human nature. The necrophilic personality is a sadistic lover and, as a political ruler, gains pleasure from controlling and brutalizing others. But unlike Camille Paglia, who finds sadism to be an inescapable part of human life, Freire believes that freedom from sadism is possible by raising levels of consciousness through an education based on his principles of a problem-posing dialogue.

In summary, Paulo Freire tries to answer the question: Why do the oppressed of the world accept their conditions in a state of silence? His answer is that the oppressor dominates the conscious of the oppressed and, consequently, creates a necrophilic personality in the oppressed that desires and loves to be dominated. His answer is similar to the one given by Wilhelm Reich in a discussion about the differences between social and reactionary psychology. In the situation in which people steal bread because they are hungry and go on strike because they are exploited, reactionary psychology, Reich argues, tries "to explain the theft and the strike in terms of supposed irrational motives; reactionary rationalizations are invariably the result." In contrast, Reich argues, social psychology does not feel it necessary to explain why some people steal when hungry or strike when exploited but tries to explain "why the majority of those who are hungry don't steal and why the majority of those exploited don't strike."[10] While Reich found his answer in the authoritarian personality, Freire finds it in the necrophilic personality.

Paulo Freire, similarly to many philosophers discussed in this volume, holds out the promise that a particular educational method will lead to freedom, equality of political power, and a loving personality for the oppressed of the world. And, similarly to other philosophers, his method depends on unproven theories about the human personality. Do we know for a fact that critical consciousness results in a biophilic personality? Is one's level of consciousness a reflection of one's sex life? If Freire is wrong about the relationship between Eros and consciousness, then his argument collapses. On the other hand, Western thought from the time of Socrates has suggested that there is a relationship between the two. In fact, this tradition supplies a possible answer to the general issue of why humans are motivated to learn and create. Similarly to Freire's revolutionary leader, who is driven by Eros to free people through education, it is possible that Eros provides humans with feelings of delight and pleasure while they learn and create.

NOTES

1. Paulo Freire, *Pedagogy of the Oppressed* (New York: Herder and Herder, 1970), p. 64.
2. Ibid., pp. 152–153.
3. Ibid., p. 59.
4. Ibid., p. 150.
5. Ibid., p. 111.
6. Ibid., p. 108.
7. Allan Bloom, *The Closing of the American Mind* (New York: Simon and Schuster, 1987), p. 79.
8. G. Stanley Hall, *Adolescence* (Englewood Cliffs, N.J.: Prentice-Hall, 1904), Vol. I, p. xv.
9. Henry A. Giroux, *Schooling and the Struggle for Public Life* (Minneapolis: University of Minnesota Press, 1988), pp. 87–91.
10. Wilhelm Reich, *The Mass Psychology of Fascism* (New York: Farrar, Strauss and Giroux, 1970), p. 19.

CHAPTER 11

An Education in Human Rights

How do you educate students without restricting their intellectual and political freedom? How do you ensure that education does not serve as an instrument of control by authoritarian institutions and people? The answer for Paulo Freire is a method of instruction designed to raise levels of consciousness. However, Freire's method is based on a questionable theory of human motivation and consciousness. There is no proof of a relationship between a biophilic personality and critical consciousness. Certainly, I would like to believe that people who have reached levels of critical consciousness are driven by desires to free themselves and other people. Yet, there is still the possibility that critical consciousness might be linked to a necrophilic personality which desires to control and destroy rather than provide freedom. Followers of Freire might respond to my doubts by claiming that a biophilic personality is part of the definition of critical consciousness. But this response focuses on an arbitrary definition. We are free to give any meaning to concepts, such as critical consciousness. However, a definition is not a proof; it is only an assertion of meaning.

Focusing on the content of education is another method of resolving the conflict between authoritarian and democratic education. Concentrating on content circumvents the problem of finding proofs for methods of instruction based on psychological theories, such as those advocated by Dewey, Neill, and Freire. In this context, the goal is to identify subject matter for instruction that is inherently anti-authoritarian and demands of the student a commitment to freedom of thought and action. If this subject matter can be found, then the next question is this: Can government school systems be required to teach this body of knowledge?

THE RIGHT TO AN EDUCATION IN HUMAN RIGHTS

I propose that education for political power and freedom of thought and action can be achieved by making it a duty of governments and individuals to ensure a right to an education that includes an education in human rights. This proposal does involve the planting of "a wheel in the head." However, this "wheel in the head" provides protection against authoritarian ideas and domination. A knowledge of human rights, I maintain, provides protection against "wheels in the head" that control and exploit the individual.

Most governments are primarily concerned with social control of the population. Very few government-operated schools, if any, teach students how to protect themselves from political and economic despotism. My experience with college students in the United States is that while they receive cursory instruction in the U.S. Bill of Rights in elementary and secondary schools, they are seldom taught that they have a right and duty to ensure the enforcement of these rights. In fact, students seldom understand their rights as students under the U.S. Constitution. In addition, I believe that the U.S. Constitution and Bill of Rights provide only limited protection of human rights. A human rights education should encompass a broader range of rights than that found in the U.S. Constitution and Bill of Rights.

I would include in human rights instruction the right to an education and the right to an education in human rights. However, this proposition generates two important questions: What is the right to an education? What is an education in human rights? I am basing my concept of a right to an education and human rights on the 1948 United Nations' "Universal Declaration of Human Rights." Article 26 of the Declaration states the following:

1. Everyone has the right to education. Education shall be free, at least in the elementary and fundamental stages. Elementary education shall be compulsory. Technical and professional education shall be generally available and higher education shall be equally accessible to all on the basis of merit.
2. Education shall be directed to the full development of the human personality and to the strengthening of respect for human rights and fundamental freedoms. It shall promote understanding, tolerance and friendship among all nations, racial or religious groups, and shall further the activities of the United Nations for the maintenance of peace.
3. Parents have a prior right to choose the kind of education that shall be given to their children.[1]

I propose changing the wording of Article 26 to emphasize the human rights aspects of education and eliminate the statement on merit regarding higher education. Also, parental choice must be limited to ensure that every child receives instruction in human rights. I would also remove the wording on tolerance and support of the United Nations. The problem, as I will discuss below, is the potential conflict between human rights and cultural tolerance. There are cultural practices that are violations of human rights. My version of Article 26 is as follows:

1. Everyone has the right to education that includes an education in human rights. Education shall be free, at least in the elementary and fundamental stages. Elementary education shall be compulsory. Technical, professional, and higher education shall be equally accessible to all.
2. Education shall emphasize the duty of individuals and government to protect human rights.
3. Parents have the right to choose the kind of education that shall be given to their children. However, parental choice is limited with regard to an education in human rights. All forms of education will include instruction in human rights.

The Universal Declaration of Human Rights contains 30 articles that could serve as a basis for human rights instruction. Of particular importance are articles stressing equality before the law, intellectual freedom, the right to life, the right to participate in government, and the right to economic security. As compared to the U.S. Constitution's Bill of Rights, the Universal Declaration of Human Rights provides more economic rights, such as the right to an adequate standard of living, the right to work, the right to form trade unions, the right to equal pay for equal work, the right to reasonable working hours, the right to adequate medical care and housing, and the right of mothers and children to special care and assistance.

An education in human rights would teach students that they had the right and duty to protect freedom of ideas and expression in educational classrooms, textbooks, society, and political life. For instance, requiring instruction in human rights would overcome the problems inherent in Amy Gutmann's proposal that a "democratic professionalism" protect freedom of thought in public schools. Gutmann's approach relies on a teacher's commitment to allowing students to deliberate among the different concepts of the good life (nonrepression). A human rights education would teach students that they had a right and duty to maintain nonrepression in the classroom. Of course, teachers would receive the same human rights instruction. Consequently, both teachers and students would consider it a duty or a "wheel in the head" to ensure the operation of Gutmann's principle of nonrepression. This common sense of duty to maintain human rights would have a stronger impact on the classroom than a simple commitment of teachers to protect nonrepression.

However, advocacy of a human rights education for all people requires an examination of the following questions:

- What is a human right?
- Are there universal human rights?
- Is the right to an education a universal human right?
- Is the doctrine of human rights a form of cultural imperialism?

HUMAN RIGHTS

There are different classifications of human rights including claim rights, liberty rights, power rights, and immunity rights.[2] For my purposes, I am considering human rights to be claim rights. Claim rights impose a duty on society and government to ensure that people have the ability to exercise a right. In contrast, liberty rights provide the right to do something without the obligation of ensuring that a person can actually exercise that right. Liberty rights only require that individuals and government do not interfere with the exercise of liberty. For instance, the right to an education as a liberty right guarantees that individuals will not be interfered with as they pursue an education for themselves or their children. It does not guarantee that a person or child can actually receive an education. As a liberty right, the right to an education places no burdens on society or government to ensure that all people receive an education.

On the other hand, the right to an education as a claims right places a duty on society and government to ensure that everyone can exercise that right. If I am taught human rights as claim rights, then I am taught that I have a duty to ensure that all people have the ability to carry out their right to an education. It is my duty and the duty of all people to guarantee that all people can acquire an education. A claim right places a general burden on society and government. If the right to an education includes an education in human rights, then, as a claim right, everyone has the duty to unite in a common struggle to ensure that everyone has the opportunity to exercise this right.

By creating duties for individuals and government, claim rights require all people to protect human rights. Claim rights require human activity to protect human rights in contrast to liberty rights which require only passive non-interference in the liberty of others. For instance, consider Article 19 of the Universal Declaration of Human Rights.

> Article 19. Everyone has the right to freedom of opinion and expression; this right includes freedom to hold opinions without interference and to seek, receive and impart information and ideas through any media and regardless of frontiers.[3]

As a liberty right, Article 19 only requires that government and society do not interfere with freedom of opinion and freedom to seek, receive, and impart information. As a claims right, Article 19 makes it a duty of government and society to ensure that individuals are able to exercise the right. For instance, I might have the right to impart information through any medium, but my ability to exercise this right is seriously limited by lack of access to television programs, particularly news programs. As a claim right, Article 19 would require that society and government find some means of allowing access to television programs for the expression of my interpretation and others' interpretations of news events. If Article 19 is taught to students as a claim right, then students would be taught that they have a right to freedom of expression and a duty to ensure that all people can exercise that right. This duty would require students to actively guarantee freedom of expression in the classroom and in society.

Some human rights education proposals do not emphasize the duty to protect all human rights. For instance, the report of the International Congress on the Teaching of Human Rights discusses methods of instruction in the language of "respect" as opposed to "duty." The report states, "It should be recognized that true respect for human rights is nothing less than a way of life . . . ."[4] Respect connotes passive action or human rights as liberty rights. Respecting someone else's right to free speech implies that I simply do not interfere in his/her exercise of that right. I would change the wording to emphasize duty over respect. For instance, the report suggests beginning human rights education in infancy and early childhood because, "Concepts of self-esteem and respect for others, the very foundation of human rights, are first communicated within the family."[5] I do not object to the basic premise that families should be models of human rights practices or showing respect for others. However, showing respect for others connotes passive action. I would change the wording to, "Concepts of self-esteem, respect for others, and <u>a duty to protect the rights of others</u> . . . ."

UNIVERSAL HUMAN RIGHTS

A criterion for identifying universal human rights must be established before specifying the content of a human rights education. A criterion is also necessary to establish as a universal human right the right to an education that includes an education in human rights. By universal, I mean rights that are appropriate for all humans despite differences in cultures. I believe that universal human rights should take precedence over cultural practices. In making this statement, I realize this creates a conflict between the desire to protect cultural differences and universal human rights. This is an important issue which I will address later in this chapter.

My criterion for identifying human rights is based on the work of philosopher Alan Gewirth. Gewirth equates human rights with the necessary conditions for human action. All humans have the right to act. He provides four major justifications for this approach to human rights. First, he argues, the existence of conditions for human activity are "undeniably of supreme importance."[6] Second, he contends, "to tie human rights to the necessary conditions of action is to connect the rights directly with morality, since action is the common subject matter of all moralities."[7] In other words, for a person to be moral or engage in moral activities they must be able to engage in purposeful behavior. Thirdly, he argues, human rights considered as necessary conditions for human action allow for more specific identification of human rights in contrast to human rights being based on concepts "like 'dignity' and 'flourishing'."[8]

Gewirth's fourth justification emphasizes the importance of the duty of all individuals to protect the human rights of others. In his concept of human rights, "duty" becomes a "moral duty." Gewirth contends that grounding human rights in the necessary conditions for human actions provides the possibility of moral activity.

> All the human rights, those of well-being as well as of freedom, have as their aim that each person have rational autonomy in the sense of being a self-controlling, self-developing agent who can relate to other persons on a basis of mutual respect and cooperation, in contrast to being a dependent, passive recipient of the agency of others.[9]

This concept of human rights strengthens the idea of claim rights. It supports the idea that humans must act to ensure that everyone can exercise his/her rights as opposed to everyone passively not interfering in the rights of others. For human rights education, this means that students should be taught that they have a "moral duty" to ensure that there exists the necessary conditions for human activity so that all people can exercise their rights. Human rights, in this context, becomes the focus of "moral action."

THE RIGHT TO AN EDUCATION AS A PRIMARY RIGHT

Human rights can be prioritized according to their importance in maintaining the necessary conditions for human action. Classification of rights into primary and secondary can aid in resolving conflicts between rights and providing a plan of action. For instance, the right to adequate medical care is more important than the right to equal pay for equal work. Also, individuals must make decisions about which rights should first be achieved. People should struggle for a right to an education that includes an education in human rights before they struggle for secondary rights, such as the Universal Declaration of Rights Article 15 that states the following: (1) "Everyone has the right to a nationality. (2) No one shall be arbitrarily deprived of his nationality nor denied the right to change his nationality."

The right to an education that includes an education in human rights is a primary right if human rights are derived from the necessary conditions for human action. By primary, I mean that it is more important than certain other rights, such as the right to organize trade unions. In the present world, education is necessary to sustain life and it is necessary for human activity. A certain level of education about germs, disease, personal health, and nutrition is necessary for sustaining life. In our present cash economy, basic levels of reading and arithmetic are necessary for the purchase of foods. Other types of human activity, such as the expression of opinions and the gathering of information, requires, in the present world, the ability to read. It is not difficult to argue that in the present world some level of education is a necessary condition for human action and, therefore, is a primary human right.

A similar argument can be made regarding the necessity of human rights education for human action. If human rights protect the necessary conditions for human action, then the moral duties imposed by human rights education are necessary for the continuation of human action. For instance, if the right to life is a primary human right and necessary for human action, then the continuation of this right depends on people and governments protecting the right to life. In this regard, the goal of a human rights education should be to teach people that they have a right to life and that they have a duty to ensure that other people have a right to life. Human rights education is essential for the protection of all human rights.

PRIMARY AND SECONDARY HUMAN RIGHTS

I propose that a human rights education should be based on the following restatement of the Universal Declaration of Human Rights. These rights are presented as claim rights that impose a moral duty on all people to ensure that everyone has the right to exercise his/her rights. I have divided the rights into primary and secondary based on Gewirth's concept of what is necessary for human action.

Originally, I thought of creating another distinction between rights that place claims on people and government and rights that are specifically related to government action. For instance, a right to life places a claim on people and government to protect life, while the right to a fair trial appears only to place a claim on the government. However, I realized that by making that distinction I was negating the moral duty implied in claim rights. It is the moral duty of all people to ensure that government provides a fair trial. Therefore, a claim right specifically directed at government action still requires all people to assume a moral duty that the right is enforced.

I have rewritten some of the original articles of the Universal Declaration of Human Rights so that they more clearly conform to Gewirth's concept of rights. As originally written, the Declaration was based on the concept that rights were derived from "human dignity." The "Preamble" of the Declaration begins: "Whereas recognition of the inherent dignity and of the equal and inalienable rights of all members of the human family is the foundation of freedom, justice and peace in the world."[10] I propose the following preamble and list of rights as the basis of a human rights education that would be included in the right to an education.

The Content of a Human Rights Education

Whereas human rights derived from the necessary conditions for human action for all members of the human family is the foundation of freedom, justice and peace in the world,

Whereas it is the duty of all members of the human family to ensure that government and society protect human rights,

Then, the following human rights will serve as the content of human rights education. It is understood that it is the duty of all members of the human family to protect their own rights from being violated by governments or other members of society. It is also the duty of all members of the human family to protect the rights of other members of society from violation by governments and individuals.

Primary Rights

1. All human beings are born free and equal in rights.
2. Everyone has the right to life, liberty, and security of person.
3. Everyone is entitled to all human rights without distinction of any kind, such as race, color, sex, language, religion, political or other opinion, national or social origin, property, or birth and other status.
4. No one shall be held in slavery or servitude.
5. (1) Everyone has the right to education that includes an education in human rights. Education shall be free, at least in the elementary and fundamental stages. Elementary education shall be compulsory. Technical, professional, and higher education shall be equally accessible to all.
   (2) Education shall emphasize the duty of individuals and governments to protect human rights.

(3) Parents have the right to choose the kind of education that shall be given to their children. However, parental choice is limited with regard to an education in human rights. All forms of education will include instruction in human rights.

6. Everyone has the right to freedom of opinion and expression; this right includes freedom to hold opinions without interference and to seek, receive, and impart information and ideas through any medium and regardless of frontiers.

7. (1) Everyone has the right to a standard of living adequate for his/her health and well-being and the health and well-being of his/her family, including food, clothing, housing and medical care and necessary social services, and the right to security in the event of unemployment, sickness disability, widowhood, old age or other lack of livelihood in circumstances beyond his/her control.

   (2) Motherhood and childhood are entitled to special care and assistance. All children, whether born in or out of wedlock, shall enjoy the same social protection.

8. Everyone has the right to freedom of movement and residence.

9. Everyone has the right to seek and to enjoy other countries' asylum from the violation of their human rights.

10. No one shall be subjected to arbitrary arrest, detention, or exile.

11. No one shall be subject to torture or to cruel, inhuman, or degrading treatment or punishment.

12. All are equal before the law and are entitled without any discrimination to equal protection of the law. All are entitled to equal protection against any discrimination in violation of their human rights.

13. Everyone has the right to take part in the government of his/her country, directly or through freely chosen representatives.

14. (1) Everyone has the right to freedom of religion as long as the chosen religion does not violate human rights.

    (2) The right to freedom of religion includes the freedom to change religions.

15. Everyone has the right to freedom of peaceful assembly and association.

16. No one can be compelled to belong to an association.

17. Everyone has the right to maintain and strengthen his/her distinct political, economic, social, and cultural characteristics so long as these characteristics do not violate human rights.

Secondary Rights

1. Everyone has the right to work, to free choice of employment, to just and favorable conditions of work, and to protection against unemployment.

2. Everyone, without discrimination, has the right to equal pay for equal work.

3. Everyone who works has the right to just and favorable remuneration ensuring for herself/himself and her/his family an existence worthy of human dignity and ensuring adequate housing, nutrition, and health care.

4. Everyone has the right to form and to join trade unions for protection of his/her interests.

5. (1) Everyone has the right to own property alone as well as in association with others.

(2) No one shall be arbitrarily deprived of her/his property.

6. Everyone has the right to rest and leisure, including reasonable limitation of working hours and periodic holidays with pay.

HUMAN RIGHTS, RELIGION, AND CULTURAL DIFFERENCES

Human rights doctrines are a double-edged sword respecting religion and culture. On the one hand, an appeal to human rights can be a means of protecting cultures from outside interference. There is a long and sad history of eradication of religious and cultural practices by European and U.S. colonial policies. The history of Native Americans provides many examples of government attempts to destroy languages, cultures, and religions. Today, these actions would be considered violations of human rights doctrines.

On the other hand, human rights is a Western concept. For instance, Chinese-Confucian traditions place the responsibility on wise rulers for ensuring the moral actions of the citizenry. In this tradition, citizens are not given any rights to restrain the action of rulers. Human rights doctrines also violate many religious beliefs. Christian and Moslem religions rely on the authority of the Bible and Koran to determine moral actions. In addition, both religions do not recognize the right to change religions. Some cultural practices clearly violate primary human rights. For instance, Saudi Arabia objects to "freedom of religion, freedom from sexual discrimination, and freedom to participate politically."[11] David Forsythe, who argues for the internationalization of human rights, wonders whether "cultural relativists feel any unease when Saudi Arabia stones a woman to death for adultery?"[12] I find that defenders of cultural relativism have difficulty responding to Forsythe's question, "Do we not need to recognize rights against clitorectomies [widely practiced in African countries, such as Egypt], infibulation [sewing closed the vulva of young women to guarantee virginity at marriage], and child marriages on a universal scale regardless of state-approved law and state practice at any given time."[13]

The growth of a global economy and international law provides one justification for declaring that human rights should take precedence over cultural differences. "International human rights," declare lawyers David Weissbrodt and Teresa O'Toole, "is the first universal ideology." They trace the beginnings of this universal ideology to the international effort to abolish slavery and slave trade. In fact, as they point out, "In joining the United Nations, every government undertook to promote 'universal respect for, and observance of, human rights and fundamental freedoms without distinction as to race, sex, language, or religion'."[14] Also, the United Nations endorsed the proclamation of the 1968 International Conference on Human Rights. The proclamation states that the, "Universal

Declaration of Human rights states a common understanding of the people of the world concerning the inalienable and violable rights of all members of the human family and constitutes an obligation for the members of the international community."[15] David Forsythe makes the same argument in *The Internationalization of Human Rights*. Forsythe argues that there already exist treaties and quasi-international government organizations that protect human rights regardless of religious and cultural practices. International law already forbids slavery, piracy, the slave trade, genocide, torture, aerial hijacking, and major war crimes.[16]

In addition, the growth of the global economy requires protection from exploitation by multinational corporations and economic organizations such as the Organization for Economic Development and Cooperation, the International Monetary Fund, and the World Bank. Multinational corporations and international economic organizations do not respect national boundaries or cultural differences. Their primary goal is to create a world that will yield the most profit and spur rapid economic growth. Without the protection of international human rights doctrines, the individual citizen and worker is helpless against these economic forces.

Of course, the existence of international laws and economic cooperation does not provide proof that human rights doctrines should supersede religious and cultural practices. I am making a simple assertion that the growing closeness of international social and economic relationships justifies the existence of universal human rights. Freedom of religion and culture would be guaranteed under these rights as long as they do not violate other human rights.

Another response to the issue of cultural imperialism is that human rights doctrines provide a means of protecting cultures. Certainly, current human rights doctrines would not permit the cultural destruction that occurred with European colonialism. An example of this argument can be found in the United Nations' "Draft Declaration of Indigenous Peoples Rights." This document focuses on the violation of cultural rights that are also a violation of human rights. The Declaration expresses concern,

> That the indigenous peoples have been deprived of their human rights and fundamental freedoms, resulting . . . in their colonization and dispossession of their lands, territories and resources, thus preventing them from exercising, in particular, their right to development in accordance with their own needs and interests.[17]

This statement relates cultural rights directly to human rights. Cultural rights are violated when there is a violation of human rights. The Declaration also highlights cultural changes that reflect the acceptance by indigenous people of human rights doctrines:

> Welcoming the fact that indigenous peoples are organizing themselves for political, economic, social and cultural enhancement and in order to bring an end to <u>all forms of discrimination and oppression wherever they occur</u> [my emphasis].[18]

In addition, Articles 1 and 2 of the Declaration extends human rights to indigenous peoples.

Article 1. Indigenous peoples have the right to the full and effective enjoyment of all human rights and fundamental freedoms recognized in the Charter of the United Nations, the Universal Declaration of Human rights and international human rights law.

Article 2. Indigenous individuals and peoples are free and equal to all other individuals and peoples in dignity and rights, and have the right to be free from any kind of adverse discrimination, in particular that based on their indigenous origin or identity.[19]

In these Articles, human rights doctrines are appealed to as a means of protecting cultural differences. If human rights is a means of protecting cultural and religious differences, then that protection depends on the recognition of human rights. The acceptance of human rights means that cultural and religious practices should not violate human rights.

Therefore, human rights protect cultural and religious differences, while, at the same time, require that cultural and religious practices do not violate human rights. The Declaration already appeals to human rights for protection of culture and religion. In addition, I would change the wording of some articles in the Declaration to indicate the inclusion of human rights in cultural and religious practices. For example, Article 12 opens, "Indigenous peoples have the right to practice and revitalize their cultural traditions and customs."[20] I would add a qualification to that statement, "as long as these traditions and customs do not violate human rights." I would also change Article 15 which states,

Indigenous children have the right to all levels and forms of education of the State. All indigenous peoples also have this right and the right to establish and control their educational systems and institutions providing education in their own languages, in a manner appropriate to their cultural methods of teaching and learning.[21]

I would add to Article 15 a requirement that education include an education in human rights.

In summary, human rights doctrines do require that cultural and religious practices do not violate human rights. In this sense, human rights are a form of cultural imperialism. On the other hand, the problem in recent centuries is protecting cultures and religions from eradication from outside forces. Human rights doctrines provide protection from these destructive forces. However, this protection does require conformity to human rights doctrines.

HUMAN RIGHTS AND MORAL DUTIES: A WHEEL IN THE HEAD

Instruction in human rights as claim rights creates a wheel in the head that ensures freedom of thought and democratic action and creates a moral duty that serves as the basis for human relationships. It resolves the problem of how to teach political ideas without those ideas becoming a source of outside control. Unlike the patriot who is taught to die for the state, the first lesson in human rights is the right to life. A student is given the moral duty of protecting other peoples' rights to life, while, at the same time, ensuring their own right to continue living. H education resolves the problem bothering so many past educators th primarily exists as a method of social control by those with power.

An education in human rights as claim rights would also provi to the concern of conservatives, such as Allan Bloom, with the decline of the family as a center for teaching human relationships. Allan Bloom believes that natural rights doctrines are disappearing because of commercialization of sex and because women's rights are destroying the family. However, Bloom uses a natural rights tradition that focuses on the right to property but does not include economic rights. Consequently, humans compete to acquire and maintain property but they do not assume a duty for the economic well-being of others. Bloom believes that the alienating qualities of economic competition should be balanced by the human relationships of the family. The lessons in human relationships learned in the family will balance the desire for property with a sense of responsibility to serve the poor and unfortunate. For Bloom, individualism and individual competition for property is regulated by the human relations lessons of the family. Therefore, according to Bloom, commercial sexuality and women's rights undermine the family and leave society to the ravages of greed.

However, I would argue, human relationships are maintained by considering human rights as claim rights and by adding economic rights. Yes, people still have the right to pursue property, but they also have a moral duty to ensure that all people have housing, medical care, nutrition, leisure time, work, reasonable wages, reasonable working hours, and the right to organize and join trade unions. Budding capitalists also have a moral duty to ensure that everyone has the right to security in the event of unemployment, sickness, disability, widowhood, old age, or other lack of livelihood in circumstance beyond his/her control. All the members of society have an obligation to ensure that everyone is treated equally before the law and that everyone has the right to life, liberty, and security of person. Everyone would be called on to fight discrimination based on race, color, sex, language, religion, political or other opinion, national or social origin, property, and birth and other status.

The right to an education which includes an education in human rights is fundamental to centering human relationships on a moral duty to protect and maintain everyone's human rights. Do human rights become a wheel in the head? Yes, they do become a wheel in the head, but it is a wheel that drives everyone to work for the necessary conditions that allow human action in a world of freedom and economic security.

CONCLUSION: HUMAN RIGHTS AND DESPOTISM OVER THE MIND

Government-provided human rights education overcomes the problem of rulers using schools to promote their own political power. Of course, governments can distort or eliminate human rights education. However, a human rights education places a duty on citizens to ensure that governments do not distort or neglect their human rights responsibilities. In the United States and other countries this could be accomplished by an amendment to existing constitutions. Preferably, it could be accomplished through international treaties. Treaties would make it a duty of all countries to ensure that other countries provide a human rights education.

The model for the legal implementation of a right to an education that includes an education in human rights is the International Covenant on Economic, Social and Cultural Rights adopted by the U.N. General Assembly in 1966. The purpose of the Covenant was to translate the Universal Declaration of Human Rights into a legal language that could be used for international treaties and government laws. The problem with the Covenant is that it appeals to the "dignity of the human person" rather than to the necessary conditions for human action. Consequently, I would change the Preamble from "Recognizing that these rights derive from the inherent dignity of the human person" to "Recognizing that these rights are necessary conditions for human action."

I would also change the language of Article 13 to emphasize human rights education and human rights as claim rights. In addition, I would introduce language that would protect schools from exploitation by corporations, special interest groups, and politicians. Despite the fact that an education in human rights contains its own protection from the use of education as economic and political control, there still needs to be some explicit language barring outside influence on the school curriculum. The following statement could be used as a model for international treaties, constitutional amendments, and government laws.

INTERNATIONAL COVENANT ON EDUCATION AND HUMAN RIGHTS

1. The States Parties to the present Covenant recognize the right of everyone to education that includes an education in human rights. They agree that education shall be free, at least in the elementary and fundamental stages and that elementary education shall be compulsory. They further agree that technical, professional, and higher education shall be equally accessible to all.
2. The States Parties to the present Covenant agree that education shall emphasize the duty of individuals and government to protect human rights.
3. The States Parties to the present Covenant agree that parents have the right to choose the kind of education that shall be given to their children as long as their choice includes instruction in human rights.
4. The States Parties to the present Covenant agree that the "The Content of a Human Rights Education" outlined in this chapter will serve as a guide to an education in human rights.
5. The States Parties to the present Covenant agree that students should be taught in elementary education that governments do not have the right to violate their human rights. They further agree that students should be taught that governments do not have the right to require an education that does not include an education in human rights.

6. The States Parties to the present Covenant agree to eliminate authoritarian forms of education designed to prepare people to serve political rulers and private businesses.
7. The States Parties to the present Covenant agree to eliminate all forms of patriotic and nationalistic education.
8. The States Parties to the present Covenant agree to make diversity of thought as opposed to conformity to a common creed the hallmark of a democratic education.
9. The States Parties to the present Covenant agree to make instruction consciously political and moral in the sense that children learn how to protect and enhance their freedom, political power, and rights.
10. The States Parties to the present Covenant agree that education shall help students to understand the political, economic, and social forces that affect their lives and the organization of society.

NOTES

1. A copy of the Universal Declaration of Human Rights can be found in *The Universal Declaration of Human Rights 1948–1988: Human Rights, the United Nations and Amnesty International* (New York: Amnesty International, 1988), pp. 111–116.
2. James W. Nickel, *Making Sense of Human Rights: Philosophical Reflections on the Universal Declaration of Human Rights* (Berkeley: University of California Press, 1987), pp. 23–27.
3. *The Universal Declaration of Human Rights 1948–1988* . . . , p. 114.
4. *International Congress on the Teaching of Human Rights September 1978* (Paris: UNESCO, 1980), p. 45.
5. Ibid., p. 42.
6. Alan Gewirth, *Human Rights: Essays on Justification and Applications* (Chicago: The University of Chicago Press, 1982), p. 5.
7. Ibid., p. 5.
8. Ibid., p. 5.
9. Ibid., p. 5.
10. *The Universal Declaration of Human Rights 1948–1988* . . . , p. 111.
11. David Forsythe, *The Internationalization of Human Rights* (Lexington, Mass.:Lexington Books, 1991), p. 3.
12. Ibid., p. 3.
13. Ibid., p. 10.
14. David Weissbrodt and Teresa O'Toole, "The Development of International Human Rights Law" in *The Universal Declaration of Human Rights 1928–1988* . . . , p. 17.
15. Beth Andrus, "The Universal Declaration of Human Rights," in *The Universal Declaration of Human Rights 1928–1988* . . . , p. 5.
16. Forsythe, pp. 1–26.
17. The "United Nations Draft Declaration of Indigenous Peoples Human Rights" can be found in Alexander Ewen, *Voice of Indigenous Peoples* (Santa Fe, New Mexico: Clear Light Publishers, 1994), pp. 159–174.
18. Ibid., p. 160.
19. Ibid., p. 162.
20. Ibid., p. 165.
21. Ibid., p. 166.

Index